Is This a Great Game, or What?

Praise for *Is This a Great Game, or What?*

"A book that covers almost all angles of the major leagues."

—*Publishers Weekly*

"Must reading for baseball fans." —*The Boston Globe*

"One of the few baseball books worth a look these days."

—*St. Louis Post-Dispatch*

"Although more books have been written about baseball than any other team sport, relatively few are memorable. . . . Now I'll have to make room on my list for a new entrant—and you should, too. . . . *Is This a Great Game, or What?* is an informative and entertaining joy from start to finish. In fact, I wish it were twice as long. . . . One thing is for sure—read Tim Kurkjian's book and you will appreciate baseball more than you did before." —*The Washington Times*

"Is this a great book, or what? Hilarious, irreverent, informative. ESPN's Tim Kurkjian has finally collected all his great stories for everyone to enjoy. I can't wait for volume two."

—Dan Shaughnessy, columnist, *The Boston Globe*, and author of *Curse of the Bambino*

"During a long—and, happily, continuing—career covering baseball, Tim Kurkjian has collected more delightful and insightful stories than anyone since Casey Stengel. And whereas Stengel was often unintelligible, Tim is a lucid and engaging storyteller. This book—the first, I hope, of many such—is like a leisurely lunch with Tim. Bon appetit."

—George F. Will, *The New York Times* bestselling author of *Men at Work: The Craft of Baseball*

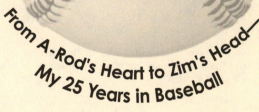

Is This a Great Game, or What?

From A-Rod's Heart to Zim's Head— My 25 Years in Baseball

Tim Kurkjian

 St. Martin's Griffin ☙ New York

www.stmartins.com

Design by Phil Mazzone

Library of Congress Cataloging-in-Publication Data

Kurkjian, Tim.
    Is this a great game, or what? : from A-Rod's heart to Zim's head—my 25 years in baseball / Tim Kurkjian.
        p.   cm.
    ISBN-13: 978-0-312-36224-9
    ISBN-10: 0-312-36224-2
    1. Kurkjian, Tim.   2. Sportscasters—United States—Biography.   3. Baseball—United States—Anecdotes.   I. Title.

    GV742.42.K87 A3 2007
    796.092—dc22
    [B]   2007008637

First St. Martin's Griffin Edition: June 2008

10 9 8 7 6 5 4 3 2 1

To Pop. This is in honor of my father.

Contents

Is This a Great Game, or What?

Introduction

The day I graduated from Walter Johnson High School in Bethesda, Maryland, in 1974, I decided I wanted to be a baseball writer, a decision made easier by two unavoidable factors (*a*) I was seventeen years old, five foot three, 120 pounds, which meant my playing days in baseball and basketball were over, and (*b*) I went to a high school named after the greatest pitcher in baseball history, where I wrote for the school newspaper (*The Pitch*, how clever). Really, what *else* would a little guy, hopelessly dependent on baseball, do with his life?

I was certain of my decision six years later when I was working as a utility infielder, a Tony Graffanino if you will, covering all sports for *The Dallas Morning News*. I'd been in Dallas about a week when we got a tip that Ron Meyer, the football coach at Southern Methodist, was going to be the next coach of the New England Patriots. Our SMU guy wasn't to be found, so I had to do the story. No one answered the phone at Meyer's house, so I was dispatched to his North Dallas home to find him. Mind you, I didn't know how to get to my house, let alone his house, and I didn't know Ron Meyer from Oscar Mayer.

I knocked on the door. Remember, this was 1981, I was twenty-four, I looked about thirteen, and I wasn't much bigger than when I graduated from high school. Meyer answered the door.

"Hi," I said. "I'm Tim Kurkjian from *The Dallas Morning News*."

"OK," he said. "I'll get you your money."

I didn't know whether to laugh or cry.

"You're collecting, aren't you?" he said.

That did it. To be twenty-four and mistaken for the paperboy while doing a football story about a coach I'd never heard of, and a college I'd never been to, drove me back to my favorite game, the best game. That is where I've been the last twenty-five years. It has been a good friend, this baseball.

The game has been challenging. It has tried to run me off several times. I covered the 1982 Rangers, who lost thirteen in a row in May, fired the general manager, held the press conference in the dugout, and briefly named owner Eddie Chiles the GM. I covered the 1988 Orioles, who demolished the record for consecutive losses (21) at the start of a season. I wrote, by my unofficial count, the second-most losing-game stories of any beat man in America in the 1980s.

Life on the road has been a challenge, also. On Opening Day in 1982, I sent my laundry out during a snowstorm in New York, the first time I had ever done that. The nasty man from the New York Hilton returned that evening with my underwear folded and my socks on hangers.

"That will be one eighty-four," he said.

I thought it was a delivery fee. I gave him $5 and told him to keep the change.

"It's *a hundred and eighty-four*," he screamed.

In 1983, Dave Smith, my sports editor, screamed at me for flying commercial instead of on a Rangers team charter that nearly crashed. "But if it had crashed, I would be dead," I said. And he said, "But what if you were the only survivor? Imagine the story you would have."

The writing has been challenging. In 1984, Rangers outfielder Larry Parrish became a father and missed a game. "What is the baby's name?" I asked Doug Rader, the manager. "Buford," he said. What? No one names his son Buford. "I swear on my mother's grave, that's his name," Rader said. So I wrote it. Parrish returned to the team the next day, found me, pulled me aside, and said, gently, "Tim, the boy's name ain't Buford."

I asked Rader how he could do that to me. "I didn't think you *believed* me," he said.

The players have been a challenge. In 1986, I went to spring training as the new baseball beat writer for the *Baltimore Sun*. On the plane ride to Florida, Richard Justice of *The Washington Post* introduced me to Oriole infielder Floyd Rayford.

"Eddie isn't going to like you," he said, referring to star first baseman Eddie Murray.

Why?

"Your head is too big," he said.

With a head that's too big and a body that's too small, I stayed with baseball because I knew it was the only game for me for a million reasons, many of which will become clear in the chapters ahead. Over the last twenty-five years, I have covered every World Series game, every All-Star game, Mark McGwire's sixtieth, sixty-first, and sixty-second home runs, Cal Ripken's 2,131st consecutive game played, two no-hitters and a perfect game, and the only game in history in which one team hit ten home runs. I have met people that I never thought I would meet, I have been to places I never thought I'd go, and I have seen things that I will never, ever forget.

The game has changed dramatically since 1980, but it remains the best game. It has always been so for me. I grew up in a baseball house with a father who loved the game more than anyone I know and could still hit in his late sixties, with two brothers who are now in the Catholic University Hall of Fame for baseball, and with a mother who took me to every game I played in my pedestrian career. When I wasn't playing baseball, I was playing tabletop baseball games, APBA with my brothers, or Strat-O-Matic alone, while my friends went drinking. I did ten years on the baseball beat, eight years of baseball at *Sports Illustrated*, and the last ten years at ESPN. It has been a great job and a great life, thanks to a great game.

And, for me, it officially started with *The Pitch* at Walter Johnson High School.

1

My Mom Was My Catcher

It is the best game. Ask anyone who follows it. Ask George Will; he says, "Baseball is the background music in my life." Ask Billy Crystal; he got chills the first time he met Ted Williams. Ask Jon Miller, the best broadcaster in the game today. I once went to his room at midnight in Minneapolis after he had called an Orioles-Twins game. He was playing Strat-O-Matic by himself. "I love the Blue Jays bullpen," he said. Ask the president of the United States. As I went through the receiving line at the White House in 2003, Mr. Bush whispered in my ear, "Who hit the home runs for the Yankees today? Did Ruben hit one?"

It is the best game because once it grabs you, it never lets go; it is so seductive, it really *is* important for some to know whether Ruben Sierra hit a home run today. I am so incurably hooked by my passion, I check Sierra's batting line first thing every day for a far more important reason: to see if he was hit by a pitch. He has not been hit by a pitch since 1990. How pathetic am I? The daily ritual of devouring box scores at the breakfast table is a rite reserved only for baseball, and intriguing box score lines don't just appear—such as Ben Petrick's 3–0–0–4 or Curtis Granderson's 5–0–5–0—they fly off the page and hit me in the face. And to be sure I absorb them, I have cut out every box score from every game for the last eighteen years, like a seven-year-old doing a current events assignment with scissors and tape.

"You know you can get all that on the Internet," said my wife, Kathy.

"I know," I said, "but I remember it better when I do it by hand."

It is the best game because the players look like us. They are not seven feet tall, they don't weigh 350 pounds, and they don't bench-press 650. We can relate to them. We can see them—they're not obscured by some hideous face mask, and they don't play behind a wall of Plexiglas—we can touch them and we can feel them. I see Greg Maddux with his shirt off, with his concave chest and no discernible muscles, and I marvel: *This* is one of the six greatest pitchers in the history of the game? I see Tony Gwynn with his shirt off and I see a short, fat guy with the smallest hands I've ever seen on an athlete, and I wonder: "*This* is the best hitter since Ted Williams?" This game is open to all shapes and sizes, including the Cardinals' David Eckstein, who is five feet six; he can't throw, he gets hit by a pitch thirty times just to get on base, and he was the shortstop for the World Champion Angels in 2002 and the World Champion Cardinals in 2006. Pedro Martinez told me that when he was in the minor leagues, he weighed 138 pounds and threw 93 mph. How can that be? Mets reliever Billy Wagner is five feet nine and throws 100 mph. "The first time I met him," said six-ten pitcher Randy Johnson, "I thought, 'This guy is a foot shorter than me, and he throws harder than I do.'"

Phillies pitcher Jamie Moyer doesn't throw harder than anyone—about 83 mph—yet he has been one of the game's most consistent pitchers over the last ten years. On the ride home from the ballpark one night after a game he pitched, one of his young sons asked him, "Dad, can't you throw just one pitch 90 (mph)? Just one?" To which, Jamie Moyer said, "Son, that's not how I pitch." As they drove on, Moyer's son noticed how fast his dad was driving. "Dad," he said, "you are driving the car faster than you throw a baseball."

The players, at least most of them, and their stories, are so human. Former pitcher Pete Harnisch helped work his way through Fordham University by appearing in police lineups. "Twenty-five bucks for a regular case," he said. "Fifty bucks for a murder case." Ex-Twins first baseman Kent Hrbek was the only player who showed up for World Series parties in 1987 and '91 because the food and beer were free. In 1990, he met White Sox rookie Craig Grebeck, who wore number 14, same number as Hrbek, and was roughly half his size: 280 pounds to 140 pounds. "You're too small to wear that number," Hrbek told him. "Put a slash between the 1 and the 4 and be 1/4." Hrbek went camping with Andy Van Slyke. "Around the campfire," Van Slyke said, "he played a tape recording of his favorite farts."

They are regular guys, at least most of them, who just happen to be really, really good at something that everyone else is not. Padres outfielder Ryan Klesko was a terrific high school pitcher. He had a mound in his backyard. His *mother* often caught him. "She wore a mask," Klesko said, "but no shin guards." The mother of former major-league infielder Casey Candaele played in the Women's Professional Baseball League, which was glorified in the movie *A League of Their Own*. "She had a better swing than mine," Candaele said with a smile. "She was the only mother ever to be banned from playing in father-son baseball games at school because she was too good." Orioles pitcher Mike Flanagan's seventy-two-year-old grandfather was his catcher in the backyard. "If I threw too far inside or too far outside, he couldn't reach it," Flanagan said. "And if he missed it, he would have to chase it. So I had to learn how to hit the target."

Normal guys? Rangers outfielder George Wright went three for five on Opening Day 1982. "Did you have fun today?" I asked. He said, "Yeah, I'd never been to a major-league game before." Amazing: the first major-league game he had ever seen, he played in and got three hits. Former reliever Bob Patterson used to fix the gloves of teammates as he sat in the bullpen during the early innings. Teammate Gary Redus called him Dr. Glove. In the minor leagues, he was nicknamed Emmett after the fix-it man on *The Andy Griffith Show.* "He's coming over Saturday to upholster my couch," said Rich Donnelly, one of his coaches. The day Keith Hernandez left home after being drafted in 1975, he packed his Strat-O-Matic in his suitcase. "You're not taking that," his father said. "You're a professional ballplayer now.'" Hernandez said, "But, Dad, I'm halfway through the '72 season!"

Human? Brewers third baseman Jeff Cirillo made the 1997 All-Star team. As he was stowing his overhead luggage in the plane on his way to the game, a man behind him asked, "Aren't you Jeff Cirillo?" Cirillo was shocked that anyone recognized him. "Yes, I am," he said proudly. The man said, "Aren't you going to the All-Star game?" Cirillo said yes.

"This plane is going to Detroit," the man said.

Even the best players, at least some of them, are genuine. There is no finer person, no more unpretentious superstar, than Hall of Fame third baseman Brooks Robinson of the Orioles. When Robin Roberts came to Baltimore late in his career, he unsuccessfully tried to field a bunt down the third-base line, preventing Robinson from making his trademark barehand catch-and-throw play. Robinson patted Roberts on the butt and said, "Let me have that one the next time; I'm *good* on that play." In the late '70s, Gordon Beard, a sportswriter in Baltimore, made a speech at one of the retirement functions for Robinson. "In New York," Beard said, "they named a candy bar after Reggie Jackson. Here in Baltimore, we name our *children* after Brooks Robinson."

It is the best game because it's a romantic game. Our finest essayists write poetically about it, yet ultimately they're all wrong. In truth, it is a hard game played by hard men; the romance disappears when that ball is traveling at your face at an incomprehensible rate of speed. It is, without question, the hardest game in the world to play, yet it looks so easy on TV. It isn't. My wish is for everyone in America to get one at-bat in a major-league game against Randy Johnson, and to stand even with third base when Albert Pujols hits a rocket down the line. Then everyone would appreciate what I appreciate: the speed of the game and the danger involved. It is a game that requires tremendous skill, athleticism, and courage. It is golf, except with running, jumping, throwing, sliding, and an overwhelming fear of the ball. PGA Tour players are amazingly skilled and disciplined, but imagine hitting an eight-iron into a green with a baseball that's hard as a rock and coming at you at 95 mph, or, after finishing your swing, having to avoid a 225-pound man in metal spikes who is coming at your knees at full speed. How hard is it? Ask Danny Ainge, perhaps the best all-round athlete of the last twenty-five years. There wasn't a sport that he couldn't play, and he did play in the major leagues, but when Orioles pitcher Tippy Martinez was asked what he threw to get Ainge out, he said, "Strikes."

How hard? Ask Michael Jordan. His greatest feat was not leading the NBA in scoring by more than eight points *and* winning Defensive Player of the Year in the same year, it was hitting .202 in Double-A ball after having not played baseball since high school, sixteen years earlier. It was a miracle that he hit that high. I thought he would hit .050, and I wasn't alone. Jordan will tell you that hitting a baseball is a lot harder than hitting a jump shot. A great NBA shooter misses ten shots in a row and he can't wait to shoot the eleventh because he *knows* it's going in. But a major-league hitter goes twenty at-bats without a hit, and he's a mess. Hall of Famer Frank Robinson, who had one of the greatest rookie seasons ever, and is the most confident hitter I've ever met, told me "I went something like 0 for twenty-five during my second year and I honestly thought I'd never get another hit." Dante Bichette was a really good hitter for nearly ten years, but he told me, "Every day I come to the park I wonder if it's the last day I'll be able to hit in the big leagues."

How hard? The Yankees' Alex Rodriguez has been the game's best player for the last ten years. His talent level is astonishingly high, far higher than that of Derek Jeter. Someday, he might be the all-time home run king, and could have the best numbers this side of Babe Ruth.

And yet, due to his failures in the postseason for the Yankees in 2004–06, critics have questioned his ability, his courage and his heart. He has been savaged by the press in New York and the fans at Yankee Stadium, where he has been booed liked an itinerant player with no track record rather than a two-time MVP, and the only in-fielder ever to win a Gold Glove in a 50-homer season. Only in baseball can the most gifted player on the field perform like the worst player some nights. That can't happen in basketball. On a bad night, Larry Bird was the best player on the court, the guy who always took the last shot.

There's nothing wrong with A-Rod's heart. It's his head. "The guys who are most affected by slumps are the bright guys who think so much and care so much," says veteran outfielder Jeff Conine. A-Rod cares too much about things around him, especially his image, and he thinks way too much. In 2006, he spoke on the phone for ninety minutes with ESPN basketball analyst Dick Vitale looking for answers for his hitting woes, as if Dickie V. might actually say something that would help A-Rod hit a 98 mph heater. Basketball players just react, they let their bodies take over because there's no time to do anything else. In baseball, with so much time to think, a player can think himself into trouble.

"You know what he's thinking right now?" a former teammate of A-Rod said after A-Rod made the final out of the eighth inning of a playoff game against the Tigers in 2006. "He's thinking 'great, I don't have to bat in the ninth inning?'" What? That's what a scared, overmatched, ten-year-old thinks! How can a guy with 500 home runs at age thirty-one think like that? It's baseball. It will strangle you if you let it. That's what makes it the best game.

How hard? Of all the stupid hypothetical questions I like to ask, my favorite is, "How many hits would you get in a hundred at-bats against Randy Johnson?" The answer for me is simple: *zero*. Any other fifty-year-old who hasn't played since high school, and thinks it's higher than zero, has no idea what he's talking about. Why? Because Johnson would sense my fear, he'd buzz the tower my first time up, and I'd never get back in there, and neither would you. I told this to ESPN's Dan Patrick on his radio show, explaining that he, too, would get zero hits in a hundred at-bats against Randy Johnson. Patrick is a good athlete, so he disagreed. I told Dan that he would get zero hits in a hundred at-bats against 200-game winner Jamie Moyer, whom I chose only because he's left-handed (Dan hits right-handed) and is a finesse pitcher who throws 83 mph, and not quite as scary.

"I'd get a hit off Jamie Moyer," Patrick said.

The next day, Jamie Moyer came on his radio show.

"You would *never* get a hit off me," Moyer said.

It is the best game because of its unpredictability. Every day you go to the ballpark, you might see something you've never seen in your life. How many other people can say that about their jobs? I saw Brad Komminsk disappear over the eight-feet-high fence in left-center field at Memorial Stadium after making a spectacular catch; his hand, with the ball in it, eventually reached over the top of the fence. I saw Bo Jackson run *up* the same fence, like a skateboarder on a banked turn, after making a great running catch. I saw

Bert Blyleven strike out nine batters in one game, all called third strikes. I saw a deranged fan jump out of the upper deck and land on the netting behind the plate at Yankee Stadium. I saw Jeff Stone make an out at all four bases in one game. Think about that one.

Unpredictable? Look, no one loves basketball more than I do. But in many basketball games, you know who is going to win, and how the game is going to be played, before it starts. When the Clippers would go to Chicago to play the dynastic Bulls, they *couldn't* win. That's never the case in baseball. No team in baseball goes 39–2 at home. Only in baseball can someone—in this case, me— pick the Angels to win the seven-team American League West in 1991, and the Twins to finish last, then have the Twins finish first and the Angels finish last. And I wasn't the only dope who made that call. In basketball, Michael Jordan is Michael Jordan, and Paul Mokeski is Paul Mokeski, and it *never* changes. The best player always dominates the game. The last guy on the bench never takes the game-winning shot. But in baseball, the best player might not even be a factor in the game, and his team can still win. The last player on the bench, be it Tom Lawless or Lenny Webster, or Geoff Blum in Game 3 of the 2005 World Series, might win the game. Francisco Cabrera was the second to last guy on the bench for the Braves in Game 7 of the 1992 National League Championship Series against the Pirates. His only expected role that night was to catch the ceremonial first ball before the game, yet his two-out, two- run single off Stan Belinda won the game and ruined the Pirates for what is now fourteen years: It remains the only postseason Game 7 ever to end on a two-out hit that took a team from behind to ahead.

It is the best game because of its rich history and tradition, from the seventh-inning stretch to my wife's favorite: the simple tossing of a baseball to the first baseman as he runs in after each in- ning so he'll have a baseball in his mitt for the next inning. It is a game of copiously kept statistics that have real meaning; they allow us to compare eras. At the 1999 All-Star game at Fenway Park, Ted Williams, who was introduced as The Greatest Hitter Who Ever Lived, sat in his wheelchair next to the pitcher's mound before the game. At the subtle urging of Tony Gwynn and Cal Ripken—no surprise it was those guys—the rest of the All-Stars surrounded Williams to talk to the great man. "Can you smell the smoke on your bat when you really hit one?" Williams asked Mark McGwire. The current All-Stars revered Williams because they knew if he were playing today, he would be the best hitter on the field. And they would be right. If this had been a gathering of NBA basketball players, and that had been George Mikan, the first great big man in the league's history, sitting at center court, with all due respect, Shaquille O'Neal probably would have thought, "Man, I'd dunk every time on this guy," and he would be right.

Baseball is the only major sport in which some of the standard-bearers have been dead for fifty years, and a team that hasn't played in eighty years, the 1927 Yankees, are still mentioned in casual conversation, as in "The Indians are a good hitting team, but they're not the '27 Yankees." It is the only sport in which we can argue who was better, Walter Johnson or Roger Clemens, Babe Ruth or Barry Bonds. Johnson was the best ever, and not because I'm biased because I went to his high school, but because he threw 113 shutouts, more than Roger Clemens, Greg Maddux, and Curt Schilling combined. Who is better, Bonds or Ruth? Entering the 2006 season, Ruth had as many career shutouts as Pedro Martinez (17). When Bonds becomes a pitcher, then we'll talk about who is the greatest baseball player of all time.

It is the best game because it begins in the spring, a time when the flowers are blooming, the snow has melted, and summer is ahead. People build their vacations around baseball trips. Countless times I have met a family that is in the middle of a two-week odyssey in which they are visiting ten different major-league ballparks.

They don't do trips like that in the NFL, do they? Baseball fans spend March going to every spring training site. Do football fans spend August visiting every NFL training camp? You're not even allowed in those places for fear that you might steal a team's game plan for next week. Does anyone really say, "We *have* to go to Arco Arena" in Sacramento? No. Why? Because NFL stadiums and NBA arenas are largely the same. The dimensions of the field and the court are always exactly the same. But in baseball, they're all different. When my family visited Wrigley Field in 2003, my wife, no big baseball fan, was dazzled by the ivy on the outfield walls and the hand-operated scoreboard. Every ballpark is different in its own way. I know. I've covered a game in forty-eight of them.

It is the best game because it is a family game, one that begins every spring with a father, or Ryan Klesko's mother, taking a son to the backyard for a game of catch. The Bell family is a three-generation family of big leaguers. Gus Bell, then with the Reds, would watch his son Buddy play as a kid, but so as not to draw any extra attention, Gus would sit alone in his car beyond the center-field fence. "If I made a good play," Buddy said, "he'd honk his horn once. For a great play, he'd honk twice." The Tyler family works in Baltimore. Jimmy runs the Oriole clubhouse. Fred runs the visiting clubhouse. Their dad, Ernie, is the umpire attendant. He has not missed a home game since he took the job in 1960, a Ripkenesque streak. There are thirteen Tylers, Ernie, Mom, and eleven kids. They once all lived in the same house at the same time. A baseball family indeed.

It is the best game because it's a daily game with great rhythm and flow to it. The game writes itself, and, if you're paying attention, it never disappoints. There are few days off, and, thankfully, fewer off-day stories to write. When Tracy Ringolsby, a Hall of Fame baseball writer, filled in briefly on his newspaper's NFL coverage years ago, he asked a question of Chiefs coach John Mackovic, who scolded him, saying, "Today's Monday; that's a Tuesday question." In football, coaches can't completely comment on a game "until we've seen the film." In baseball, there is enough time between plays, between pitches, you have time to analyze it. In baseball, you don't wonder if the home run is going to be called back because of a penalty. You don't have to wait for the referee to stare into the replay monitor for twenty minutes to determine that, yes, now you're allowed to celebrate. And, in baseball, the ground can indeed cause a fumble.

It is the best game because it has the best broadcasters. We go to bed with them every night; they are our eyes and ears, members of the family. Their call is soft and soothing, not like the frenetic, apocalyptic call of a basketball game. Is there anyone softer and more soothing than Ernie Harwell? When Tiger Stadium was vacated in 2001, Ernie wanted a piece of a memorabilia from the park, so he chose one of the urinals from the visiting clubhouse. Why? I asked. "It's personal," he said. "Every great visiting player in the American League history used it. I'm going to clean it up and make it into a planter for my wife."

Jon Miller is as good a broadcaster as there is in the game today. When he was the play-by-play guy for the A's in the 1970s, they played the first game of a doubleheader at Tiger Stadium. The stands were virtually empty. The radio booth is right on top of home plate there. The A's Gene Tenace fouled a ball off his foot. Jon Miller, speaking on the radio, said something like, "Boy, that has to hurt." To which, Tenace, hobbling around home plate, looked at the broadcast booth and shouted, "You think so? And thanks for telling everyone!"

The only thing better than listening to Jon Miller call a game is to go out with him for pizza afterward. There is no one in the world funnier than Jon Miller. He can do any dialect, imitate any play-by-play guy, any public address announcer. When he does the venerable Bob Sheppard, the Yankee PA man, ordering breakfast—*Good morning, ladies and gentlemen, and welcome to my table. I'll have the Number 2, Two Eggs, Over Easy, With Toast, Number 2*—I laugh so hard, I cry. When he does Sherm Feller, the once great PA man at Fenway Park, in a fictional *Leave It to Beaver* episode—*Good morning, Miss Landers, boys and girls, today's lesson . . .*—I have to leave the room.

Well, maybe Bob Uecker, the Brewers broadcaster, is funnier. When Johnny Carson asked Uecker for his biggest thrill in baseball, he offered two: He saw a fan fall out of the upper deck in Philadelphia, and he got out of a rundown against the Mets. Uecker was the master of ceremonies at the Brewers' winter banquet one year. He winged the whole thing, and he was hilarious. The banquet was held soon after the Brewers had made a controversial trade of popular Jeromy Burnitz. "Look, people have differing opinions on many issues," Uecker told the crowd. "Take my career. Half the people thought I was the worst player they've ever seen, and the other half thought I was a disgrace to the uniform."

It is the best game because it has the best Hall of Fame. There is nothing better than a summer weekend in historic Cooperstown, New York, especially on induction weekend when you can walk down the street and run into a Hall of Famer. It's as if you've gone back in time. There is no better tour in this country than the Hall of Fame Museum, but the best tour ever is the basement of the museum, which houses, among other things, some old-time baseball gloves that are no more substantial than one you would use to shovel snow.

It is the best game because it has the best nicknames. Catcher Doug Gwosdz was Eye Chart. G-W-O-S-D-Z. Rockies pitcher David Lee was Diesel. Something happened to the bus driver in spring training 1999, so Lee had to drive the team bus. He pulled into a gas station and pronounced, "We need some diesel!" And there was minor leaguer Pork Chop Pough. "When I was eight, my nickname was Pokie," he said. "We had another kid on our team named Pokie, but I was much bigger than him, so everyone started calling me Pork Chop. Teachers in high school called me that. They didn't even know my name was Clyde."

It is the best game because it's the only one with a simple yet intricate system of keeping score. My sixteen-year-old daughter Kelly *has* to score every game she goes to. Most everyone knows how to keep score, but Tim McCarver didn't know until he went to the broadcast booth. Don Zimmer, who has been in the game for over fifty years, still doesn't know how. "I know that a double is two lines," he said. "But if I had to score a fielder's choice I'd have no chance. Hey, I've been in uniform my whole life. Who keeps score when you're in uniform?" No two people keep score exactly the same way. Is a called third strike a backward K, a K-C, or something else? Bob DiBiasio of the Cleveland Indians used to a run a seminar on keeping score at the club's winter banquet. As he was at the podium explaining the scoring of a complex play, a *nun* stood up in the back of the room and said, "That's not how you do it. Let me show you how *I* score that play."

It is the best game because the best in the game never forget anything, partly because the game moves at a pace that allows you digest all that is happening. "My wife says I can't remember the name of someone I met five minutes ago," said former Rangers manager Buck Showalter, "but I can remember pitch sequences from five years ago." Jim Palmer never gave up a grand slam in nearly 4,000 innings, amazing considering that Chan Ho Park gave up two in one *inning*, and, in 2005, Braves reliever Joey Devine became the first pitcher ever to give up a grand slam in his first two major-league appearances. I asked Palmer what was the closest he came to giving up a slam, and, twenty-five years later, he took me through an inning, pitch by pitch, from a game in 1973 in Cleveland. "Rico Carty hit a ball over the fence, but [Al] Bumbry reached over and caught it," Palmer said.

Pitch count? I met Billy Crystal, a New York native and a huge Yankee fan, for the first time on the field at Yankee Stadium before Game 1 of the 2003 American League Championship Series between the Red Sox and Yankees. I asked him, on live television, about his first recollection of the Red Sox-Yankees rivalry. "I was sitting right up there [first-base side, upper deck]," Crystal said. "Second game of a doubleheader, Ted Williams strikes out against Bobby Shantz. Thirty years later, I meet Mr. Williams. I said, 'I have home movies of you striking out against Bobby Shantz in the second game of a doubleheader at the Stadium.' He looked at me and I swear, Tim, he says, 'Curveball, low and away.' He said, 'Ellie [Yankees catcher Elston Howard] dropped it and tagged me, right?' I said, 'Yes, *that's it!*' "

It is the best game because the equipment used is so personal and so important to the players. Tony Gwynn has been to the Louisville Slugger factory, run by Hillerich and Bradsby, to pick out the billets of wood used to make his bats; he could close his eyes and, from the feel, pick out his bat from a teammate's bat that was the exact same weight and length. "I broke a bat that I used for a whole year," Gwynn said. "I almost cried." Then there was former Reds outfielder Glenn Braggs, who brought twelve bats on one road trip, and broke ten without making contact. Braggs was so strong, he'd whip the bat with such force on his follow-through that the bat would snap when it hit his left shoulder. "I broke three like that in one game," he said.

Gloves are even more personal than bats. Future Hall of Fame second baseman Roberto Alomar wouldn't let anyone touch his glove for fear that any hand not his own would wreck the perfect form of his glove. "Who had his hand in my glove?" he yelled at no one in particular in the Indians clubhouse one day. "My glove is ruined." Former infielder Rene Gonzales would carry his glove in a Wonder Bread bag. Why? I asked. "Their slogan is 'No holes,' " he said. Former shortstop Walt Weiss was equally protective of his glove, mainly because he had used it since high school. It was so beat up, strings and such hanging from it, he called it "the Creature." Then there was Indians utility man Jeff Manto, who used to carry thirteen gloves with him on every trip, including two catcher's mitts, two first basemen's mitts, and a miniature glove that made him concentrate even more when catching the ball. "The guys call me " 'Store,' " he said. "The equipment man hates me."

It is the best game because it contains so many elements and nuances, so much happening behind the scenes; it lends itself to strange circumstances, events, and plays, things that can only happen in baseball, things that make me smack myself in the forehead and say, "How great is *that?*" I did a story on the position of third base for *Sports Illustrated.* Why is it so hard to play? Why are there fewer third basemen in the Hall of Fame than any other position? Why have so many teams had such a hard time filling that position for a long period of time? The common answer I got from those who played the position was I Don't Know, which happens to be the name of the third baseman in the great Abbott and Costello routine "Who's on First?" Speaking of which, how great was the night that Glenn Abbott pitched for Detroit and Marty Castillo caught, making the battery of Abbott and Castillo? Or the night that Bud Black pitched and Steve Decker caught, a Black-and-Decker battery. Steve Rushin, the brilliant writer from *Sports Illustrated*, wrote that Decker wore the *power tools* of ignorance.

Strange things? How can it be that pitcher Dennis Eckersley could go four years between pickoffs, then the first guy he picked off in 1982 was the last guy he picked off in 1978, Kenny Williams.

(At least Williams redeemed himself: he was the general manager of the 2005 White Sox, who won the franchise's first World Series in eighty-eight years.) In 1983, the Orioles' Tippy Martinez picked three runners off first base in the same inning. His catcher was Lenn Sakata, an infielder who had never caught, but had to that night because manager Earl Weaver had used up the whole bench trying to get the score tied in the ninth. So, with a second baseman behind the plate, three Blue Jays were a little too anxious leading off first, and Martinez nailed them all—a first, and surely a last, in baseball history. "Tippy had the worst pickoff move of any left-hander I've ever seen," teammate Mike Flanagan said. "I bet he never picked off another runner before or after that." Of course, Sakata hit the game-winning home run in that game, later voted by Oriole fans as the greatest game in club history. When Memorial Stadium closed in 1991, and many former Orioles were brought back to say goodbye, they went to the positions that they played for the Orioles. Sakata didn't go to second base, he went behind the plate. And every fan in the ballpark got it.

A lot of people get it. They get baseball. And they will always get it. They're the lucky ones. They know, and always will know, that baseball is the best game.

2

Business . . . But It's a Pleasure

Peter Gammons and I were walking through the White House in March 2003 as part of a luncheon for Hall of Fame players. As we toured the halls of one of the most hallowed places on earth, past the historic photos of presidents and their families on the right, and the Rose Garden on the left, I asked Peter what the Red Sox were doing at second base in spring training. He said there were several options, but thought they would go with Pokey Reese.

"Guys, we're in the White House," said my wife, Kathy. "Is this the time or place for Pokey Reese?"

For baseball writers, it is always the time and place for Pokey Reese, and all things baseball. We are seamheads; we are the un-laundered, often overweight, usually unathletic baseball nerds who are trained only to cover baseball. We have covered winter ball games, Instructional League games, Arizona Fall League games, sim-ulated games, and we have traveled two hundred miles to watch a "B" game on a back field in spring training. The White House? We know more about pitcher Grover Cleveland Alexander than we do about Grover Cleveland. The opera? When you say Placido, we think Polanco, not Domingo. I can't name the nine Supreme Court justices, but I can name the nine players who have won the Triple Crown.

We do what we do not for the love of the written word or the writing process, which is hard, but for the love of the game, which is easy. If we didn't love the game, why would we spend 150 days a year on the road, writing five stories daily for three deadlines, for editors who change our words with utter disregard, and all while dealing with players who make five hundred times what we make, who have no problem lobbing soiled underwear in our direction, and who think our sole existence involves loitering in their clubhouse with a pen and a notebook, with the singular purpose of bothering them? And yet we do what we do mostly because we know, despite our complaints, that we have the best gig in the world. Many years ago, the effervescent John Lowe, who covers the Tigers for the *Detroit Free Press*, checked into the Bond Court Hotel in Cleveland at 2:00 A.M. following a harrowing flight in the middle of a killer road trip for a Tiger team that was on its way to losing a hundred games. The clerk asked him if he was in town for business or pleasure.

"Business," he said, "but it's a pleasure."

The last twenty-five years have been a pleasure for me. I have seen things I will never forget. I covered the Buckner game, the David Henderson game, the Kirk Gibson game, the Joe Carter game, Game 7 of the 1991 and 2001 World Series, the Pirates-Braves Game 7 in 1992, the McGwire-Sosa weekend in 1998, and Cal Ripken's 2,131 celebration, none of which need further elaboration. For ten years, I voted for the annual awards—Most Valuable Player, Cy Young, etc. And since I covered baseball for a daily newspaper for ten consecutive years, I have filled out a Hall of Fame ballot for the last eighteen years—that's more than pleasure, that is a privilege—I have a lifetime honorary Baseball Writer's Association of America card that will get me in to any major-league regular season game for free for the rest of my life, a fact that was wonderfully contorted by a fourth-grader after I spoke to his class. "Mom," Jeremiah said, "I want to be a baseball writer when I grow up. Mr. Kurkjian has a credit card that allows him to get anything for free the rest of his life!"

I have met people that I never thought I'd meet. "Would you like to meet the old man?" said George W. Bush, the owner of the Rangers. George Herbert Walker Bush landed in a helicopter and visited the Rangers' spring training site, where I shook his hand. I did so with two other presidents, and with Billy Crystal, Bill Murray, Steve Martin, and Steven Wright. I met singer Bruce Hornsby, who is a friend of ex-Angels pitcher Mark Langston, and, one night in Baltimore, he played and sang at the hotel bar for a circle of friends.

I have interviewed hundreds and hundreds of major-league baseball players over the last twenty-five years, though I'd like to forget the night I woke up irate pitcher Hoyt Wilhelm in his hotel room, which I had rung without answer every five minutes for two hours, only to be told by the idiot woman working the switchboard, "Sorry sir, I've been connecting you to the wrong room. It seems we have *two* Hoyt Wilhelms in the hotel tonight." But for every bad interview, there have been a hundred good ones, including all of those with ex-pitcher John Burkett, who is a great bowler. "In high school," he said, "I bowled forty games in one day. My right arm got tired, so I bowled the last ten games left-handed."

I interviewed then the three greatest living players, Hank Aaron, Willie Mays, and Ted Williams, in a five-minute stretch at the Hall of Fame. I met Joe DiMaggio in the bathroom at Baltimore's Memorial Stadium. He took the last urinal, saying, "I have to go worse than you do." I batted against Bob Feller, one of my father's baseball heroes. I was covering Class A baseball in Alexandria, Virginia, at Four Mile Run Park (which writing colleague Peter Mehlman, who went on to write and produce *Seinfeld*, once called

Three Mile Island Park in one edition of *The Washington Post*). Mr. Feller, then sixty years old, traveled around the country putting on pitching exhibitions. He threw to the local writers. I was twenty-two years old, and he was throwing 50 mph. A monkey could have hit him, so I hit a couple of balls hard, and he wouldn't throw me any more strikes, just breaking balls off the plate. Afterward, all the hitters received a certificate stating that they had batted against Bob Feller. In large print on the bottom of the page was the disclaimer: The above-named slugger realizes that batting against Bob Feller during his prime would have been considerably more of a challenge and the results would have possibly been different." Yeah, like I thought I'd have lit him up in 1940.

I have met so many great baseball writers, especially the venerable ones who wrote so beautifully so many years ago. Shirley Povich of *The Washington Post* once told me that "Walter Johnson is the fastest pitcher I've ever seen, and that includes Nolan Ryan." When I asked Burt Hawkins of the *Washington Star* to name the greatest player he had ever seen, he said, "Buddy boy, I'll take Babe Ruth, and you can have the next three." Those writers had a style and a language all their own, including the wonderful Lou Hatter of the *Baltimore Sun*, who would occasionally write that a player who was thrown out at home plate "expired at the cash register."

Baseball writers don't need much to be happy, just a phone and a computer that works. In the old days, back in the 1980s, neither was a nightly guarantee. For several years, I used a computer called a Teleram Bubble, which was the size of a Samsonite and had the capacity for maybe five feature-length stories; that's it. It had couplers built into the top, and you'd stick the phone into the couplers to send your story. When the signal was too faint, you would have keep the phone pressed firmly into the couplers for the entire transmission. But you needed two hands to hold down two buttons simultaneously on the computer to send, so I briefly became adept at holding the phone in the couplers with my forehead.

Baseball writers are an unusual lot. There is Hall of Famer Tracy Ringolsby, who wears cowboy hats, does smokeless tobacco, and used to be a taxidermist. There is Randy Youngman, who, when connecting through his hometown of Chicago, would order a pizza from his favorite place, Gino's East, which would deliver to the terminal at a cost of roughly $100. There is Joe Goddard, who didn't use a reporter's notebook; he wrote on little slips of paper that he kept in his pocket. There is Bob Klapisch and Joe Sexton, who, when covering the Mets for competing papers, wrote each other's stories one night, in each other's distinctive style. There is Gene Collier, who went from baseball writer to columnist, but still kept track of multi-hit games by pitchers years after he got off the beat. And there is Jayson Stark, who has compiled more useless information than any baseball writer in America. For the last fifteen years, he has recorded every pitching line of every nonpitcher who has pitched in a major league game, and has interviewed almost every one of them.

"I have stuff rattling around in my brain that I can't get out," Stark said. "I can still remember Bob Forsch's pitching line from 1989: 7–18–10–10–0–3. And I still remember a writer saying to him, 'But at least no one walked,' and Forsch said, 'Why would anyone want to?'"

And then there's me. My day begins at 5:30 A.M. with the devouring of box scores and the completion of my day-by-day book. Every day, like Raymond Babbitt in the movie *Rain Man*, I write down, among other things, every score, with the winning pitcher of every game of the previous day, the pitching lines for most starting pitchers, 10-strikeout games, multi-home run games, four-strikeout games by hitters and 10-, 15-, and 20-run games by teams, which came in handy in 1999 when a team scored 20 runs in a game nine times: it happened five times in the decade of the 1960s. Every day, I cut out every box score and tape them in a binder, which are stacked in order at the top of my closet. I have done the same drill for the last seventeen years without missing one day, a streak that is longer than Cal Ripken's, and, I must say, is far more impressive. It is a labor of love; it takes forty-five minutes a day, not counting the daily drive to the gas station to buy the late edition of the paper for West Coast scores. My wife thinks I'm a complete idiot.

"I have not risen to the level of complete idiot," says Ray Ratto, columnist for the *San Francisco Chronicle,* and a former baseball writer. "My wife thinks I have a condition for which there is no medication. She shakes her head as if to say, 'I married a moron.'"

Ratto makes me look normal. He keeps most of what I keep, but he keeps the pitching line of every starting pitcher, every closer, and selected setup men. This takes him ninety minutes daily, but he does a similar book for the four major professional sports, college football, and college basketball. In April, when four sports are going, it takes him two and a half hours a day to complete.

Ratto has been reminded by his wife, as I have by mine, that he can get all this information off the Internet, and can get it quicker, but, like me, he says, "I remember it better when I write it down. Anyway, one guy in a crowded press box spills a Bailey's and rum on your computer, and you are hosed. Look, we're sportswriters. We spill often."

Ratto's obsession with completeness, neatness, and accuracy extends to the keeping score of a game, for which he uses six to eight different colored pens. When he writes out his lineup, blue is for right-handed hitters, red is for left-handed hitters, and green is for switch-hitters. Outs are written in black, hits are written in red, and walks are written in green. "When I have twenty minutes to write, I want to be able to look at my scorebook and know what I'm looking at," Ratto said. "This comes from twelve years of Catholic schooling, too many irons from Sister Mary of Discipline. No Protestants or Jews do this. I have been mocked everywhere I go, but one color just doesn't work for me. I've seen guys whose scorebooks look like they've held a Flair pen in their mouth and coughed. They seem to be able to make sense out of it, but I can't. That's just the way I am. Basically, you would need a tractor to pull a needle from my ass, that's how anal retentive I am."

But he's not changing. "Baseball writers especially aren't wired correctly," says Ratto. "We are not paid commensurate to the time that we put into the job. We have to talk every day to people that we don't like, we know they are lying to us, but we put what they say in the paper the next day, and the fun is to figure out when they're lying. People who do the beat for ten years deserve a medal for socialist labor. The demands are extraordinary. If you're in Cancún with your wife, and Barry Bonds robs a liquor store, you're filing from Cancún; drop the piña colada. It's a neurotic business, and it's not as much fun as it use to be. For some of us, like myself, bitching about things is aerobic exercise. But what we do, basically, we do just to stay out of the cubicle. And we all love it."

Nobody loves it more—no one has ever loved it more—than Peter Gammons. "I've never met anyone who loves anything as much as Peter loves baseball," said Bob Ryan, a former colleague of Gammons's at *The Boston Globe*. And that's why he's the best at what he does. Most people know him as a TV analyst on ESPN, but as Dan Shaughnessy wrote in *The Globe* when Gammons was inducted into the writer's wing of the Hall of Fame in 2005, "That's like knowing Joe DiMaggio as Mr. Coffee." Gammons was one of the greatest baseball beat writers of all time. No one wrote a better, more entertaining game story; he had everything from sliders-on-the-black to Latin phrases to politics to rock-and-roll references. He perfected, if not invented, the baseball notes column that ran every Sunday, a gossipy, humorous, inside look at the game that became required reading not only for every baseball writer in America, but for every baseball executive. The game has made some writers bitter, cynical, and disinterested after ten years. Gammons has done it for nearly forty years and still has the same joy and passion.

No one, in any business, works harder than Peter Gammons. He is on the phone constantly; his contacts and sources in the game are unmatched. He knows everyone; everyone knows him. He will routinely say, referring to some obscure minor-league player, something like, "Yeah, he painted my house at the Cape." Gammons has always been incredibly charitable with his time and with his information. When he covered the Red Sox in the mideighties, I was covering the Rangers. I knew my team was on the verge of making a trade; I could sense it, but I couldn't figure it out. I called Peter. "Oh, you guys are getting Cliff Johnson from Toronto," he said. Later that day, the trade was officially announced: The beat guy for the Red Sox knew more about my team than I did. That's Peter.

Gammons taught so many of us how to cover baseball. He taught Dan Shaughnessy, who mentored me at the *Washington Star* 1979–81. "What are you doing?!" Shaughnessy yelled at me as I drew my scoresheet by hand on a large, yellow legal pad before an Oriole game. He got me a scorebook, a little one, with enough pages to cover the entire season. A beat writer's scorebook is his most important possession; I know, I lost mine temporarily at Milwaukee's County Stadium in August 1989. I was literally headfirst in a Dumpster, tearing open bags of garbage, as if I had lost my wife's wedding ring. The writer who found it under a chair returned it before the start of the next night's game.

Few write better, or faster, than Shaughnessy, and no one is more fearless, which is why he is, in my mind, the best daily sports columnist in America. He can make you cry with what he writes, but mostly he can make you laugh, and he can make those he covers mad. He called former Red Sox Carl Everett, on first reference in *The Globe*, "Jurassic Carl" because Everett said he didn't believe in dinosaurs (or that men landed on the moon). He once wrote that Red Sox reliever Steve Crawford "was as useless as a bag of doorknobs," then swears that shortly after writing that, Crawford was seen at a Home Depot having just bought a bag of doorknobs. Shaughnessy used to call Red Sox reliever Tim Lollar "the anti-cigar" in print because when he came into the game, it meant that the Red Sox had lost, the opposite of former Celtic coach Red Auerbach's victory cigar. Shaughnessy once called to tell me, "You're not going to believe this, but Tim Lollar was a forestry major at Arkansas!"

"So?" I said.

"Don't you get it?" he said. "He's been setting fires all across the American League!"

"Did you write that?" I asked.

"Of course I did," he said.

At *Dallas Morning News* in 1981, I replaced their baseball writer, Randy Galloway, who was promoted to columnist. It was like following John Wooden. Galloway was a great reporter, a great runner, and a great drinker, a man who once told me, "Timmy, the key to life is vomit." He'd go out drinking with the manager or the players or both, learn what was going on inside the team, arise the next day and run ten miles, puke his guts out, then go to the park to explore what he had learned the night before.

"What is *that*?" Galloway asked me as I did my Rangers day-by-day book, in which I recorded the daily results of the hitters and pitchers. "Timmy," he said, "when I covered this team, some days, I didn't even keep score." The first story I broke at *Morning News* was the trade demand of star outfielder Al Oliver. Galloway did all the reporting; I got the byline. "There's nothing harder than covering baseball," he said. "It's like being in the jungle. Once you've covered baseball, you can do anything at the newspaper."

It is the hardest, but most rewarding, job I've ever had. No one except those on the team knows more about the team than the beat writers. They go wherever the team goes, which is what separates them, especially in the minds of the players, from, say, the local radio guys, who don't travel with the team and therefore can't possibly know what's going on when the team returns from a fourteen-day road trip. The 1989 Orioles were miraculously in first place late in August 1989, a season in which everyone, myself included, figured they would finish last and lose a hundred games, as they had the year before. The team was in Cleveland late in the season when a local radio guy told me he had picked the Orioles to win the division.

"Really?" I said, not believing him. "How could you have picked them?"

"I've followed them for a long time, I know them, I just had a feeling," he said.

Then he paused and said, "I need to do some interviews now. Which one is Cal Ripken Jr.?"

The job is so hard, so time consuming, that most newspapers today put two guys on a beat because it's simply too much work for one. I did the beat alone for eight years, which was how it was done in the 1980s. For a 7:30 P.M. game, I usually arrived at the ballpark at 2:30 P.M. Reporters were allowed in the clubhouse at 3:30 P.M., and we'd stay there, or on the field, until about 6:30 P.M., during which we would gather material for our daily notes.

"Gammons ruined the business," Ratto said, laughing. "His Sunday notes columns were so good, writers had to write notes every day." Mark Hyman of the Baltimore *News American* used to say, "The two worst words in the English language were 'Oriole Notebook.'" I was with him that morning in the Seattle airport in 1986 when we found out that his newspaper had folded, and suddenly, he was out of a job. "That's all right," he said, dryly as always. "I didn't have a very good lead note for tomorrow anyway."

After your notes are filed by, say, the second inning, you start writing the game story, what we called "running." For morning papers, for which I worked for twelve years, running stories are due as soon as the game is over, which means you have to write during the entire game. But as so often happens in baseball, the story of the game changes in the tenth inning, and it has to be rewritten immediately. My story was ready to go at 12:15 A.M. for Game 6 of the 1986 World Series, but amazingly the Mets rallied, the ball went through Buckner's legs, and I had ten minutes to rewrite the biggest story I had ever covered. And it wasn't made easier when I was doused with beer by maniacal Mets fans as I sat typing hysterically in the auxiliary press box at Shea Stadium.

After you file for the first edition, you have to run down to the clubhouse, talk to the players and managers and the rest about what happened in the game, then run upstairs to the press box and write for the next edition, the home edition, the edition that is delivered to your doorstep at 5:30 A.M. Sometimes, you had thirty minutes to do all this, and if it still wasn't how you liked it, you'd rewrite for the final edition, which about ten people read. And you would do the same routine every night. One year in Texas, I did it for all 162 games, which is nothing: Sheldon Ocker of the *Akron Beacon Journal* covered all 162 Indians games for fifteen consecutive years.

If you don't try, or you don't know what you're doing, you will get your brains beat out by the other writers on the beat, as I did in 1982 covering the Rangers. I tried, and I understood the game, but I didn't understand the intricacies of the beat, and I didn't know the players well enough to develop a trust where they would tell me what the hell was going on with the team. For ten years on the beat, I'd wake up and read the competing papers, but I'd never read them in the company of anyone for fear that they would have something that I didn't have and, out of embarrassment or anger, I would hurl the paper across the room. I will never forget that terrible feeling in the pit of my stomach when I missed a big story. It is a feeling so horrible, it makes every beat guy make the extra call every night.

It makes for an interesting dynamic: competing hard with other guys on your beat, yet remaining friends. There have been fights between beat writers, and situations where two guys didn't speak to each other for years. I traveled on the Orioles beat for four years with Richard Justice of *The Washington Post,* who always will be my friend, but was a challenging companion at times. During a rain delay in Chicago, Justice, Ken Rosenthal of *The Evening Sun,* and I did a segment on the Orioles' flagship radio station, WBAL, to fill some time. Jack Wiers, the host of the show, first asked what stories we were working on. Justice said, "We're working on one about Tim here being gay."

Alarmed, I asked, "Are we on the air?"

"Yes," said Weirs, "we are."

Justice apologized the next day, but not before a caller had called in on another WBAL show and said, "Hey, Tim is a good writer; it doesn't matter what his sexual preference might be."

I spent more time with beat writers than with my wife in those ten years. The drive from Miami to Fort Myers on old Alligator Alley was endless, and led to indescribably stupid discussions, most of which were initiated by me. How many hits would you get in a hundred at-bats in the major leagues? (Zero.) Could you score a point if you played forty-eight minutes in an NBA game and your only goal was to score a point? (Yes.) How long would you last in a boxing match with Mike Tyson? (Ten seconds.) Who would win in a fight to the death, you or a killer Doberman? (Doberman.) We picked the greatest player for each number in baseball history; it took a good two hours to even come up with a candidate for number 38, which later became easier with the success of Curt Schilling. Then we expanded the argument to include the greatest player for each numbers for all sports. The fights over number 4—Lou Gehrig or Bobby Orr?—and number 9—Ted Williams or Gordie Howe?—were legendary.

As a young, single guy, traveling was an adventure. I would fly all over the country, go to ballparks that I'd never seen and stay in first-class hotels. It was a marvelous life, but after marriage, and especially after having children, the time away from home became very difficult, and the travel got even harder, or, as Alex Wolff, one of my basketball writer colleagues at *Sports Illustrated*, once said, "Traveling is a violation."

The $184 laundry bill I naively ran up in New York made it into many baseball notes columns that Sunday, under the heading, "Look what the idiot rookie writer from Texas did." So did the story many years later when Kent Baker, my colleague at the *Baltimore Sun*, left a note on my hotel room door one morning: "Tim, I'm writing the Dodgers for the early [edition] today . . . by the way, the rental car has been stolen."

During one of my trips to Cleveland, the Bond Court Hotel was hosting a convention for recovering drug addicts. I stood in the elevator next to a guy who looked right at me and screamed, "I love Reese's Peanut Butter Cups!" looked away, and didn't say another word. I checked in to that same hotel once after midnight and the lobby was empty except for one guy. He got on the elevator with me, didn't press a button, got off on my floor, and followed me directly to my room. I slammed the door in his face. Then he called my room.

"What do you want from me!" I screamed.

"Just a little company," he said.

A number of baseball writers took the same flight during the play-offs many years ago. It was, as always, a packed flight. Three of the largest baseball writers in America—their combined weight was close to a thousand pounds—were sitting in a row across the back of the plane. One of them, Marty Noble of *Newsday*, decided this arrangement wasn't going to work. So he made a trade. He found me—I weigh 140 pounds—sitting in another middle seat, in between two normal-sized people. One of the big guys traded seats with me and I sat between the two fat writers, greatly lessening the weight in that row.

The traveling was worth it as long as your story got in the paper, and it was acceptable to read, which wasn't always the case with stories that were written in ten minutes. Or if some editor changed a word or a phrase that made you scream. No really terrible edits happened to me, but a friend at the *Fort Worth Star-Telegram* once wrote that the Royals weren't going to trade pitcher Larry Gura "because he's a five-and-ten man," that is, the last five years with the same team, and ten years in the major leagues. His editor rewrote it to say the Royals weren't going to trade Larry Gura "because he is five feet ten."

Dealing with editors is easier than dealing with players. Thankfully, I have had very little trouble with them. Hall of Famer Eddie Murray, whom I covered in Baltimore, didn't speak to me (or others) for years because he didn't like something I had written. As I approached him, he would routinely wave me off and say, "Not today." He never yelled at me, but the Orioles' Rick Burleson, out of character, screamed at me for a solid three minutes in the clubhouse one night, in front of everyone, because he didn't like the way my newspaper had played my story in which he ripped into teammate Alan Wiggins. Reggie Jackson publicly humiliated me not once, but twice, for no apparent reason. "Look at this guy [me]," Jackson once said to a group of writers who were huddled around him. "He walks in in the middle of the crowd and asks that question. I've already answered it three times." Someday, I'll forgive him for that.

Despite the hard travel, the hard competition, the hard deadlines, and the hard players, the baseball beat is the most satisfying job I've had in journalism. To cover a team on an everyday basis is like writing a book, with every game and every player a chapter. And even if that team is really bad, as were many that I covered, you are a part of the story that unfolds, and often changes, every day. Every day, you are the readers' eyes and the ears, and every morning, they light up to see what you have written . . . at least so I thought.

"I haven't seen Tim Kurkjian in the paper lately," a caller to a Baltimore talk show once said.

"He went to *Sports Illustrated* three years ago," the host said.

I spent eight of my proudest years at *SI*. When you write a bad story for a newspaper—and we all did—you can always make up for it the next day. It's like being a baseball player; there's always another game tomorrow. At *SI*, I became a football player, who wrote once a week, meaning there were no excuses about strict deadlines. You write a bad story there—and I know I did—and the editors would take one look at it and say, sometimes, aloud, "You had a week to do this, and *this* is the best you could do?" (The pressure is even worse at *ESPN The Magazine*, which publishes every two weeks.)

SI is an amazing place, one that strives for excellence, and almost always achieves it. Still, there were moments that made me wonder how it ever got into print. One of the baseball editors at *SI* went to the 1990 World Series. The Reds' Billy Hatcher got hits in seven consecutive at-bats in that series. It was announced in the press box that Hatcher became the first player since Goose Goslin in 1925 to get seven consecutive hits in the World Series.

"I never knew Goose Gossage was that good of a hitter," the editor said.

"Yeah," one writer said, "that was the year he was the DH when he didn't pitch."

"Oh yeah," said the editor. "I remember that."

For four days, I reported a story for *SI* about the resurgent Red Sox, but when I was ready to write, I was told not to, there was no room for it. About twenty-four hours later, suddenly the editors needed the story, but there was no time for me to write, so they had me send my notes to the office and an editor would write it. So, dutifully, I did. As I walked through an airport four days later, I picked up *SI* on a newsstand and read the lead to the Red Sox story.

"Wow, this is really good," I thought. "Who wrote this?"

I looked at the byline and, alarmed, said, "*I* wrote this!"

Since I had done the reporting, I got the byline. Steve Wulf, a better writer than I'll ever be, wrote it. Imagine getting a byline for a story that you didn't even write.

No one writes better than *SI*'s Steve Rushin. He is the smartest and funniest person I've ever met. He is the only person I've ever known who I really believe is a genius. And he can really shoot a basketball. He came to *SI* in the late eighties partly because he wrote such a clever letter to Alex Wolff, our basketball writer, urging him to come to watch the three-on-three basketball tournament that Rushin ran. Wolff helped get Rushin a job at *SI* after graduation. For two years, he mostly checked facts; that is, he read stories such as mine and made sure everything was accurate. It's a thankless job, but it's what young guys and women do at *SI* until they get their chance to write. For two years, a senior editor didn't even know Rushin's name; he called him "Stretch" because he was tall.

Finally, they gave Stretch something to write, and it was brilliant. Another story. Brilliant. Then another. Brilliant. They took him off fact-checking and made him a staff writer. After a year or so, his stuff was so funny, so inventive, a staffer from the *David Letterman Show* called and asked if he was interested in writing for their show, and could he write a couple of scripts and a couple of

Top 10 lists. So, he did. And they were better. They wanted him to write more, but Rushin said no. Make an offer or leave me alone.

They left him alone. He became one of SI's baseball writers; his story on the 1991 World Series is one of the finest pieces I've ever read. Traveling with him in the postseason, as I did for three years, was hilarious and educational. As we sat next to each other in the press box in Atlanta for Game 7 of the National League Championship Series in which Francisco Cabrera hit the two-run single with two out in the ninth, turning a loss into a miracle win, Rushin looked at me ten seconds after it had happened, as Atlanta Fulton County Stadium exploded around us, and said, "*Abra Cabrera*." I could have thought about that for ten years and not come up with that line. He had it in ten seconds.

Rushin moved on to other things; mostly he writes amazingly clever one-page columns in *SI*. Most baseball writers stayed put, mainly for the love of the game, for the people they meet, the things they see and the places they go. I am one of them, and I wouldn't have it any other way.

Only through baseball could I have met the aforementioned Pokey Reese, whose life story is why we cover the game. He was so poor as a teenager in South Carolina in the late eighties, he didn't have indoor plumbing. They had an outhouse in the backyard and a well for drinking water in his grandfather's yard next door. "We had Christmas," Reese said, "but we didn't have no Nikes." He lived on biscuits, and he got in trouble with his grandmother when he took her flour and used it to line the baseball field in the lot near his house.

I told that story that day at the White House to the two men who sat next to me at lunch, Brooks Robinson and Stan Musial, two of the greatest players and greatest gentlemen in baseball history.

At the urging of President Bush, Musial played "Take Me Out to the Ball Game" on the harmonica. It was a marvelous day, a day I experienced only because I cover baseball for a living. That day, it was OK to talk about Pokey Reese at the White House.

3

I'll Beat You Playing from My Knees

The tunnel that leads from the visitors' dugout to the clubhouse at the Metrodome in Minneapolis is long and steep—eleven steps, then a landing that's six feet deep, eleven steps, a landing, eleven steps, a landing, and eleven more steps. Oriole shortstop Cal Ripken would finish his pregame infield and sprint up the stairs. The idea, which only he would invent, was to get to the top in the fewest strides. Ripken could do it in six strides, which was positively Bob Beamonesque. But before one game, teammate Rene Gonzales made it in six. That was unacceptable to Ripken. He couldn't stand to not be the best, not even for one night, so he went back to the bottom, did it again, and made it in five.

Why? Why would a guy who was closing in on Lou Gehrig's record of 2,130 consecutive games feel the need to play such a stupid, childish, meaningless game forty-five minutes before the start of a major-league game? What if he turned an ankle as he lunged on that last flight? The tunnel game was about the love of competition, the common denominator shared by all the greatest players. They are exquisitely skilled, underrated athletically, durable, and prepared. They are driven by the fear of failure and embarrassment, but mostly, no matter the sport or game, they have to play it correctly, and they *have* to win.

"I've never seen anyone who wants to win more than Albert Pujols," said Cardinals manager Tony LaRussa of his first baseman, whose first six seasons might have been the best first six seasons by any player in history. "We play an intrasquad game in spring training—an intrasquad game!—and he's jumping off the bench yelling for a guy on his team to go from first to third on a single." On the final day of the 1987 season, a cold, rainy Sunday morning in New York, Yankee great Don Mattingly was taking batting practice alone at 9:15. It was an insignificant game, he was hitting .327, there was no batting title to be won that afternoon, and he would be going home that night for the off-season.

"I had a couple of bad swings yesterday," he said. "I couldn't go home swinging like that."

In the tenth inning of Game 7 of the 1991 World Series, Twins manager Tom Kelly went to the mound to take out his starter, Jack Morris. Kelly reconsidered after talking to Morris, seeing that look in his eye, that unmistakable look of a competitor, that look that all the great ones have had their whole lives. Morris got out of the inning, the Twins won the game, 1–0, and the World Series, in the bottom of the tenth. "There was no way Jack was coming out," said Twins teammate Randy Bush. "If TK had tried to take him out, Jack would have killed him right there on the mound."

Future Hall of Famer Greg Maddux was invited to dinner one night at Ruth's Chris SteakHouse by Hall of Fame pitcher Don Sutton, but Maddux gracefully declined, saying, "I've got a pizza that I didn't finish from last night, and I've got a video game that I can't beat, but tonight I'm going to beat that game." In the final season of Hall of Famer George Brett's career, he was asked what he would like his last at-bat to be like. Maybe a signature ringing double to right center, or a rocket single to left? Brett said, "No, I want to hit a hard ground ball to the second baseman, and run as hard as I can to first base so every young guy on our team will know that that's how the game is supposed to be played."

Hall of Famer Nolan Ryan's team, the Rangers, had lost eight in a row. He stood on the top step of the dugout before the top of the first inning, looked at his teammates, and said, "This stops *right now!*" then proceeded to throw a two-hit shutout with fifteen strike-outs. Braves pitcher Tim Hudson weighs 155 pounds, but you wouldn't want to mess with him. Late in 2000, with the A's in an important game against the Mariners, he gave up two runs in the top of the first inning. He came into the dugout and screamed, "Get me three runs because I'm not giving up any more fucking runs." He didn't. The A's won, 3–2.

That kind of competitive spirit exists in most baseball players, who, when challenged, never back down. Former Orioles center fielder Brady Anderson was in a restaurant in 1992, a year in which he was an MVP candidate for most of the summer. A guy proclaim-ing himself to be a former high school sprint champion in Pennsyl-vania approached Anderson and challenged him to a race, saying, among other things, "I'll blow your doors off." So Anderson went to the parking lot, took off his shirt, and, in the middle of a season in which he was bidding for MVP, raced the guy three times, and beat him each time.

That spirit lives within Derek Jeter every day of his life. "You can *hear* him run down the first-base line every time," said former Blue Jays manager Buck Martinez. "That's how hard he runs, and that's why he's the captain of the Yankees." Major-league players are proud guys with quick tempers and short memories—show them up, humiliate them, throw at them, cheap-shot them or a team-mate, and they will respond with an anger. If Terrell Owens did the baseball equivalent of disrespecting the star at the fifty-yard line at Texas Stadium, Roger Clemens would have hit him in the head with a 95-mph fastball. And the next time he faced him, he would have hit him again. So would Nolan Ryan. "He threw at me just for taking a big swing against him," said former Mariner Harold Reynolds. "I didn't even *hit* the ball, but he didn't think anyone as small as me, and as young as me, should be taking that big of a swing against him."

Vengeful? Short memory? Former reliever Ed Farmer gave up a home run one year to Wayne Gross, who, according to Farmer, disrespected him by taking far too long circling the bases. Farmer vowed to get Gross for that, but being a reliever in a different division, he didn't face Gross again until three years later, and this time they were teammates. So, in batting practice in spring training, Farmer hit Gross in the middle of the back with a pitch.

"What was that for?" Gross yelled.

"That was for three years ago," Farmer yelled.

"OK," Gross said.

The level of that competitive spirit, the daily need to win and to be great, is often what separates good players from Hall of Fame players. Early in center fielder Jim Edmonds's career, there was a question as to how interested he was in playing his best every night, "but on the *ESPN Sunday Night* game," said former teammate Tim Salmon, "no one was better than Jimmy." Jim Leyland quit as the manager of the Colorado Rockies in 1999 in small part because he had "the best player I've ever seen" on his team—Larry Walker—but he was never sure if Walker was going to play that way every day. Fred Lynn had Hall of Fame ability, but injuries cost him a spot in Cooperstown. He played hurt, and he was tougher than people think, but when I told him that he was better at 80 percent than most players are at 100 percent, he said, "I know, but so much has been expected of me my whole life. If I can't drive that ball on the inside corner because my wrist is killing me, or I can't get to the ball in right center because my hamstring is hurt, then I can't play."

Ripken always played. In twenty-five years of writing baseball, I have never met anyone as competitive as Ripken, not just in baseball, but everything. "I would tape his ankles, and he'd ask, 'Why are you doing it that way? Why don't you do it this way?'" Orioles trainer Richie Bancells said. "Finally I told him, 'Look, I don't know. This is how I was taught in trainer's school!' So he taught himself. Now he can tape his own ankles better than I can."

There were players far more talented than Ripken; former Angels manager Gene Mauch once said that Ripken had "the worst swing of any great player I've ever seen." But he became one of the three greatest shortstops of all time because he wanted to win more than anyone I've ever met. "He doesn't ever want to lose, even in these tiny games," ex-teammate Brady Anderson said. "He makes up games, like sockball [baseball played with a taped-up sock], in the hallway during rain delays. He's sweating his butt off, then goes out and gets two hits. We play indoor hockey. He's the best. At Anaheim Stadium, there's a stretch of grass, dirt, grass. After we do our stretching, he and I *always* have to long-jump over the dirt. It's at least fifteen feet. He makes it. I said to him once, 'How did you make that jump easier than I did?' He said, 'I always assumed I could jump farther than you.'"

Ripken said it was his goal to win the *Superstars* competition, which included athletes, and skills, of all major sports. It even had an obstacle course. Ripken never got a chance to compete because the *Superstars* was canceled, but he actually trained in the off-season to win it. "In spring training [with the Orioles], we had the twelve-minute run," Anderson said. "You don't have to try. But he tries. He comes to me before the race and plans out how we're going to run it. I won it, and he got mad at me. He said I went out too fast. I ruined him. I broke him down."

Ripken and Anderson were part of a team of Major League All-Stars who played a series of games in Japan one winter. They were exposed to a strange Japanese game that was played inside a cage, involved a ball and some sort of basket, kind of a cross between basketball, polo, and Rollerball. The Japanese had a team. Ripken formed his own team that included Anderson, Mike Piazza, and only one player familiar with the game, Japanese pitcher Hideo Nomo. "Cal devised a strategy to win the game; he planned the whole thing," Anderson said. "Then we went out and beat the Japanese at their own game."

Former Orioles manager Johnny Oates remembered a day in Kansas City in 1991, but it could have been any day in any town in any year. "Cal had gone two games without getting a hit, so he wanted to take extra hitting," Oates said. "He hasn't missed an infield or batting practice in ten years. So I tell him to come out for just the last fifteen minutes and hit. He said, 'No, I want to shag, too.' After a while, I look around, and he and Tim Hulett are climbing the outfield fence, seeing who can swat away Sam Horn's home runs in batting practice."

Oriole pitcher Mike Flanagan was there that day. He has seen Ripken do some amazing things, on and off the field, all in the name of competition, and for the need to excel in whatever he tried. "I was that way until I started playing professional ball," Flanagan said. "But pro ball is so demanding, I lost some of my desire in other sports. It didn't matter any more if I won in Ping-Pong. But it matters to him. Basketball is a perfect example."

I've played basketball many times with Ripken, which surely was a raging conflict of interest, I concede, but I learned more about him playing basketball with him than I ever did watching him play baseball. For two years in the mideighties—before he reached legendary status, before he had a spectacular gym built at his house—we played in the winter in a dingy little gym in Baltimore. There were no fans, there was no money to be made, and yet he played every game like it was his last. He dived for loose balls, he admonished teammates for dribbling with their heads down, and he was the best help defender ever. He is a foot taller than me and weighs a hundred pounds more than I do, but in pickup games with nothing on the line, and no one waiting to play the next game, he would harass me defensively all the way down the court until his offensive player arrived.

"Would you leave me alone," I once yelled at him. "Can't you stop trying for one second?"

"No!" he said.

On the eve of the start of the 1995 season, the year in which he broke Gehrig's record, the Orioles were in Kansas City, where former teammate Rick Sutcliffe lived. They went to Sut's house for a cookout. There was a basketball hoop in the driveway. "Did you shoot around?" I asked Ripken the next day. "We played two-on-two," he said. Did you dunk? "A couple of times," he said. Were you wearing basketball shoes? "I was wearing loafers," he said. On the night before the start of the season in which he would break one of the most prestigious records in baseball history, Ripken played two-on-two wearing loafers, because there was a hoop and there were players. Did his team win? "We crushed," he said.

Braves pitcher John Smoltz would have done the same thing. He could have played basketball at Michigan State, and he's the second-most competitive person I've met in baseball. Like Ripken, it doesn't matter what the game, the task, he has to do it better than anyone: He purchased a sleep chamber to maximize his sleep; he even had to sleep better than everyone else. "I used to play the accordion when I was a kid," Smoltz said. "I'd practice hours and hours and hours a day." How old were you? "I was four," he said.

Four! No four-year-old can do anything for hours at a time!

"Ninety percent of the time he's a four-year-old child who's had too much chocolate," former teammate Tom Glavine said. "John ran our football pools every Sunday. He'd hand them out to us and say, 'You have no chance.' He has to win every pool. I'd say, 'John, why do we get involved when we know you're going to win anyway? It's a donation.'"

A frantic Smoltz accosted me in the Marlins clubhouse one day. "I *need* for you to find something for me: I know I've walked more times than any active pitcher," he said. "Where can I find that? Can you find that?" Most walks by an active pitcher? Who cares? Smoltz cared. I made a call to the Elias Sports Bureau, which confirmed that Smoltz, by a wide margin, had the most walks among pitchers. "I *knew* it," he said.

Another victory for John Smoltz.

Then there is golf. Smoltz is a scratch player who once beat Annika Sörenstam head-to-head. "Nothing is impossible to him on the golf course," says Glavine. "If he has a terrible front nine, he'll want to bet you that he'll go three-under on the back." One summer, he played in a Braves tournament, which, of course, his team won. But there was enough daylight left for three more holes, so Smoltz ran through the pro shop looking for another game.

"I won twenty-five bucks from Smoltzy; it was one of the greatest days of my life," said Braves bullpen coach Ned Yost. But Yost is a lousy player, so how did he beat Smoltz? "Well, I had two other guys on my team—they were really good—and we were playing John three against one," Yost said. "He was taking all comers. We split the first two holes; we won the last. It was dark at the end. Smoltzy would never be on the team of three against one. Never."

And then there was the Christmas party at third baseman Chipper Jones's house. Jones has a hoop in the backyard, so Smoltz challenged anyone to a game of H-O-R-S-E. Again, Yost agreed to play. There they were, in street clothes, playing under the lights at 10:30 P.M. Yost, who is not a good basketball player, made a couple of lucky shots from the deck and another prayer from the street. "I had him beat," Yost said. "It would have been the greatest athletic feat of my career . . . then I went into full panic mode; he made some shots and beat me." Glavine said, "If Ned *had* won, John would have stayed all night until he won. John couldn't go home on that note. John is always looking for an area where he can excel. Then he loves to tell you that he's the best." Smoltz smiled. "I only brag about things that I'm no good at," he said. "I never brag about pitching."

But he does about Ping-Pong. Smoltz played a friend, also very competitive, in Ping-Pong.

Smoltz won.

"I bet I can beat you playing left-handed," Smoltz said.

Then he did.

"I bet I can beat you playing from my knees," Smoltz said.

Then he did.

"I am not afraid to fail," Smoltz said. "I've been humbled in this game. I've experienced humility. If you want to blame me, blame me. I like the pressure. I want the pressure on me. I'm not as good when there's a mismatch, not a David and Goliath thing, but when there's a big-time challenge, I'm ready for it. All these games I play with myself, and with others, allows me to raise my game. And God gave me a gift to be calm in those big situations."

Smoltz is calm in those situations partly because he has worked so hard to be ready. That is another common thread that binds the best players: They try harder than everyone else, they are in better condition than everyone else, and they are better prepared than everyone else.

In spring training 2003, on a Sunday morning, I left my hotel at 7:30, headed for the long drive to Orlando, Florida. As I drove through the parking lot, I saw two men throwing a football. One of the guys looked like Roger Clemens. It couldn't be him, I thought. What would he be doing up this early? What would he be doing throwing a football in the parking lot? I got closer. It *was* him. On a Sunday—the only morning in which Clemens's team, the Yankees, didn't have to be at the ballpark until 11:00 A.M.—Roger Clemens, age forty, was working with his personal trainer at 7:30 in the morning.

"I once checked out of the Grand Hyatt at 7:00 A.M.," former Orioles owner Edward Bennett Williams once told me. "As I was leaving, Roger Clemens was coming in. He had run the streets of New York. And he had pitched the night before . . . I guess that's why he is so great."

Clemens learned from his idol, Nolan Ryan. No one worked harder than Ryan. He was one of the first players, and maybe the first pitcher, to lift weights. He did exercises and routines to make him stronger and more flexible. He spent more time on an exercise bike than Lance Armstrong. After Ryan's record seventh no-hitter, which he threw at age forty-four, a large group of family and friends were waiting outside the clubhouse to congratulate him. He told them that he would be with them soon. Then he went in the clubhouse and rode the exercise bike for forty-five minutes, because that's what he did after every start, and it didn't matter that he had just thrown a no-hitter at age forty-four. For Ryan, the work was always a priority.

Future Hall of Famer Tony Gwynn was much the same. No one spent more time with his craft than him. He hit off a tee more than a PGA Tour player. He watched more film than Roger Ebert. He spent more time in the cage than a Gunther Gebel-Williams of Ringling Bros. circus. He studied, studied, and studied; he was prepared to the point where he could look into the glove of pitcher Shane Reynolds, see what grip he was using, and know a split-fingered fastball was coming.

"Can anyone else see that?" I asked.

"No," he said.

Mets reliever Billy Wagner grew up poor, and right-handed, in rural Virginia, but he broke his right arm so badly as a kid, he switched to left-handed. He became one of the best closers in the game, and the hardest closer to hit in baseball history. He developed his arm strength by throwing baseballs as far as he could across the field behind his house. He would throw, then walk or run the 300 or so feet, then throw it back. He did this for hours.

"You had a whole bag of balls?" I asked.

"No," he said. "I only had one ball."

I once arrived at Veterans Stadium, the old home of the Phillies, at 12:30 P.M for a 7:30 P.M. game. Then-Marlins leadoff hitter Juan Pierre was on the field, rolling a baseball down the first- and third-base lines. He had never played in the ballpark before, and, being a great bunter, he wanted to see how the lines played so he knew where to bunt a ball that night.

"It's 12:30," I said.

"I know," Pierre said, "I got here late today."

There has never been a more prepared player or harder worker than Ripken because he knew he didn't have Gwynn's hands or eye at the plate, he didn't have Ryan's robotic arm, he didn't have Pierre's speed. In the gymnasium at Ripken's house, he would invent games that made his training more fun, but also served to make him a better, more complete baseball player. He set up an oscillating tennis ball machine that shot out ground balls, rapid-fire, to his right, his left, up and back. It was his way to improve his range.

Ripken had total recall on games and situations. He always knew the count, the hitter, the pitcher, and the pitch. He knew, with a breaking ball coming, against a certain hitter, he had to be positioned more toward the hole. One year, he even called pitches for some of the Oriole pitchers while he was playing shortstop. He didn't keep a little black book; it was all in his head. He had a mental scouting report on every pitcher he ever faced, and every hitter.

One day in his gym, he played a game of one-on-one with his wife, Kelly. "Watch," he said gleefully, "she always fakes to her right, then turns to her left and shoots." And that's exactly what Kelly Ripken did. He even had a scouting report on his wife.

Kelly Ripken bought a trampoline for the gym. "Let's see what you can do," she said to her husband. Ripken abruptly declined, having never been on a trampoline, and, as usual, would never attempt anything without proper preparation for fear of being embarrassed, his greatest fear. "Show me a few things," Ripken said to his wife. She did. Two weeks later, Kelly entered the gym and her husband was doing jumps and backflips on the trampoline.

"You've been practicing in the middle of the night!" she said.

"No, I haven't," he said.

Kelly Ripken signed up the family dog for training classes. One night, Cal Jr. went with her to the class. She got sick during the lesson, leaving Ripken to be in charge of the incorrigible dog, which he was incapable of doing. He was unprepared; he was humiliated. Two weeks later, Ripken said that he would take the dog to the training class. This time Ripken was in charge, and the dog was trained.

"You've been training him in the middle of the night!" she said.

"No, I haven't," he said.

Besides being the most competitive and best prepared player I ever met, Ripken was also the most durable—another attribute shared by all the best players. His toughness came from his father, Cal Sr., a minor-league catcher who often caught in the bullpen without a mask, and once was hit in the face by a pitch and knocked unconscious. "When I was a kid, he would come home from playing soccer," Cal Jr. said. "He played midfield when he was in his fifties. He would have these huge blood blisters under his big toe. He'd take out a power drill, drill into the toe, the blood would come spurting out, and he'd go *ooooooooh*."

One night in Boston, Ripken Sr. was hit in the face with a line drive while throwing batting practice. Orioles trainer Richie Bancells raced to the mound, thinking Ripken was dead. "When I got there," Bancells, "Rip had gotten up and was screaming at me, 'What in the hell are you doing out here! I haven't finished my round!' Blood was spurting from his face. But he finished his round, went to the hospital, got stitched up, and was back on the field in the third inning."

Cal Ripken Jr. played in 2,632 consecutive games. Some say Bret Favre's record for consecutive starts in football (242) is far more impressive. I disagree. What Favre has done is remarkable, and commendable beyond words, but he played once a week, Ripken started at shortstop every night for fifteen years. And he never missed infield or batting practice.

"Guys are dragging, and he's in the back of the bus whooping it up," Flanagan said. "I've never seen him asleep in the corner." Said Orioles first baseman Randy Milligan, "I've never heard him say 'I'm not feeling good today.' I say that *every* day."

On Opening Day 1985, Ripken rolled his ankle on second base while making a double play. He played the rest of the game, but after the game, his ankle was severely swollen. The next day was a day off—if there had been a game, he says he would not have been able to play. His ankle was ringed black and blue, the kind that keeps normal people out for a month. He went to the hospital after the game. The doctor gave him crutches and told him to stay off the ankle for two weeks. Ripken threw the crutches away when he left the hospital, treated the ankle and, less than twenty-four hours later, played in a big-league game.

How did he do that?

"I taped it really tight," he said.

The Orioles used to play a game to determine which player could take the most pain, and which one was the hardest to bruise, a game invented by Ripken, who, of course, was also the champion. "Ten minutes before the start of a game," former Oriole pitcher Ben McDonald once said, "a couple of our guys jumped Rip and dug their knuckles in his ribs. We had him pinned down. He was yelling, 'No! No!' but he wouldn't give up. He would rather die than give up. The next day, I had a huge bruise on my ribs, and he had a tiny red spot." McDonald smiled and said, "I can't wait until the streak is over. A bunch of us are going to pummel him. But we still won't be able to hurt him. He will not bruise."

Most of the best players of all time were incredibly durable; they always go out there, even when they're not feeling well. Hall of Famer Don Sutton made thirty or more starts in twenty-one of his twenty-two full seasons. Warren Spahn was the most durable pitcher ever; he had almost as many complete games after he turned forty as Curt Schilling (one of today's workhorses) has in his career. Tom Glavine has never been on the disabled list in any of his nineteen big-league seasons. Fragility is something that has, at least so far, kept pitchers Mark Prior and Kerry Wood of the Cubs, and many other good players, from becoming superstar players.

Baseball players have a reputation for not playing hurt, a bad rap for a variety of reasons. Being the ultimate skill sport, a baseball player's body has to be working properly if he is going to be able to play well. An NFL lineman can be wrapped in more pads than a mummy, and he can still play because he doesn't have to use his hands in any dexterous way. In 2005, Redskins offensive tackle Jon Jansen played a game with two broken thumbs in casts, which was incredibly noble and courageous, but a baseball player can't play while wearing a cast on his hands. "If you can't get a feel for a ball, if you can't get the grip, if your fingers don't work, you can't pitch," said Hall of Fame pitcher Jim Palmer.

Baseball players are a lot tougher than people are led to believe. "I learned everything I needed to know about playing hurt when I was a young player," said the Astros' Craig Biggio, one of the game's most durable players. "We were playing a doubleheader in New York. In between games, Buddy Bell, who was in the last year of his career, was in the trainer's room with a needle stuck in his knee so he could go out and play the second game."

Bell was from the same era as Hall of Famer Robin Yount. He was the Brewers' shortstop as an eighteen-year-old, and retired as a Brewer after twenty seasons. No one played the game harder than him. "One day he was hurt so badly, he couldn't even walk," said Brewers reliever Dan Plesac. "I looked at the lineup card and Robin was in it. I saw him in the outfield during batting practice and asked him, 'Why are you playing today?' He said, 'Remember when you were in elementary school, and you said you were sick so you didn't have to go to school?' I said, 'Yeah, I did it all the time.' He said, 'Remember how much easier it was to do it the second time?' I said, 'Yeah.' He said, 'Well, don't do it the first time.' "

Yount also was a tremendously skilled and athletic player, with talent and gifts that the average person cannot comprehend. The great misconception about baseball is that it is an easy game to play, because it looks so easy on TV, and because most of us played it at some level. But if you were an ordinary high school baseball player, and you think you have something in common with a great major-league player, you have no idea what you're talking about. I learned that valuable lesson as a young writer. The best player I ever played with was a little shortstop named Tommy Smith. He was drafted our senior year (1974) at Walter Johnson High School on the thirty-fifth round by the Rangers, but to us, it was like being a number-one pick. He played one year in Rookie Ball, and was released. Eight years later, when I was covering the Rangers for *The Dallas Morning News*, I found the man who released Tommy Smith. It was Rich Donnelly, a Rangers coach, who was Smith's manager.

"How could you release him?" I said.

"He couldn't play," Donnelly said.

The best player I ever played with . . . couldn't play. I learned that every town in America has a Tommy Smith. If Tommy wasn't good enough to get to A ball, and if my oldest brother, Andy, a rocket-armed, left-handed-hitting catcher who broke all the home runs records at Catholic University, didn't even get drafted, how good must the major leaguers be?

They are sensationally talented. Greg Maddux is perhaps the greatest control pitcher in baseball history. He doesn't pick up a baseball from the day the season ends until January 1, then starts his preparation by playing catch with his brother, Mike, who is a pitching coach for the Brewers. After a few throws, Mike gets down in his catcher's stance and Greg hits the target every time even though he hasn't thrown a baseball in nearly two months. I covered a game in which Maddux threw twenty-seven consecutive strikes. "Greg never throws a ball straight to the plate. He has the greatest natural movement I've ever seen by a pitcher," said ex-Braves shortstop Walt Weiss, "but when he throws to the bases, no one throws a ball straighter than Greg. He throws to the bases better than any pitcher ever."

Roger Clemens throws so hard, it has to be seen up close to be believed, but even he didn't believe it until 1986, his third year in the major leagues. He started the All-Star game in Houston, and he had to bat, which he hadn't done basically since high school. Clemens was facing the great Dwight Gooden, whose first pitch was clocked at 98 mph.

Clemens looked at the umpire.

"Do I throw that hard?" he asked.

"Yes," said the umpire, "you do."

Clemens then knew how good he was. No one, he figured, could hit anything thrown that hard.

Giants shortstop Omar Vizquel has the greatest hands of any player I've ever seen. He developed them by throwing a rubber ball up against a wall and catching it barehanded as a kid in Venezuela. Seven years into his career, I went to his home in Seattle to do a story on his great hands. It was a rainy, cold January day, and he hadn't picked up a glove for nearly three months. I threw to him in his driveway so he could show me, among other things, the famous sleight-of-hand trick that he does: The ball does not appear to go into his glove, and in an instant, it is in his hand on his way back to me. He did this so quickly, I couldn't see it, so he slowed down the process: The ball hit the heel of his glove, then he deflected the ball into his hand, which was usually at least a foot away. Fifty throws, and not one ball entered the pocket of his glove, and not once did he drop or fumble any of the throws.

"How can you do that?" I asked.

"It's *magic*," he said.

I've seen Julio Franco, ageless wonder, take batting practice with a weighted batting donut on his bat, and hit line drive after line drive. How can he do that? "I have no idea," said manager Bobby Valentine. Magic? That was George Brett at the plate. Brett once badly sprained his ankle, which prevented him from playing in the Royals charity golf tournament. But he went anyway, and was playfully putting on the eighteenth green when a teammate in the group behind him hit a shot that was headed directly at Brett. He dropped his crutches and, using his putter as a baseball bat, hit the flying ball 150 yards back down the fairway.

"Remember," he said, "that was 1980. I hit .390 that year."

Tony Gwynn hit .394 in 1994. In 1998, he was in the World Series, playing the Yankees in New York. He was upset with his batting practice, which, as always, I thought was tremendous, another hitting clinic up close. He was thirty-eight years old and he was bitching and moaning.

"I can't see like I used to," he said.

"So, what are you, 20–20 now?" I asked.

"No," he said, "I'm 20–15, but I can't see like I used to."

Gwynn was a great basketball player at San Diego State; he

once held the school record for career assists. Baseball players, I believe, are the most well-rounded athletes in any major sport, and I don't mean that literally, as in the case of, say, David Wells and Cecil Fielder, both of whom could dunk a basketball despite their girth. Almost all major-league players excelled in two sports in high school, some played three sports, including Mariners first baseman Richie Sexson, who was, obviously, a great baseball player, but also was an all-state (Washington) wide receiver and averaged 27 points per game on the basketball team. Rangers outfielder Brad Wilkerson was all-state in Kentucky in *four* sports: football, baseball, basketball, and soccer. He was Mr. Baseball in the state, and runner-up Mr. Soccer. And his best sport before he got to high school might have been tennis.

I've picked the ten-man all-basketball team from current major-league players, and all ten played in college or in the NBA, led by Kenny Lofton, Mark Hendrickson, and Tony Clark, who scored 44 points a game in high school, and played at San Diego State. I've picked the all-football team from current major league players, and it's filled with players who were recruited to play big-time college football—such as Tampa Bay outfielder Carl Crawford, who was headed for Nebraska—or played big-time college football (former Tennessee quarterback Todd Helton) or in the NFL (Brian Jordan). Former Michigan quarterback Drew Henson played several years as a third baseman in the Yankees minor-league system before giving it up for football. Why didn't he make it? "He's got heavy legs," one scout said. "He's kind of slow, not that athletic." But athletic enough to play quarterback?

I have tremendous respect for athletes in other sports, especially basketball players, but I've seen Chris Webber and Patrick Ewing attempt to take batting practice, against a coach who was throwing 50 mph, and it was pathetic. I didn't see Tiger Woods take

BP, but a player who was there told me he had a tough time even getting the ball out of the cage.

Michael Jordan is the greatest athlete that I've ever seen, but ask him why he didn't make it in baseball—it was a miracle, a tribute to his competitive nature, that he did as well as he did—and he'll tell you it was partly because he wasn't as strong in his wrists and forearms as most of the players on his team, guys who weren't even close to being at his level as an athlete.

Cal Ripken is incredibly strong in his hands, wrists, and forearms. "I can lift more weight than he can," said Brady Anderson, who weighs 200 pounds, "but when he gets me in a bear hug, I can't get free." It's that strength, and the necessary skill sets, that made Ripken, and so many other baseball players, so great. That, and the tremendous love of competing, and winning.

"I wouldn't want to be his kid," Johnny Oates, a former manager, once said. "He might play checkers with his child, and Rip would get upset because he didn't crown him soon enough."

To that, Ripken smiled. "I split my head open playing checkers, I was six years old," he said. "I set up the girl next door with a six-jump move. She fell for it. I was so excited, I jumped up in the air and banged my head on the concrete windowsill and needed stitches."

Six jumps to victory. Just like the tunnel game at the Metrodome. Some things never change.

4

Phil Niekro's Teeth

Toronto pitcher Mike Flanagan was driving to Exhibition Stadium with former teammate Mike Boddicker in a Blue Jays rental car, with the Blue Jays insignia splattered all over it. New players to the team drove these rentals until their cars arrived. Flanagan spotted me as I was walking to the ballpark, lugging my computer and oversize bag of books. He gave me a ride.

"This was Phil Niekro's car," Flanagan said of the ancient pitcher, who had just been released.

"How do you know it was his car?" I asked.

"I found his *teeth* in the glove compartment," he said.

Baseball is a funny game. It is the funniest game; it always has been, even before the days of Jackie Price, the strange shortstop from the 1940s who could throw and catch a baseball while standing on his head (unlike NHL goalies, he really *could* make a stop standing on his head), and taught himself to hit a baseball while suspended upside down from a trapeze, bringing new meaning to the term "hanging curveball." Has the word "flake" ever been used of an athlete other than a baseball player? Mitch Williams was a flake. He said he pitched "like my hair was on fire," he wore number 99 in Philadelphia " because that's how fast I do everything in my life" and his nickname was "Wild Thing" for several reasons, mostly his legendary lack of control: I once saw him miss the batting cage with a pitch. "My brother Bruce was worse," Mitch told me, laughing. "We'd go out in the front yard to play catch in high school, and mothers would run out of their houses screaming, 'Everyone off the street, the Williams boys are playing catch!' "

Baseball is the funniest game because it presents so many opportunities for humor; it has props that other sports don't. It has walls to run into, mounds to run over, dugout toilets in which a player can get locked, and fans that are nearly in play: In what other sport could Larry Walker toss a baseball to a kid in the stands after making a catch, realize there were only two out, grab the ball back from the startled child, and throw it to the plate? There is ivy on the outfield fence at Wrigley Field; Michael Jordan never had to frantically search for a basketball in the ivy before taking a jump shot. There's a hill in play in center field at Houston's Minute Maid Park; Jerry Rice never had to climb a hill to make a catch. "I took a header on that hill a couple of times," said the Astros' Craig Biggio.

The funniest bloopers come from baseball. The clip of third baseman Lenny Randle on his stomach, *blowing* a bunt into foul territory, will live forever. As will the fly ball that hit right fielder Jose Canseco in the head and bounced over the fence for a home run. "The World Cup is coming to Dallas," said Rangers teammate Jeff Huson. "Jose was just practicing."

The funniest superstitions come from baseball. Wade Boggs ate chicken before every game. Pitcher Turk Wendell ate black licorice during every appearance, and often brushed his teeth after every inning so his teeth wouldn't stain. Former Twins pitcher Scott Erickson ate spaghetti before every start; he wore all black on days he pitched. Teammates knew not to talk to him on those days, and he sat alone in the corner of the dugout between innings. "We called it," teammate Kevin Tapani said, "the Day of Death."

The funniest promotions come from baseball. The minor-league St. Paul Saints had Two Dead Fat Guys Night, which commemorated the lives of Elvis Presley and Babe Ruth, who died on the same day, August 16. Every team plays a Throwback Game where players wear uniform styles from as much as a hundred years earlier. "The image was kind of ruined," said the Rangers' Huson, "when Jose [Canseco] drove into the parking lot in a Testarossa." A fan in Milwaukee won a free oil change performed by Brewers second baseman Jim Gantner, who owned a lube-service business. But the Orioles blew a great opportunity after acquiring pitcher Daniel Boone, a direct descendant of *the* Daniel Boone. "I suggested instead of Cap Night, we have Coonskin Cap Night," said Doug Melvin, then the Orioles' assistant general manager. "I was told to stay out of marketing."

They don't have Haircut Night in the NFL, but for several years in Seattle, they had Jay Buhner Buzz Cut Night, honoring the Mariners right fielder who was losing his hair, so he had it shaved off. One night, 426 people sat in a barber's chair at the Kingdome. "Hair was flying everywhere," Buhner said. "I should have collected some in case I need a weave someday."

They don't have cow-milking contests in the NHL, but Pirates Jay Bell and Stan Belinda, who grew up on a farm, engaged in one. "Jay lost by a quart," teammate Andy Van Slyke said. "It wouldn't have been that close except Jay was pumping skim milk and Stan was doing whole milk." They don't have bubble-gum blowing contests on the PGA Tour, but Indians pitchers Jesse Orosco, Steve Olin, and Kevin Wickander took part in one that was eventually won by Orosco, who jammed thirty-six-pieces of Bazooka bubble gum in his mouth and blew a bubble that Olin said "was only slightly smaller than a hot air balloon."

The Pirates' Mike LaValliere was a short, stout catcher nicknamed Spanky. In his catching gear, he looked like Leonardo, one of the Teenage Mutant Ninja Turtles of '90s fame. He was made an honorary Ninja Turtle in a pregame ceremony at Three Rivers Stadium. "Spanky loved it" said Pirates third-base coach Rich Donnelly said. "He got to the ballpark early and swam for two hours in the whirlpool, then ate a goldfish, just to get ready." LaValliere received an honorary plaque at the induction. "People send me stuff all the time," LaValliere said, laughing. "Some lady even sent me a picture of a real turtle."

Former Astros pitcher Jim Deshaies is from Massena, New York, hometown of Hal Smith, the actor who played Otis the Drunk on *The Andy Griffith Show*. In 1991 at the Astrodome, Deshaies was made an honorary citizen of Mayberry, Texas, by the local chapter of the Andy Griffith Show Fan Club. A Barney Fife look-alike was on hand, among other dignitaries. "I even got one of Aunt Bee's cookbooks," Deshaies said. "It was a special night."

The best postgame celebrations happen in baseball. When was the last time you saw an NBA player get hit in the face with a pie during a star-of-the-game interview? Giants manager Bruce Bochy has a size 8 head. He caught for three teams in his major-league career, and each time he joined a new one, he brought his helmet with him because it was the only one that fit. His new equipment manager would spray-paint it to match the new team's colors. "One night, Boch hit a walk-off home run," said former Padre catcher Terry Kennedy. "We ran a red carpet from the door of the clubhouse to his locker. In his locker, we put a six-pack of beer, with ice, *in his helmet.* You might be able to get a six-pack in some other guy's helmet, but only in Boch's could you put beer *and* ice."

The substitution system in baseball—once you are out of a game, you can't return—is unlike any other sport's, and has resulted in humorous situations, such as a first baseman catching for the first time in his life, a shortstop having to pitch, or a pitcher having to play second base. It would be very funny if seven-foot-seven center Yao Ming had to play point guard, but it would never happen, but five-foot-seven center fielder Doug Dascenzo pitched in a game. "I really was a short reliever," he said.

The absence of a clock in baseball can make for some long, funny games. On a Saturday night in June 1989, the Dodgers and Astros played twenty-two innings, a seven-hour, fourteen-minute marathon that ended at close to 3:00 A.M. Several Dodgers slept in the clubhouse that night because they had a day game Sunday. "It was so long," said the Dodgers' Mickey Hatcher, "I went on the fifteen-day disabled list before the game and was eligible to come off after it."

The weather is funnier in baseball. During rain delays, Orioles catcher Rick Dempsey, the son of vaudeville performers, would stuff a pillow under his jersey and do a pantomime of Babe Ruth hitting a home run, finishing with Dempsey's hilarious headfirst splash on the tarp into home plate. The wind blew so hard in Toronto one night, Rangers manager Doug Rader chose to start 250-pound Jim Bibby over scheduled starter Charlie Hough "because Charlie is old, he'll blow away, and Bibby is the largest man in North America." In the first inning, a fly ball to shallow left field wound up in the first base dugout for a foul ball, and the game was called off in the second inning. The wind whipped so violently one day at County Stadium, goofy Rangers center fielder Mickey Rivers said, "The wind was blowing sixty-three degrees today. I felt like the Lost Mohican out there."

The Lost Mohican?

The equipment is funnier in baseball. Ex-Brewer B. J. Surhoff confirmed that teammate Kevin Reimer broke twelve bats in one day: four in batting practice, four in the game, and four that he angrily snapped the handles off of after making each of his four outs.

In 2005, Dodgers pitcher Duaner Sanchez threw his glove at—and hit—a batted ball, resulting in a triple for Luis Terrero. When a baseball lodged in the webbing of pitcher Terry Mulholland's glove, he threw the glove to first baseman Bob Brenly for the out. "You blew it," teammate Mike Krukow told Brenly, "you should have whipped it around the infield."

The baseball has plugged in a catcher's mask. In 2006, a baseball separately found its way inside the jersey of the Reds' Ryan Freel and the Orioles' Ed Rogers. The same baseball has ended up in the uniform pocket of players, but there was no room in the pocket of former outfielder Rico Carty. "He carried his money and his wallet in his uniform pants during games," said former teammate Dusty Baker. "That's why he never slid because he had his wallet in his pants. When he rounded third, his coins would be jingling. He sounded like Santa Claus."

Even religion is funnier in baseball. One Sunday morning in the tiny home clubhouse at Fenway Park, the Red Sox were having chapel. An unfortunate writer accidentally leaned against the door and stumbled into the middle of the service. Red Sox right fielder Dwight Evans, infuriated, screamed, "Can't you see we're having fucking chapel in here!"

Baseball is the funniest game because it moves at such a deliberate pace, there is so much time to think about funny things, things that NBA players don't have time to think about as they fill the lane on the break, and NFL players don't have time to think about as they wait to field a punt. "My son, A.J., who is ten, wants to be an architect," Pirates outfielder Andy Van Slyke said, years ago. "I told him he has to be a baseball player because there's so much time to sit around and play cards." And as they play cards, the players often are surrounded by members of the media, whose access time in the clubhouse—nearly three hours before every game, and another two afterward—is so much greater than in other sports, and therefore offers more opportunities to talk to the players, meaning more chances for humor. In comedy terms, baseball players do four sets a night. Football players do maybe two.

In baseball, there is so much time to observe and absorb what's going on around you, especially for pitchers in the bullpen, and for starting pitchers, who have little to do in between starts except watch and wonder. As pitcher Dennis Lamp watched teammate outfielder Luis Polonia butcher another fly ball, he decided, "If you hit Polonia a hundred fly balls, you could make a movie out of it, *Catch-22*." As teammate Steve Stone was headed for a twenty-five-win season in 1980, Flanagan, a starting pitcher, developed the different stages of Cy. He was Cy Young because he was the reigning American League Cy Young winner. Jim Palmer, a three-time winner, was Cy Old. Stone was Cy Present. Storm Davis, who had great promise, was Cy Future. "After you get hurt and have to rehab your arm," Flanagan said, "you become Cy Bex. When you retire, you're Cy Onara."

Rene Gonzales didn't play much during the 1991 season in Toronto, so he stared a lot at the roof of the SkyDome and, bored out of his mind, devised a way to kill time: bunji jumping. "It would be a first-ball ceremony," he said. "I'd drop down, leave the ball on the mound, and bounce back up." Van Slyke, who played center field for over ten years, said there was even time between pitches to ponder the fate of the world. When asked about his team's 6–18 record at the Astrodome over a three-year period, he said, "When Bush and Gorbachev have their summit meeting, they should agree on a missile test—one missile each. We test ours wherever we want in Russia. But they have to test theirs at the Astrodome."

Ex-White Sox reliever Ken Patterson, a geophysics major from Baylor, spent a lot of time examining the dirt in the bullpen in the early innings. "I can pick up a rock and tell my teammates what kind it is, and no one cares," he said. "I can tell everyone how the earth looked before the continental drift, and they say, 'Man, what are you talking about?' "

Larry Andersen played all over the major and minor leagues, including one season in Reno. "Our clubhouse guy quit midway through the season, so, for an extra $10 a week, I was the clubhouse guy," he said. "I was a starting pitcher, I had time on my hands. But I'd be on the mound in the fourth inning wondering, 'Did I take the jocks out of the dryer?' "

Time on his hands? In 1991, Indians pitcher Rod Nichols didn't get in a game until May 5, a month into the season. Twice he was sent to Florida for extended spring training. "I thought I'd at least get frequent flier points," Nichols said. "But they sent me on different airlines."

Baseball is the funniest game because the season is so brutally long, the daily grind is so tiresome, and the game is so indescribably difficult to play, with failure a part of every day, if you don't have fun with it, if you don't giggle along with it at times, it will squash you like a cockroach, which, by the way, former Blue Jays catcher Mike Maksudian once ate, as well as a locust, a cricket, and a three-inch lizard, all in the name of laughs. "I've never been one to turn down a dare," Maksudian said. "I'll do just about anything short of suicide."

Red Sox reliever Rob Murphy had a rough eighth inning one night in 1990 in Seattle, so he shaved off his beard after the inning and returned in the ninth to record his first save of the season. "I went through four razors, but I came out a new man," he said. "I added a foot to my fastball." A bar in Seattle called Swannies had a promotion for most of one season: Every Tuesday from 7:00 P.M. to midnight, certain drinks would sell for whatever Mariners catcher Dave Valle's batting average was that day. For a good portion of the year, and the promotion, Valle was hitting around .150. "We would like him to raise that average a little," said the owner of Swannies.

Brady Anderson, who was going badly at the plate, was a passenger in a car driven by teammate Rene Gonzales, who was going dangerously fast in a rainstorm. "If I wasn't hitting .178," Anderson said, "I'd ask you to slow down."

Junior Ortiz, a backup catcher for several teams, had a son named J.J., which he said—I should have known—"stands for Junior Junior." Ortiz was a terrible hitter with an even worse stutter. When he extended his hitting streak to three games one season, he said, "Only fifty-eight more and I break Lou Gehrig's record." (With Junior, I was never sure if he was kidding.) In 1990, his Twins teammates gave him a T-shirt that read I Can't Hit, I Can't Throw, I Can't Run, What I Am Doing Here? And yet Junior was the catcher in Cleveland on a Sunday in 1991 when the Twins extended their winning streak to fourteen games. After the game, Ortiz gave the famous Lou Gehrig speech: *Today, I consider myself the luckiest man on the face of the earth,* stammering all the way through it. "If we had lost today," Ortiz said, "the guys would have beat the hell out of me. I was afraid I would jinx us. I thought *I* was the only way we could lose this game."

Dann Bilardello was a well-traveled backup catcher; Mets broadcaster Ralph Kiner, the king of the mangled name, once called him Don Bordello. Bilardello wasn't nearly as good as Junior Ortiz. "I want my stats taken off my baseball card; that's my goal," Bilardello said. At one point in 1990, the Pirates were 9–2 in games that Bilardello caught, but he was one for thirty in those starts, an oddity that he analyzed thusly: "When I start, the other guys know there are really only seven hitters in the lineup. So they concentrate more on getting a hit. I'm trying not to put too much pressure on myself, but I think I'm overcompensating. I'm putting too much pressure on myself to not put too much pressure on myself."

When Oriole first baseman Sam Horn struck out six times consecutively in a game in 1991—the first time in American League history that a nonpitcher had done that—I asked Flanagan for perspective. "Well," he said, "three strikeouts is a hat trick, four is a sombrero, five is a golden sombrero, and, from now on, six forever will be known as 'a Horn.'"

And seven would be?

"A Horn Aplenty," he said.

Angels pitcher Jim Slaton didn't win a game for several weeks, so his brother, Frank, decided that he wouldn't eat anything except soup until his brother won another game. Jim didn't even get into a game for nearly two weeks, during which Frank lost sixteen pounds. Frank wanted his father to join in the fast for Jim. Dad said, "I love my son, but I'm not crazy."

Crazy? The five-hour plane flights, two-week road trips, and endless string of hotels can make you crazy unless you laugh along with the monotony. The Pirates once took a fourteen-day trip to St. Louis, Chicago, St. Louis, San Francisco, San Diego, and Los Angeles. "Our next stop is Guam for two games," said Pirates third-base coach Rich Donnelly. "On this trip alone, I've spent $1,200 on tips to the bellman to take my luggage to my room."

Daily grind? Hank Greenwald was the radio play-by-play guy for the Yankees for several years in the late eighties. Every home game, he went to the same entrance at Yankee Stadium at the same time and had to show the same photo ID to the same security guard, who surely knew who Greenwald was after a while, but made him go through this insulting exercise every day. Finally, Greenwald had had enough. Greenwald, a white man, pasted a head shot of Giants outfielder Jeffrey Leonard, a black man with the nickname Penitentiary Face, over his face on his photo ID.

"Let me see your ID," the security guard said.

Greenwald did.

"OK, go ahead," he said.

The following day, Greenwald pasted a headshot of Secretariat—a horse—over his face on his photo.

"Let me see your ID," the security guard said.

Greenwald did.

"OK, go ahead," he said.

Baseball is the funniest game because it lends itself to so many funny game situations. None was better than minor-league outfielder Rodney McCray running through the wooden wall in right-center field in 1991 trying to make a catch. He suffered a bloody nose and some cuts on his forehead, but was able to finish the inning. "The first thing I thought of was 'Man, I just ran through the wall,'" McCray said. "Then I thought about the movie *The Natural*. The guy that ran through the wall and died. I'm not dead, though. I'm built pretty good. I've got three percent body fat and a really hard head. I stayed down for a minute behind the fence, but only because I fell in a mud puddle back there."

In 2004, the Triple-A Indianapolis Indians first baseman Jeff Liefer got locked inside a dugout bathroom, forcing a twenty-minute delay in the game against Louisville. The handle on the inside of the door didn't work, so maintenance workers opened a vent above the door and handed Liefer tools to unscrew the handle. When Liefer and the Indians ran back onto the field, a gift of toilet paper was waiting from the Louisville dugout. "They announced that an Indians player was being temporarily detained in the clubhouse, which can be interpreted in a million different ways, I suppose," said Liefer. "The place just erupted when I came back out on the field. Everyone knew what had happened. But I don't want to be remembered as the guy who got stuck in the bathroom."

It is always amusing when a nonpitcher pitches, which happens maybe three or four times a year. In 1989, Pirates five-foot-seven outfielder John Cangelosi was brought in to pitch in a blowout in

Los Angeles, another classic case of the short reliever. His catcher was six-foot-four first baseman Dave Hostetler, who had never caught in his life. "He looked like he was wearing the gear that a ten-year-old would wear," said Donnelly. "His shin guards didn't even cover his shins." The mound at Dodger Stadium is known for being really high and really steep. "When Cangy walked off the back of the mound to pick up the rosin bag," Donnelly said, "he disappeared from view. All you could see of him was the top of his cap."

That same year, a Brewers-Angels game began without a center fielder on the field. Angels center fielder Devon White was in the clubhouse making a phone call when Jim Gantner grounded out to second base on the first pitch of the game. But the play was replayed after White had finished his phone call and made it to his position. After the game, Angels right fielder Chili Davis was asked if he had noticed that there was no center fielder. "I yelled to the umpire," Davis said, "but not only are they blind, they're deaf, too."

The center fielders for the Giants and Mets—Willie McGee and Vince Coleman—shared a glove for a three-game series at Shea Stadium in 1992. "And it was a *blue* glove," said Giants catcher Terry Kennedy. "They should be beheaded." McGee's three gloves had been stolen from the visitors' clubhouse, so he borrowed from Coleman, a former teammate. They left the glove in center at the end of each half inning. They weren't decapitated by teammates, but "they were fined by their respective kangaroo courts," said Kennedy. "We fined Willie $2 an inning. The Mets fined Vince $5 for each catch Willie made."

In the early 1990s, a man locked his keys in his car, which was parked beyond Fenway Park's Green Monster in left field. He was frantically trying to find a way to open his locked car. He was giving up hope when the A's Mark McGwire hit a majestic home run that cleared the Monster and smashed a hole in the guy's windshield. He retrieved his keys and had the ball delivered to McGwire, complete with the story. McGwire autographed the ball.

The Pirates' Kirk Gibson was on first base one day in Chicago when Jay Bell singled behind him to right field. Gibson's helmet, as always, went flying off as he went tearing toward second base. The ball hit the helmet and ricocheted to second baseman Ryne Sandberg, but Gibson didn't see any of this, so he rounded second and took off for third. Sandberg threw to third baseman Chico Walker, who threw to shortstop Luis Salazar, who tagged out Gibson. After the game, Van Slyke said, "Score that putout 7¼ to 5 to 6."

In spring training 1982, Rangers pitcher Dan Boitano stood on the mound during a drill, pointed to the sky, and said, "I'm going to whirl around, throw, and hit that seagull," and then did precisely that. The gull fell thirty feet from the air and landed dead on the infield dirt. "That's what happens," pitcher Charlie Hough said, "when you don't wear a helmet."

Baseball is the funniest game because it has so many characters, including pitcher Kevin Appier. He is such a clean freak, and so neurotic, teammates with the Royals called him "Bob" after the Bill Murray character in the movie *What About Bob?* "We also called him Buffy because he would buff himself with his towel until he was red after a shower," said former teammate Brian McRae. "As he left the shower, we would throw a dirty towel behind him, and he'd go back in the shower and stay there for another forty-five minutes."

Characters? Charlie Hough was old, had a bad body, and threw a knuckleball. "Some things strike me as funny," he said. "*I'm* one of those things." When Rangers pitchers started throwing footballs before each game to strengthen their arms, I asked Hough if it was doing any good. "I don't know," he said, "but we lead the league in third-down conversions." Former outfielder Brady Anderson always struck me as funny also. I told him in 1989 that he had more extra-base hits than any leadoff man in the league, and he responded,

"I floss more than any leadoff man in the league." And, he swears, the first time he met O. J. Simpson (pre-murder, of course) on the running track at USC, he told him, "O.J., *loved you* in *Towering Inferno.*"

I covered Flanagan for five years in Baltimore, which means I laughed for five years. After Oriole pitcher Mike Boddicker threw a good game one night in Toronto, he told the press, "My fastball was clocked at 87." Flanagan walked by, said, "That's 82 Canadian," and kept on walking. In his career, Flanagan met several presidents, Canadian prime minister Brian Mulrooney, and the queen of England. "She left in the third inning; everyone else left in the fifth," Flanagan said of a terrible game that featured seven walks and three errors. "Maybe she was more accustomed to baseball than we know." On Opening Day 1991, when he returned to pitch at Memorial Stadium, Flanagan received three standing ovations. "I got a bigger hand than the Defense Secretary," he said, referring to Dick Cheney, who attended the game. "And he had a better spring than I did."

Larry Andersen was comedian Steven Wright with a slider. "Why," he wondered, "do we park in a driveway and drive on a parkway?" and "Why is there an expiration date on sour cream?" Andersen once said of Fernando Valenzuela, after yet another comeback in the early 1990s, "If he's only thirty-three, then I'm the president of the Hair Club for Men." Andersen was a terrible hitter, but one season, he miraculously got two hits in his first two at-bats. "If one for one is a 1.000 batting average, then at two for two, I should be hitting 2.000," he said. "That way, if I made an out, I'd only drop to 1.500." By September that year, he was still hitting .400 (two for five). "This [Houston] is a terrible baseball town," he said. "We've got a guy hitting .400 in September, and no one has written a word about it."

In the eight years I wrote for *Sports Illustrated*, the "They Said

It" feature of the magazine could have been called "Andy Van Slyke Said It." After a game in which the fans threw debris on the field, Van Slyke said, "Fans are mad at us because we make so much money, then they throw *money* at us—quarters, nickels. Why? Throw me a tax audit. Throw me your electric bill." One spring training, he told me, "I just got my W-4 tax forms, and I'm nervous. It should be called a W-4 million form." In the early '90s, Van Slyke played a word association game with Dan LeBetard of *The Miami Herald*. The first name LeBetard said was baseball commissioner Fay Vincent, who wore thick glasses and had a size-8 head. Van Slyke said, without hesitation, "Mr. Potato Head."

Today's players aren't as funny or as outrageous as they used to be partly because they make so much money and they're so famous, doing or saying something really funny no longer helps them, and it might hurt if it's taken the wrong way. The last of the great fun-loving teams was the 1993 Phillies with Mitch Williams, Andersen, John Kruk, Lenny Dykstra, and others. I miss the days when I would enter that clubhouse at 9:30 A.M., Williams would be walking around in his underwear, eating a burrito the size of a brick, and pitcher Curt Schilling would warn me, "Watch out, the animals are out of their cages today."

There is hope, however, with young players such as the Indians' Travis Hafner. His original nickname with the Indians was Shrek because he has such a big head, and kind of looks like the Disney Ogre. His nickname was changed to Pronk, which is a cross between Project and Donkey, "I was a project, and you call all big, clumsy guys like me 'Donkey,'" Hafner said. He looks like a pretty dumb guy, but he's actually one of the smartest players on the Indians. In Jamestown, North Dakota, he was valedictorian of his high school class.

"How many people were in your senior class?" I asked.

"Eight," said Hafner. "Four boys and four girls."

Eight?

"The only thing easier than finishing in the top ten," he said, "was getting a date for the senior prom."

Baseball is the funniest game because most of the players aren't as smart as Hafner, or aren't smart, period, or, to be kind, often say or do dumb things. Former first baseman Steve Balboni is one of the nicest, quietest people in the world, a marvelous guy, but apparently, he has a bad memory. He hit a grand slam one night. After the game, the press huddled around him. A writer incorrectly told him it was the first grand slam of his career.

"Yeah, your first grand slam is a big thing," Balboni said. "It's something I'll never forget."

"But Steve," said another writer, "you hit a grand slam last year."

"Oh yeah," Balboni said, "I forgot."

Balboni apparently was a bad speller, too. After retiring, he wanted to be a coach, so, in a letter to a general manager, he wrote, "I want to be a couch." He didn't get the job, coach or couch.

Scott Sanderson nearly threw a no-hitter for the Yankees. After the game, a writer asked Yankee catcher Matt Nokes if he had ever caught a no-hitter. "Jeez," he said, "I don't know." I don't know? Wouldn't a catcher remember the feeling of jumping into the pitcher's arms after the final out? Another writer, with a memory as bad as Nokes's, wondered if Nokes had caught Tiger Jack Morris's no-hitter during the first week of the 1984 season. Nokes was a former Tiger, but in 1984, he was a minor leaguer with the Giants.

"Yeah, I think I did," Nokes said.

I *think* I did?

Pat Zachry, a smart guy, got confused one night pitching for the Mets. They've been in existence since 1962, and no Met has thrown a no-hitter, but on April 10, 1982, at Wrigley Field, Zachry had one going with two outs in the eighth when it was broken up by

Bob Molinaro. After the game, he told Marty Noble of *Newsday* "you can't write this, but I'm kind of glad that it was broken up." Why? Noble asked. "Because I thought the eighth inning was the ninth inning." Zachry said. Which means, if he had gotten the last out of the eighth, he might have leapt into the arms of the catcher. How embarrassing would that have been? Many years later, when another Met nearly threw a no-hitter, Noble called Zachry for permission to write the story.

"It's okay to tell it now," he said.

Boston Globe columnist Dan Shaughnessy hammered Red Sox pitcher Bob Stanley in the newspaper after he lost a game in Texas in the mideighties. The next day, Stanley approached Shaughnessy in the clubhouse. He was really mad.

"My wife told me you called me an ape in the paper today," Stanley said.

"I killed you, Steamer, but I didn't call you an ape," Shaughnessy said. "I'll get the papers flown in and I'll take a look." The paper arrived, and Shaughnessy found the problem.

"You see, here in the third paragraph, I called you a buffoon." Shaughnessy showed Stanley. "And maybe your wife thought I called you a 'baboon.' But I just called you a buffoon."

"Oh, OK," Stanley said.

I promised never to reveal the name of the player who was told in the early 1990s that Major League Baseball might be moving a team to Washington, D.C. And the player said, "The league can't give Washington a team. It already has two teams, Baltimore and Seattle."

That guy wouldn't do well in the geography category on *Jeopardy*, but *Jeopardy* was on TV in the Charlotte Knights (AAA) clubhouse one September day in 1994. I was doing a story on the minor-league play-offs since there were no play-offs in major leagues due to the players' strike. I was watching the show out of the corner of my eye. The Final Jeopardy category was Poetry. Suddenly, a Knights' player ran out of the player's lounge screaming as he if had won the lottery.

"Did he get the Final Jeopardy answer in *Poetry?*" I asked, incredulous.

"Oh no, that's not how we play," said Tim Jones, a Knights infielder. "The way we play, if you guess the Final Jeopardy *category*, you win. Hey, we're baseball players."

And there have been few baseball players in history quite like Red Sox pitcher Dennis "Oil Can" Boyd, who had a language, and a thought process, all his own. A Red Sox game in Cleveland was postponed because of fog in the late 1980s, to which the Can said—I'm not making this up—"That's what happens when you build a ballpark on the ocean."

In spring training one year in Winter Haven, Florida, Oil Can rented several adult movies from a local video store. It was nearly time to break camp and head north when the Can was detained because he hadn't returned the movies. It became a story for the enterprising Boston writers, one of whom went to the video store to get the facts of the story, including verifying the specific titles of the porn movies. *Writer: Is* Debbie Does Dallas *on the list? Clerk: Yes sir, it is.* The problem was cleared up, the movies were returned, and Boyd was allowed to leave with the team, but not before Chuck Waslesski, a statistical guy who worked for the Red Sox, came up with the funniest line ever in a sport that always has provided the funniest of lines: He called it the Can Film Festival.

5

I'm Old, I'm Fat, I'm Bald, I'm Ugly, I Have a Plate in My Head

My relationship with major-league managers officially began on a spectacularly sunny day in Baltimore in April 1980. It was the day that I met Earl Weaver, one of the greatest managers in baseball history, a cross between John McGraw and Mickey Rooney. I was introduced by Dan Shaughnessy, our baseball writer at *The Washington Star*.

"Earl, this is Tim Kurkjian, he's going to be covering some games for us," Shaughnessy said.

"Fuck you, Tim," Earl said, and walked away.

I was twenty-four and ready to cry when Shaughnessy laughed and said, "Don't worry. That's just Earl." A few minutes later, Weaver returned. "Why do you want to do this with you life?" he asked. "It will kill you. Look at me." And then he sat for an hour with the writers, telling stories and talking about baseball. He was, all at once, brilliant, hilarious, charming, acerbic, rude, and crude, and, when it was over, I had learned so much about the game. I was hooked. I could have listened to him forever. Some days, it seemed like I did.

Managers are among my favorite people in baseball because

their love for the game runs so deep. Most of them played in the major leagues, but that wasn't enough; they needed more. Some look ridiculous in uniform, waddling to the mound to remove a pitcher—see seventy-four-year-old Jack McKeon of the 2005 Florida Marlins—but they can't take that uniform off because they've worn one for so long. I have met hundreds of major-league managers over the last twenty-five years, and even though they do the same job, they're all different.

There was the elegant Cito Gaston, and there was the aptly named Stump Merrill, who—I am not making this up—was seen flossing his teeth with his soiled sanitary socks after a workout.

There was Gene Mauch, who never undressed in front of anyone, and there is Lou Piniella, who, after a game in 2005, paced around his office, butt naked, while eating a piece of fried chicken and screaming about the umpires, who had missed a blatant balk.

There was Doug Rader, who read more books than most writers, and there was Joe Altobelli, who said he'd read one book in his life, *The Gordie Howe Story*, to which ex-Pirate Andy Van Slyke said, "Boy, I bet *that one* kept him up all night."

There is Eric Wedge, who is so committed to managing the Indians, he moved to Cleveland year-round, and goes into the Indians offices nearly every day in the winter. And there was Billy Hunter, who, after the season ended, would go home from Texas to Baltimore, and in the four months of the off-season, wouldn't chew tobacco and wouldn't swear.

There is Jim Tracy, who is so proper and so dignified, and there was Rader, who in April 1983 entered the lobby of the Boston Sheraton, where dozens of runners were stretching in preparation for the Boston Marathon. So Rader, dressed in street clothes, got down on the floor and, holding a draft beer in one hand and a lit cigarette in the other, at nine o'clock in the morning, began stretching among the marathoners. He would later insist that bowlers were better athletes than marathoners because bowling requires hand-eye coordination.

There is Charlie Manuel, whose wardrobe, body language, and diction scream unorganized, and there was Johnny Oates, who was as neat as a cat, the desk in his office was so meticulously laid out, "if you moved a pen two inches," said Doug Melvin, his general manager in Texas, "he would come into the room and say, 'Who moved my pen?'"

There are managers whose lineup cards are unreadable, and there is Jerry Narron, who writes out his lineup card in calligraphy so stylish, it looks like the menu at a pretentious French restaurant. He says he can write with that penmanship "in the same time it takes me to scribble," and he includes a special dot on the lowercase *i*'s for future Hall of Famers.

There is Joe Torre, whose arguments with umpires are rational discussions, and there is the great Weaver, whose apocalyptic rants were legendary. Weaver would turn his cap backward so the bill of his cap wouldn't hit the umpire when Weaver got nose to nose. When umpire Larry Barnett once entered an argument saying, "I'll take charge of this," Weaver said, "The last time you did, you fucked it up, and I ended up kicking a hole in my television."

There was blue-collar Cal Ripken Sr., who once shot a groundhog by lying in his tomato garden in camouflage fatigues, at 5:00 A.M., and who delayed his job interview with Orioles owner Edward Bennett Williams by one day "because I was painting the house on Tuesday." And there is Bobby Valentine, whose shirts have been dry-cleaned since he was sixteen.

There was Terry Bevington, who was so uptight his meetings with the press were like inquisitions, and there was the laid-back Roger Craig, who once relived the day that he threw out the first pitch to commemorate the twenty-fifth anniversary of the Mets, saying, "They should have had the bases loaded, because every time I pitched for them, that's what happened."

And there is Don Zimmer, who has worn a major-league uniform for over fifty years. His 1982 Rangers were in the midst of a thirteen-game losing streak when I staggered in to his office.

"What's wrong with you?" he asked.

I told him that I wasn't enjoying covering his horrible team, that the relentless losing was getting tiresome, and that my love for the game, however strong, was starting to wane. "Quit complaining," Zimmer snapped. "Look at you. You're young, you have your whole life ahead of you. Look at me. I'm old, I'm fat, I'm bald, I'm ugly, I have a plate in my head, and I have this team to manage. I'm the one with the worries."

It was then that I decided to shut up and write. It was that year—after watching what Zimmer endured, the disgraceful manner in which he was fired—that I realized how difficult a job it was to manage a major-league team, especially a bad one. During that thirteen-game losing streak, Zimmer was ordered to meet individually with all his players to discuss short-term goals, an insulting directive that came from a front office numbskull who said that marketing a baseball team was the same as marketing a tube of toothpaste. Zimmer had to ask his players how many hits they thought they'd get in their next twenty-five at-bats.

Outfielder Leon Roberts, who was hitting under .200, told Zimmer, "I think I'll get seventeen hits."

"That's a lot of hits," Zimmer said.

Zimmer was fired on a Monday morning, but was asked as a favor to Rangers owner Eddie Chiles to manage the team Monday, Tuesday, and Wednesday night because Chiles didn't have a replacement. Amazingly, Zimmer agreed. I didn't think he'd manage again, not after that latest indignity. He had been through it all in Boston, where some still refer to him as the Gerbil, and still think he's an idiot. He managed again, and after taking the Cubs to the play-offs in 1989, he was fired two years later. It didn't end well in

Chicago, as if it ends well anywhere. I asked Zimmer why he put himself through that torture again.

"I can't help it," he said. "I love it."

You have to love the game to be a major-league manager. It is a difficult, stressful job. It is not Wilford Brimley sitting on the bench, arms crossed, spitting tobacco and waiting for Roy Hobbs to arrive in *The Natural*. A manager's job is a lot harder than it appears, especially given the primary responsibility of manager today: keeping players happy and playing hard. "I have to put out a couple of fires here every day," Mike Hargrove said when managing the Albert Belle–Manny Ramirez–Kenny Lofton Indians in the '90s. Firefighter Terry Francona did the same for the 2004 Red Sox, led by Manny.

Stressful? I have known Tony LaRussa for twenty-five years, he has won over two thousand games, and he still answers my benign pregame greeting—How are you doing?—the same way every time: "I'll tell you in four hours." That is, I'll tell you after the game when I know if we won or lost. Former Orioles manager Johnny Oates, who was wound tighter than a juiced baseball, told me in 1994 that he was so burdened by managing, so afraid of being fired, that after being ejected from a game at Yankee Stadium, he sat alone in the dark tunnel that leads from the third-base dugout to the visitors clubhouse, bowed his head, and said, "Lord, I give up. Help me, *please.*" Hall of Fame manager Sparky Anderson is a gregarious guy on the outside, but, in season, he never filled his coffee cup more than halfway because it shook so when he picked it up. "This is twenty-five years of managing," he said. "Two weeks after the season, the shaking stops. When the season starts, it starts."

Astros owner Drayton McLane once gave his manager, Art Howe, motivational tapes of General Norman Schwarzkopf in hopes of rallying his team, which apparently didn't work, because Howe was fired at the end of the season. Unbowed, McLane told

Howe's replacement, Terry Collins, to watch the movie *Twelve O'Clock High* for a lesson in leadership. Collins appreciated the gesture, but told McLane, "Do you know what happens at the end of the movie? Gregory Peck cracks. He couldn't get in the plane."

"Are you going to crack?" McLane asked Collins.

"No," Collins said.

McLane, who is in the food-services industry, sent Collins with virtually no notice to Chicago one winter to give a motivation speech to 15,000 convenience store workers. "How was I supposed to motivate them?" Collins said. McLane's company was promoting a new chili that the convenience stores were going to carry to make chili dogs. "So there I was, *in my uniform*, talking to these people about chili," said Collins.

It didn't do him much good. Collins was fired two years later.

"If everyone in this country had to manage a major-league team, there would be no need for Social Security—the job takes ten to fifteen years off your life," said Rich Donnelly, a major-league coach for nearly twenty-five years. "I've seen it do some strange things to people. If you don't smoke, you will. If you don't drink, you will. And if you do drink, you'll stop." The pressure to win today is greater than ever; there's no time for rebuilding: win or you're fired. Owners think they know baseball, but they don't, yet some call their manager to discuss game strategy. General managers, some of whom didn't even play in high school, like to tell the manager how to manage. The media, which has become so large and so intrusive in the last twenty years, takes up so much of a manager's time and energy. And the players, with their money, fame, and sense of entitlement, think they're in charge.

"*Think* they're in charge? They *are* in charge," said former Nationals manager Frank Robinson.

It didn't used to be that way. Twenty-five years ago, the manager was the boss. When he spoke, players listened. And he wasn't interested in their feelings. He would blast a player publicly, or bench him, or, in the case of Billy Martin, pull Reggie Jackson off the field in the middle of an inning because he didn't hustle. That never happens today. In 1994, when young Padres manager Jim Riggleman yanked Phil Plantier off the field for not hustling on a fly ball, one of Riggleman's coaches told him, "You can't do that. The guys will quit on you." Can't do that? Isn't that what a manager is *supposed* to do?

Old-school guys such as Dick Williams, who managed from 1967 to 1989, "wouldn't even talk to the players," said Harold Reynolds, who played for Williams in Seattle. "I'd walk by him and say, 'Hey, Skip,' and he wouldn't say a word. He'd keep on walking. I'd go a month without talking to the manager." Ralph Houk, an ex-Marine, was nicknamed "the Major" because he was in charge, and everyone knew it. So was Bill Virdon, and Frank Robinson.

And Weaver. He tore into his players, but even when he did, he played them if they could help the Orioles win. When I told Weaver I was writing a story on third baseman Doug DeCinces, he said, "Great, Doug'll love you and the other twenty-four guys will hate you." When catcher Rick Dempsey went to the plate against Ferguson Jenkins, who he could not hit, Weaver once told him to "just go up there take three pitches" because he wouldn't look as stupid as when he swung and missed. Weaver once said that pinch hitter supreme Terry Crowley "would be working in a beer hall if not for me." Crowley nearly cried after reading that, and was certain that Weaver had been misquoted, but Earl looked at the story and said, "No, those are my quotes." (Weaver did apologize; he needed Crowley at his best.)

Pat Kelly, one of Weaver's outfielders, decided that he was going to join the ministry while he was still playing for the Orioles. It was a big decision in his life, so he went to Weaver.

"Earl," he said, "I'm going to walk with the Lord."

Earl said, "I'd rather you walk with the bases loaded."

A writer asked Weaver one too many times what the Orioles were going to do until star outfielder Al Bumbry came back from a major injury. "Stop asking," Weaver yelled. "As far as I'm concerned, Bumbry is dead! I only deal with the living!" To Weaver, the DL was the Dead List.

Frank Robinson is an old-school guy. In 1988, he took pitcher Jay Tibbs out of a game with an 0–2 count—Jose Canseco had hit two vicious line drives into the seats down the left-field line—the only time in twenty-five years of covering baseball that I've seen that. In 2005, Robinson hooked starting pitcher John Halama after only twenty-four pitches and one run allowed. That same year, when Nationals pitcher Toma Ohka turned his back on Robinson when he came to the mound to make a pitching change, a clear act of dishonor, Robinson ripped him to the writers, and, one week later, had him traded to the Brewers. In 1989, Robinson said he was concerned about the game-calling ability of backup catcher Bob Melvin.

"What's wrong with him?" I asked.

"His head is too small for the rest of his body," Robinson said.

"No, seriously," I said.

"I am serious," he said. "I worry about big guys who have small heads."

That strident style usually doesn't work today. Today, the most important part of managing is getting the players to play hard. You have to coddle some of them, pat them on the back, to get their best. You have to communicate constantly. Diamondbacks manager Bob Melvin, whose head is of normal size, no matter what Robinson said, does that well. So does Twins manager Ron Gardenhire. "We were all out one night, and my cell phone rang, so I rested my drink on the top of Gardy's head to free my hands," ex-Twins infielder Denny Hocking said. "Can you imagine doing that with TK?" TK is ex-Twins manager Tom Kelly, who won two World Series without coddling, and never having his head used as a coaster.

Tigers manager Jim Leyland, who has managed four teams, including the 1997 World Series Champion Florida Marlins, is a great communicator. "I was the twenty-fifth guy on the team; I was terrible," said ex-Pirate Dave Hostetler. "Every day, Jim would come up to me, and say something positive, anything, like 'good at-bat last night.' That made me feel good." Leyland's Tigers 2006 went to the World Series in part because of his tremendous relationship with his players. When rookie pitcher Zach Miner was called up to make his first major league start, Leyland told him "you better make sure that your family and friends get to the game early. We're playing the Red Sox. They're a really good hitting team. You might be out of there in the second inning." Miner laughed. Leyland had put him at ease.

That's how Bobby Cox works, which is one reason why, by any statistical measure, he is one of the five greatest managers of all time. Every day, he says hello to every player on his team, one reason why his players love him. He treats them like men. He never trashes them. He's intensely loyal to them, and respectful of them and their ability. "Look up 'player's manager' in the dictionary, and his smiling face is right there," says Braves third baseman Chipper Jones. "I've never heard any player say anything bad about him. He's the reason why players who leave here want to come back." Cox protects his players, as does Torre, who, like Cox, is going to the Hall of Fame as a manager. Playing in New York is difficult and draining. "You start getting ready to go to the ballpark at about noon for a night game," said former Met Mike Cameron. "By 7:30, with all you've done up until then, you're exhausted—and the game is about to start." Torre makes it easier playing in New York by deflecting unneeded attention from his players, by defusing difficult situations, especially the ones created by Yankee owner George Steinbrenner.

Managers today are always looking for ways to connect with players, and bring together the eclectic mix in a clubhouse that includes players of all nationalities and personalities. The Angels' Mike Scioscia, whose team won the 2002 World Series, had found a unique way to open the lines of communication. In spring training every year, Scioscia assigns tasks for his players, perhaps a book report, or the making of a map that displays the hometown of every player on the team. Pitcher Chris Bootcheck demonstrated how to make a golf club. The assignment must be presented in the clubhouse, in front of the team.

"It's nerve-wracking. You better do it well or Scioscia will get all over you," said former Angels shortstop David Eckstein. "When John Lackey and Frankie Rodriguez were called up late in the year, we said to ourselves, 'We know those guys.' When they got here, they felt they could talk to Tim Salmon and other veterans. . . . All Frankie had to do was stand up there and give the definition of a word that he had to research. That's too easy."

One spring, Angels pitcher Jarrod Washburn, and a couple of young players, were assigned to cover a local ostrich festival. For $150 and a couple of autographed balls, Washburn, the team prankster, convinced the workers at the festival to bring the ostrich to the Angels' clubhouse the next morning. "I told them, 'The team meeting is at 9:30 A.M., Make sure you're there,'" Washburn said. "At 9:30, in they walked with the ostrich. It was chaos. Guys were screaming with laughter." Scioscia was one of them. "[Pitcher] Ramon Ortiz jumped *in his locker*," he said. "He was holding on to the walls and yelling, in Spanish, 'Get that big chicken away from me!'" Washburn smiled and said, "It was hilarious. I don't think anything we ever do will ever top the ostrich."

First baseman Scott Spiezio did . . . in a way. "He was given the word 'erudite' to research," Scioscia said. "He got all mixed up and researched the wrong word. He researched 'hermaphrodite,' not 'erudite.' So he's up there talking about all this sexual stuff, and everyone in the room is laughing. From 'caveat' to 'hermaphrodite,' I've learned a lot of new words."

Scioscia is almost a master strategist, a managerial art that has changed significantly over the last ten to fifteen years. The game since the midnineties has been one mostly of power, not speed. Teams usually play for the big inning, not for one run. Bunting? The 2005 Rangers set the major-league record for fewest sacrifice bunts in a season (nine). The demise of little ball can mean fewer decisions for a manager, especially in the American League, and yet managers are more involved in the game than ever because of their insistence in stopping the opponent's running game: They call every pitchout, every pickoff throw, every slide step, and every step-off.

Baseball managers, perhaps more than the head coaches in any sport, are more open to being second-guessed because the game moves slowly; there's time to digest every decision, especially the bad ones. Some managers make moves because they are safe, and can't be questioned by the press, such as using his closer the same way almost every game. Some managers manage scared, to which Tom Kelly said, "If you're scared, get a dog."

No manager was more fearless than Davey Johnson, who didn't give a damn what anyone—his owner, his players, the press—thought about him or his strategy. He always knew he was right. In Game 1 and Game 4 of the 1997 Division Series against the Mariners, Johnson benched his three best left-handed hitters because the Orioles were facing Randy Johnson, a dominant left-hander. It was a huge risk, but the Orioles beat Johnson twice with Jerome Walton at first base instead of Rafael Palmeiro, who had 110 RBIs, 101 more than Walton. "Raffy told me he'd *like* to play, but said that Johnson could mess him up for a couple of weeks," Johnson said. "That's all I needed to hear."

Every manager has a slightly different philosophy on when to bunt, hit-and-run, pitch out, intentionally walk a hitter, etc. I saw Zimmer, who loved to go to the track, and managed with the same gambler's mentality, put on the hit-and-run *with the bases loaded* twice in 1982. In twenty-five years, I've never seen another manager do it even once. Former Astros manager Larry Dierker, once a terrific pitcher, said the manager, by intentionally walking a hitter, is telling his pitcher that, in most cases, he doesn't believe he's good enough to get the hitter out. So Dierker's team issued only seventeen intentional walks during the 1999 season; in 2001, Brewers manager Davey Lopes ordered 117 intentional walks. Buck Showalter, then the Diamondbacks' manager, walked Barry Bonds intentionally *with the bases loaded* in the ninth inning, cutting the lead to one run.

"I looked in for the sign the first time, then I looked again, then the third time, I realized what was going on, and I thought, 'You want me to do *what?*'" said Arizona reliever Gregg Olson. The next hitter, Brent Mayne, lined out to right field. Olson got the save.

In 2001, the Mets' Bobby Valentine tried twelve suicide squeeze bunts; another year, Lou Piniella didn't try one. In 2004, Dusty Baker pitched out fifty-six times, and Felipe Alou pitched out twice. In 2001, Jimy Williams pitched out 106 times and Dierker pitched out 12 times. To most people, there can't be anything in baseball more boring than a pitchout, but I once asked Showalter for his philosophy on pitchouts. An hour later, he was still talking, I had learned fifty things I didn't know, such as "If you're not willing to pitch out on 1–0, don't even bother on other counts."

Weaver's theories on strategy were brilliant, yet uncomplicated. He, like all managers, stressed pitching and defense, but he loved walks and three-run home runs, much like the principles that many managers work under today—only he had it pegged thirty-five years ago. Weaver was the manager who moved third baseman Cal Ripken to shortstop in 1982 because he knew he'd get 25 to 30 home runs from a defensive position. Less than week before the start of the 1978 season, looking for more offense, he moved from first base to third base and Doug DeCinces from third to second so he could get Lee May's bat in the lineup every day at first base.

It didn't work, but Weaver didn't want to give up outs, so, like many of today's managers, he used the stolen base judiciously—the risk of making an out, Weaver said, was far greater than the reward of advancing ninety feet, especially when the next guy up was capable of hitting a ball four hundred feet. Weaver rarely bunted, using the same theory: We only have twenty-seven outs, so why sacrifice one when the next guy might hit a homer? When the opposition looked to bunt, he'd tell his pitchers—sometimes, he'd yell—"They're giving us an out. Throw it over the plate!"

Some of Weaver's theories contrasted with those of another of the greatest managers ever, Gene Mauch, who loved the game more than anyone I've ever met. He was a utility infielder who played 304 major-league games, but once told me "I would have given up thirty years of my life to play a hundred games in Henry Aaron's body." No one knew the game better than Mauch, and he was willing to try anything to win, including once giving Larry Lintz, an infielder, not a pitcher, the take sign on 3–2. He was to little ball what Weaver was to power ball. When Mauch managed the Angels, he wasn't against bunting with his number-three hitter in the first inning. In 1986, Angels first baseman Wally Joyner, a middle-of-the-order guy, was one of two player to have 20 homers and 10 sacrifice bunts. The day after Mauch bunted in the first inning with his number-three hitter in Baltimore, Weaver looked at me and said, "I could lose my next 500 games and I'd still have a better record than that guy."

Weaver was always prepared, another key element in the art of managing. He was one of the first contemporary managers to platoon; he carried white index cards that included batter-pitcher matchups so he'd have the right guy for the right spot. In the eighth inning of Game 1 of the 1979 League Championship Series, the Angels brought in reliever John Montague. He had been acquired late in the season, so Weaver didn't have a white card on him. Weaver breathlessly called the press box looking for twenty-year-old intern Dr. Charles Steinberg, who was responsible for, among other things, the data for the white cards.

"I don't have Montague!" Earl yelled.

A panicked Steinberg worked quickly to look up the Montague numbers, then gave the white card to Earl's daughter, Kim, who was an Oriole BaseBell, a person who, among other duties, helped deliver things, such as soft drinks, during games. She had never delivered a key piece of information to her father during a game. So she rushed down from the press box, through the Oriole clubhouse where she'd never been allowed, past Jim Palmer, who was wearing only a towel, and into the dugout. Weaver saw it: The guy to use against Montague was John Lowenstein, who was three for four against him with two homers. When the spot came up, Lowenstein pinch-hit and belted a three-run homer to win the game.

Today, managers are provided every statistic they could possibly need and given elaborate scouting reports from advance scouts. Some managers carry laptop computers on the road to have updated data and to read the Internet, all in the name of being prepared. I've never met a better prepared manager than Showalter, who says, "When the game starts, I don't want any surprises." Before a series, for the benefit of his player, he will write on a blackboard a scouting report that is so precise, so detailed, it includes the counts on which opponents like to steal third. "Every manager does this," Showalter said. Orel Hershiser, his pitching coach, laughed and said, "*No* manager does this."

Showalter never misses a thing during a game. Neither does Valentine or Cox, and neither did Weaver or Mauch, who once showed me how to look at a box score, and, by some complicated formula involving at-bats, runners left on base, double plays, etc., I could tell who made the final out in the game, as if anyone really cared. Mauch cared. He cared about, and was intrigued by, every facet of the game. And then there was Maury Wills. When he managed the Mariners in 1980, he told local writers during that off-season, "None of you has mentioned the guy I believe will be our center fielder this year, Leon Roberts." A writer raised his hand and said, "Maury, you traded him to Texas two months ago."

It's not good when a writer tells you that your projected center fielder plays for another team, but it is good for a manger to get along with the press, especially given that the media is so much larger and more invasive than it was twenty-five years ago, before ESPN, before the Internet, before talk radio. The media used to be an annoyance, a gnat that managers would flick away, but now it has power and influence. Dealing with the media has become an enormous part of the manager's job—pre- and postgame radio shows, the daily ritual of answering questions from a mob of fifty (most managers meet with the press in some sterile conference room after every game, not in their office), and the task of being a front man for the organization who has to help promote the team. It is too big of a job for some managers. Ex-Expos manager Tom Runnels read so much in the daily papers about his team's inability to win a day game—the Expos lost their first ten day games in 1992—he held a team meeting to discuss the issue, after which he lost all credibility with the players.

Weaver handled the media better than anyone I've ever seen. He was so quotable, so funny, so irreverent, and, usually, so helpful. In the late '70s and early '80s, on a getaway night with strict deadlines and a plane to catch, he would give the beat writers "if quotes" before the game, so they would have them ready after the game. He'd say something like "If we win, I'll say, 'We won five out of six on this trip, that's a pretty good trip given the teams we played.' And if we lose, I'll say, 'Four out of six isn't bad, and now we're going home.' "

After games, Weaver was so quotable, the danger for me was depending on him to carry my story.

"Earl," I said after a game in 1986 in which rookie John Habyan, just up from Triple-A Rochester, walked the first four hitters of the game, "Habyan had a little trouble with his control?"

"Yeah," Earl said, screaming, "home plate in the minor leagues must be seventeen *feet* wide, not seventeen inches wide. And all the hitters down there must be eight fucking feet tall."

In spring training 1986, a young radio guy asked Weaver a spectacularly stupid first question. I had to leave the room; I couldn't bear to watch Weaver humiliate this kid, who deserved it. I came back five minutes later and Earl was holding the kid's tape recorder and microphone: Earl was being the interviewer and the interviewee: "First you ask me, 'So, Earl, how does your pitching look for this season?' and I'll say, 'Well, Bob, it looks really good.' Then you say, 'Earl, how does the offense look this year?' and I'll say, 'It looks great.' "

Weaver's replacement in 1987, Cal Ripken Sr., was not as quotable. He used the word "command" a lot. "I bet," Richard Justice of *The Washington Post*, said as we waited to enter the clubhouse after a game, "I can get him to say 'command' within five words." Justice's first question was "Schmidt had good command, didn't he, Rip?" Rip Sr. said, word for word, "He had good command. He had good command of his fastball, good command of his curveball, good command of his changeup, and good command."

Few commanded the media better than Sparky Anderson just by being the sociable Sparky. I spent several great afternoons in his office, but I wasn't there the day that Sparky was interviewed by one of my colleagues at *Sports Illustrated*, Steve Rushin. That day,

Sparky, unsolicited, did his impersonation of Leslie Nielsen as the umpire in the movie *The Naked Gun*, complete with the moonwalk and the yelling *Steeeeee-rike threeeee*. When Rushin asked Anderson about his Stengelesque mangling of the language, which was so comical and so charming, Sparky said, "Why do you have to know English? It's like two. There are three twos! There's tee-oh. There's tee-dubya-oh, and there's tee-double-oh. Three twos! Now, if I put any one of them down in a letter I wrote, you would know which one it is I am talking about. It's like 'there' and 'their'. What is the difference as long as you know there's a there there?"

If not for Frank Robinson's touch with the press, the 1988 Orioles would have been a nightmare to cover. They lost their first twenty-one games, demolishing the record for most losses at the start of a season. It was a dismal, horrible situation for him, the players, writers, everyone, yet Robinson's humor, competitiveness, and resounding presence carried all of us.

Consecutive loss number 19, six more than the previous longest losing streak in baseball history, came in Minnesota. Robinson, perhaps needing some support during such a horrendous time for him and the team, took the three Oriole beat writers out to dinner after the game. Halfway through the evening, I asked Robinson if anyone interesting had called to offer support, criticism, maybe a joke, whatever, during the historic losing streak.

"Yeah," he said, "the president called today."

"Of the United States?" I asked.

"Yes," he said.

Robinson was a big kidder. I pressed him several times on this, not believing him.

"Damn it!" he yelled. "The president of the United States called today."

"What? What did he say?" I asked.

"He said, 'Frank, I know what you're going through,'" Robinson said. "I said, 'Mr. President, you have *no idea* what I'm going through.'" The three beat guys ran to the pay phones in the restaurant and called in the story of President Reagan calling the Oriole manager.

In Doug Rader's first spring training as Rangers manager in 1983, Dave Smith, my sports editor at *Dallas Morning News*, came to visit. Smith wanted to set the ground rules for coverage, but no one told Doug Rader what to do, especially on his turf. I was asked by both men to sit in on the meeting. Rader was in his long underwear, no shirt, no shoes. Smith was wearing his new golf outfit, green pants, Izod shirt, Docksides. I didn't like the looks of this matchup, but it went surprisingly well until Rader said that, when the Rangers won the World Series, "We're going to give Tim a World Series ring." Smith, the most ethical newspaper man I ever met, a man who never allowed his writers to accept anything from any team they were covering, reacted badly to that, as the mischievous Rader knew he would.

"No, he won't get one!" Smith said.

"Yes, he will!" Rader said.

Back and forth they went, debating the ethics of whether a dinky sportswriter should be entitled to a World Series ring. Finally, Rader looked at the most decorated and respected sports editor in America, and said, "Eat me!" And I didn't know whether to laugh or to cry.

Rader is now out of baseball. The players have changed too much, they don't listen, they are in charge, and he couldn't take it anymore. Unfortunately, there probably won't be another one like him, or like Dick Williams or Earl Weaver or Sparky Anderson or Gene Mauch.

There is, however, hope with Ozzie Guillen, the manager of the 2005 World Champion White Sox. There is some Weaver in him, at least without the chain-smoking, the white index cards, and the

1,480 wins. But like Weaver, Guillen is in charge of his team, he is fearless, he makes the moves he wants to make, and he doesn't give a damn what anyone—his players, and especially the members of the press—thinks about it. He's honest. He blasts his own players, other team's players, and umpires, but doesn't care as long as he wins.

Guillen speaks quickly and at times incoherently; sometimes I can't understand a word he says. But I'm not complaining. I learned that lesson twenty-five years ago from Don Zimmer, who is now in his seventies; he's still fat, bald, and ugly, and still has a plate in his head. But at least his difficult, stressful days as a manager are over. And he still misses them terribly.

6

My Face Was Crushed by a Bowling Ball Going 90 MPH

A baseball is a wondrous little thing. It weighs six ounces, same as an apple, the perfect size and shape for the hand. It is the ideal home for the proudest autographs, so white and pristine, resting on the mantel or in the trophy case. A shiny new baseball is known as a "pearl," pearls are so elegant and romantic. It is what brings fathers and sons together in the backyard for a joyful, peaceful catch. It appears in springtime, like flowers and warm sunshine.

Yet when that pearl leaves Randy Johnson's hand or Albert Pujols's bat, and starts traveling at an unfathomable rate of speed . . . the romance ends and the primal fear begins. There is nothing in sports as terrifying and dangerous as a baseball flying at your head at 95 mph. You can hear it coming, the elegant pearl has become like a giant bee attacking. When it hits you, those red seams bore into your skin like the teeth of a buzz saw, leaving an imprint of the ball for days, even weeks. If it hits you in the face, God help you. One major leaguer has been killed by a baseball. The second could come at any time.

"Fear of the ball is real, dude," says former Cubs manager Dusty Baker, whether you're a Little Leaguer or "Big Papi," David Ortiz.

"The difference between life and death in this game can be an inch." Fear is why the seven-year-old child retreats to the safety of soccer the first time he's hit with a pitch or takes a ground ball off his lips. It is why the high school player decides to hit the books, not the ball, after he gets dusted a few times by someone throwing in the high eighties. It is why the Double-A kid flinches on the breaking ball, ending his career early. Fear of the ball is why base-ball is the hardest game in the world to play.

"It is there all the time, with every hitter," says former out-fielder Larry Parrish. "That was the whole idea behind Goose Gos-sage. It's why Ryne Duren took his glasses off when he pitched. It's why pitchers drop down sidearm. Anyone who says he has never been afraid up there . . . is lying." To say you're afraid is to say you're less of a man, and to show your fear is to invite a pitcher to throw at you because he knows you are intimidated. Don Zimmer, who has been in the game for more than fifty years, and was twice hit in the head so horrifically he is lucky to be alive, says, "I know guys who are retired who said they were scared every time they went to the plate. And some of them were big hitters."

White Sox announcer Ken Harrelson was a big hitter. "I played nine years with fear," he says. "Everyone has it. I can't remember a hundred at-bats when I didn't have fear. I almost quit my second year in the big leagues because I was so afraid. One day in Kansas City, Al Kaline, one of my idols, walked past me. He saw my fear. He said, 'We all have fear at the plate,' and kept on walking. That helped. In thirty-five years in baseball, I've known maybe five guys who were fearless. The only one who was totally fearless was . . . Tony Conigliaro."

Before or after his beaning?

"*Both*," Harrelson said. "He was never afraid."

Conigliaro is one of many major leaguers whose careers ended or were derailed because of the damage done by the ball, or the fear that followed. Yet for every Conigliaro, Dickie Thon, and Robby Thompson, there are players such as former Grants first baseman J. T. Snow, who was hit in the eye by a Randy Johnson fastball in March 1997, and not only recovered to have his best season, but gave up switch-hitting for other reasons, and now faces lefty Randy Johnson batting left-handed. "You don't want to be cruel, but if there's any way to keep a guy in the game after he gets hit in the head, you should do it," says former Twins manager Tom Kelly. "The longer you're out, the harder it is to come back."

Third baseman Charlie Hayes got hit flush in the face with a pitch, and played *the next day*. For the average non–baseball player, coming back is not an option. If Roger Clemens threw near my head, near your head, near the head of anyone who is not a baseball player, that person would never get back in the batter's box. "That is the fear of God," said former catcher Mike Macfarlane. "That sound you hear is the thumping of your heart." The fear of God? If you disagree, go to a batting cage and get in the box against a pitching machine that is shooting out baseballs over the center of the plate at 90 mph, an incomprehensible speed to those who haven't experienced it. Now, imagine it at 100 mph, and it might not be a strike, it might curve or drop or cut, or it might come at your face.

That is what a big-league hitter faces every night, and their ability to defeat fear is what separates them from everyone else. "Fear of the ball," says Yankees manager Joe Torre, who was badly beaned in 1968, "is the deep dark secret in baseball that players won't talk about. It is a crossroads for players. You can't have courage unless you're afraid. If you don't have fear, there's nothing to be brave about. Everyone fears that little white sports car."

Former Mets manager Bobby Valentine knows that fear. He was hit in the face so violently one night, his cheekbone was shoved dangerously close to his brain. "For all humanoids, those who breathe," Valentine said, "when someone throws a baseball from sixty feet, and throws it hard, the *first* thought is *always, always, always,* 'Do I duck or swing?' The difference is the time people take to decide whether to duck or to swing."

I'm ducking, and so are you. We all remember the fear when we faced that really big kid who threw really hard when we were ten years old. "Every town in America has a kid who was bigger than everyone, who threw harder than everyone, and who everyone feared," said Yankees pitcher Al Leiter. "In my town, *I* was that kid. And I had terrible control. I hit seven kids in one game. I could see the fear in the eyes of the hitters."

Fear of the ball doesn't just exist at the plate, there is a pitcher's fear on the mound, and an infielder's fear. I understand that fear, also. In 1982, I was invited by the trainer of the Rangers to shag during early batting practice at the Kingdome. I eventually wandered into the infield to see what it was like to stand even with third base, on AstroTurf, when Larry Parrish, one of the strongest right-handed hitters in the game, was at the plate. He hit a couple of balls past me at such indescribable speed, I had two thoughts: (*a*) if one of these missiles hit me, it might kill me, and (*b*) how could anyone catch anything traveling this fast? And yet that night, Rangers third baseman Buddy Bell caught a one-hop rocket off the bat of Jim Presley, a ball that would have sent the average nonplayer running for cover.

"Fear is the great equalizer," says Mariners manager Mike Hargrove. "If you're three feet tall and a hundred pounds, or if you're six feet ten and three hundred pounds, the fear of the ball is the same."

I don't even pretend to know what it's like to go across the middle in football and get crushed by Rod Woodson, but in football you know you're going to get hit, and you have protection. In baseball, all you have is your courage and a helmet, which a baseball will split in half when it's thrown hard enough. Ask any NFL player what would be scarier, returning a kickoff or trying to get out of the way of a 100-mph pitch at your face? I've asked a few, and they'll take the kickoff any day. Don't even ask NBA basketball players what's more frightening, standing in front of Shaq when he's taking it to the rack, or standing in the batter's box when a 100-mph fastball is coming at your head.

"What was the worst thing Michael Jordan could do to you?" says Jeff Huson, a former major-league infielder. "He can go dunk on you. So what? What's the worst thing Randy Johnson can do to you? *He can kill you.*"

A Hitter's Fear

Randy Johnson, the Yankees' six-foot-ten left-hander, is "everyone's ESPN-highlight nightmare," says J. T. Snow. And that day in Scottsdale, the Big Unit was really firing. A 97-mph fastball got away from him and sailed at Snow's face. Snow got his left wrist up in time, but the ball was deflected into his left eye. Had it hit him flush, he might be dead. Snow remembers lying in the dirt, blood gushing from his eye. "It felt like I'd been coldcocked, like in a fight," he said. "All I could hear was my wife screaming in the stands."

"It was one of the worst things I've ever seen," says Dusty Baker. "You know how a boa constrictor squeezes a mouse before he eats it? That's what J.T.'s eye looked like. It was that tight. If you had touched his eye, it would have popped out. I never thought he'd play again."

Snow was in the hospital for three days. "The first night was pretty scary," he said. "I was thinking, 'Will I ever play again? Will I ever see again?'" The eye was shut for two days, when it opened, he had double vision. By then, Snow thought, "I want to get on the field as soon as possible. I don't want this to linger." Within three weeks, he was playing in a minor-league game. His first at-bat after his accident—a big test—there was no fear, no cringing. "I didn't want to be labeled as a guy who couldn't come back from that," he says. "That pushed me." So did the actions of opposing pitchers. "When I got back, guys threw me up and in; they challenged me, to see what I got," Snow said. "I had to prove that I could stay in there, that I was not going to be intimidated, that I was not going to flinch."

Snow, the son of former Rams wide receiver Jack Snow, said being raised in a football household "really helped. You learn to play in pain, and you go back as soon as you can. Baseball players are tough-guy athletes, too. You're not going to stop me or slow me down."

There was no stopping Don Zimmer, either. In Columbus, Ohio, in 1952, he was hit in the head—no helmets back then; were they crazy?—by a Jim Kirk fastball that he never saw. When he awoke from a coma, his wife, Soot, and his parents were standing by his bed. His vision was so blurred, he saw three of each. "I thought it was the next day," Zimmer said. "But I'd been out for thirteen days." When he left the hospital after thirty-one days, he had lost 42 pounds (down to 128) and had four holes drilled in his skull. Soot had to hold his hand when he walked. On a good day, he could make it fifty yards. He almost didn't make it. Period.

"I was this close," he said, his index and middle finger were held a half inch apart.

He played the next year—and pitchers regularly threw at his head to test his courage. A hard game by hard men? They threw at a guy who almost got killed on the field a year earlier. In 1956, Zimmer was hit in the face again, this time purposely, he claimed, by Hal Jeffcoat, who never once called to check on him, he said. "My face caved in," Zimmer said. "They put a hundred needles in my face to get rid of the black blood." His retina was detached. He was blindfolded for six weeks. He had to feel for his food; many times, he stabbed his chin with his fork. His children weren't allowed to touch him; the slightest nudge could cause more damage to the eye. After six weeks, he was allowed to wear slate glasses, which had pinholes. "I was the happiest guy in the world," Zimmer said. "I could watch TV."

Zimmer came back and played the next year. He never changed his stance; he always stood on top of the plate. He played nineteen years in the major and minor leagues, and was never scared at the plate, but he says he was "lucky," not courageous. He is modest. He is wrong.

Kevin Seitzer is a modern Zimmer, only with fear. In 1989, Seitzer was hit in the helmet by a pitch from Jack Morris. It knocked him unconscious. "As I was lying on the ground, all I could think of was the movie *Ghost*," Seitzer said. "Remember, the guy is dead, he's out of his body looking at himself. I felt like I was out of my body, looking at myself laying at home plate. I was afraid to open my eyes because I thought I was dead. When I finally did, I saw Mike Stanley's shin guards. I knew I was alive."

Alive, but scared. Seitzer played the next day, but "for the rest of the season, I was petrified every at-bat. Every time the pitcher got the ball to here [release point], I saw his eyes and I thought, 'Is he going to get me?' My batting average went way down." That's the thing about fear and baseball: If you're afraid, and you're thinking safety first, and you're wondering if it's going to hit you, you're done, you'll never hit again. The next spring, Seitzer nearly quit. "I told myself, 'Get over the fear, or retire,'" he said. He got over it.

Get over it? I would have retired. And so would you.

In 1994, Seitzer was hit in the cheekbone by Melido Perez. Four bones in his face were broken, and he spent the night in the hospital. He wanted to play the next day—the next day!—but Brewers manager Phil Garner said no. The doctors warned him if he got hit in the same place, "My eyeball could drop into my cheek." Seitzer wasn't in the lineup the next day, either. "I went ballistic," he said. "I went to the trainer and screamed, 'Are you responsible for me not being in the lineup!' I played. In the on-deck circle before my first at-bat, I've never been so scared. But when I got to the plate, I felt bulletproof, invincible. I felt I could straddle the plate. I walked on four pitches. I was pissed. I really wanted to hit."

Seitzer wore a protective bar on his helmet the rest of the year. When the 1995 season began, he stopped wearing it "because I didn't want to be a wimp." Two months into that season, Minnesota's Scott Erickson hit him in the face again, this time half in the temple, half in the bone next to left left eye. "That one hurt 10,000 times more than the first one," Seitzer said. "It was like my face was crushed by a bowling ball, a bowling ball going 90 mph."

Miraculously, he played two days later—with a face mask, and without fear "because of my faith in God." More miraculously, he got eleven hits in his first nineteen at-bats after the beaning. He wore the mask to the plate every at-bat from the Erickson accident until he retired after the 1997 season. "The only people in the world who could give me a hard time about wearing it are the guys who were hit in the face twice—no one else," Seitzer said. "But for me to play eleven years in the big leagues, after what I went through, is a miracle."

One of the greatest at-bats I've ever seen came from Roberto Alomar in 1997. Roger Clemens threw the first pitch under his chin, flipping him. He threw the second pitch, another fastball, in the direction of Alomar's right ear. "I was lying on the ground thinking 'how did that miss me?'" Alomar said. "But you brush yourself off and you concentrate even more. The best way to get back at him is to get a hit." Alomar rifled the next pitch, down and away, off the right-field wall for a double. "That at-bat tells you that baseball isn't an easy game to play," Alomar said. "It is very, very dangerous game, but you can't be afraid."

John Valentin was . . . briefly. He was hit in the face by a Tim Belcher fastball in 1995, breaking a bone in his cheek. It was an unusually sunny Sunday afternoon at Fenway Park, and the ball came flying out of the white shirts in the center-field bleachers. Valentin never saw the ball. "When I came back, it helped that I never saw it," he said. "If I'd seen it, and not been able to get out of the way, then I wouldn't have trusted my reactions. I knew it was a fluke. I knew it wouldn't happen again." His next at-bat came two days later. "I've never been more scared in my life," he said. "But instead of moving farther from the plate, I moved closer. That's who I am. I knew if I moved farther away, I was done."

Pitchers are the same way. They intimidate. Their job is to get the hitter out by any means possible, and scaring the hell out of the hitter is an extremely effective way. That's what Bob Gibson and Don Drysdale did so well in the 1960s. When Nolan Ryan threw a 95-mph fastball under a hitter's chin, he called it a "bowtie." Stan Williams, a massive right-hander who pitched for several teams in the '60s, carried a list of names on the inside of his cap.

"What's that?" a teammate asked.

"Those are the hitters I have to get," Williams said. "I don't want to miss anyone."

Joe Torre was hit in the left cheekbone by Chuck Hartenstein in 1968. He broke his nose and cheekbone, and split his palate. He was out six weeks. He said he was afraid when he came back, but Torre got past his fear. "I'm a baseball player. That's all I know," he said. "You have to get over it or you'll be possessed by the thought. You want to play, but you learn how bad you want it. I didn't want to be bailing out every pitch. To me, the fear of failure, the fear of embarrassment, was greater than my fear of injury." That's the difference, that's what separates the best baseball players from everyone else in the world.

Boston's Dwight Evans was hit in the head twice in the early

'70s. He developed a fear of the ball and couldn't hit. He angrily fought that notion, but accepted it, changed his stance and improved his balance, making it easier to get out of the way of pitches at his head. He took martial arts to improve his mental discipline. He defeated fear, and had a great career. Astros second baseman Craig Biggio, who has been hit by a pitch more times than anyone in history, has fought fear by wearing an extralarge, extrathick helmet since getting hit in the head by St. Louis's John Costello in 1991. "I call it a football helmet," Biggio said. "Hey, I have a wife and children. I'd like to know them. There are some helmets you wear for protection; there are some to make you look good. If Randy Johnson hits you in the head, the helmet that makes you look good isn't going to do any good."

The big helmet may have saved Biggio when he was hit half in the face, half in the helmet, by the Cubs' Jeremi Gonzalez in 1997. "It felt like I got hit in the head with a hammer," he said. "My wife and our kids, and their class from school, were sitting upstairs in the luxury box. She was screaming *please get up!* That scared the daylights out of me. I thought, 'Another eighth of an inch, and I could be another Dickie Thon.'"

Dickie Thon, a star shortstop for the Astros in the early '80s, was hit in the head by Mike Torrez in 1984. Thon played nine more years, but he was never the same hitter. After the beaning, he was hit by a pitch once in his next 1,432 plate appearances. Near the end of his career, a reporter talked to Thon about his accident. When the reporter said the word "fear," Thon walked away and never finished the interview. "Dickie was scared," said Garner, a former teammate. "After a year, he got his courage back. But he couldn't see the ball."

Same with Conigliaro. He was hit in the right eye by Jack Hamilton in 1967 and missed the '68 season. He hit twenty homers in '69, thirty-six with 116 RBIs in '70. "Thirty-six homers with one eye," Harrelson said in amazement. "Every homer he hit was on a ball up in the zone because he couldn't see anything down in the zone." His vision worsened. He played ninety-five games the rest of his career. "Fear didn't get him," Harrelson said. "He couldn't see."

Conigliaro, Thon, Ellis Valentine, Al Cowens, Paul Blair, Doug Griffin, and dozens of others had their careers ended or curtailed by beanings. Kirby Puckett never played again after being hit in the face by Dennis Martinez near the end of the 1995 season. Puckett's vision in his left eye was blurred the following spring, forcing him to retire. Blair, hit by Ken Tatum in 1970, never overcame the fear, and it didn't help when Boston pitchers would walk by him in batting practice and say, "We're going to throw at you. You just don't know when." Blair tried switch-hitting late in his career because he couldn't stay in against right-handers. "One of the saddest things I've ever seen," said teammate Frank Robinson.

Giants second baseman Robby Thompson was hit in the face by Trevor Hoffman's 95-mph heater on September 24, 1993. His left cheekbone exploded, his eyes were blackened, his face was disfigured. Remarkably, he played eight days later, in the team's season finale, but clearly he wasn't ready physically or mentally. At the plate that day in Los Angeles, he flinched noticeably. Thompson had batted .312 with nineteen home runs that season, earning him a three-year contract with an option for a fourth year. But, says Baker, "he was never the same player." There was no one tougher than Robby Thompson, but in the spring of 1994, six months after the beaning, when he touched the cheekbone, it still hurt. He played a total of 193 games the next three seasons, and batted .217. He was done at age thirty-four.

Zimmer has seen it happen. Nothing, he says, was sadder than what happened to Lou Johnson.

"He was our second baseman in A ball, one of the toughest kids I'd ever met. He'd fight anyone," Zimmer said. "He got hit in the head, and fractured his skull. When he came back later that year, a pitch skimmed his chin. He never moved. He couldn't get out of the way. He dropped his bat at the plate, walked to the bench, and started *crying*. He said, 'I froze. I'm done.' That was it. He went home and never came back."

A Pitcher's Fear

April 4, 1994, was Mike Wilson's twenty-first birthday. He was supposed to throw five innings that day in spring training in Lakeland, Florida, but the first five went so well, his pitching coach asked if he could go the sixth to work on his changeup. "Sure," Wilson said. "What do I care?" That inning, Boo Thompson hit a changeup that was traveling 100 mph when it hit Wilson in the mouth. "I never saw the ball," Wilson said. The ball was moving with such force, it hit Wilson's mouth, then hit his glove, and still landed at home plate.

"I blacked out for ten seconds," Wilson said. "When I came to, I was lying on my back. Blood was pouring out of my mouth. It felt like there was nothing left in my mouth. It destroyed my upper bridge. It tore a hole into my nasal cavity. I put my hand to my mouth and two teeth fell into my hand. The third tooth that was knocked out landed at second base. Our second baseman brought it to me."

"Is this yours?" the second baseman asked.

Wilson was so bloody, his catcher ran off the field to vomit. Wilson walked off the field and went to the hospital in his blood-soaked uniform. His mouth and his teeth were mangled. "The oral surgeon looked at me and said, 'Oh mercy, I'm speechless,'" Wilson said. "I thought, 'Great, I can't talk, either.'" The nurse got ill looking at Wilson, and had to leave the room. "The pain was the worst I've ever felt," he said. "That night, I thought, 'Thank God, I'm alive. Two inches higher, I'm dead.' I've never seen anything in baseball as bad as what happened to me. Other players told me the same."

Wilson was in surgery for three hours ("I woke up during surgery; it was not a good day," he said). Ten days later, he was playing catch; another two weeks later, he was facing live hitters in a minor-league game. But he had lost so much strength after being hit, his velocity had dropped from 94 mph to 85. He was no longer able to throw his curveball, because he was not finishing his motion: When he was ready to release the ball, all he was concerned about was landing in proper fielding position, because, in proper fielding position, he might have been able to deflect that line drive.

Wilson's first game back, a line drive went five feet over his head. "I didn't realize it, but I was ducking," he said. "My coaches told me I was scared. I said, 'No I'm not.' I was flinching. I couldn't get over that. I had to see the tape to believe it. As I was going in to the pitch, I was not scared. But when the ball was hit back at me, or if I didn't see where the ball was hit, I'd get scared . . . you know, I've never said that before, but I was scared. Psychologically, I was scarred."

Wilson never regained his velocity or his curveball. In June 1996, he was released by the Tigers. "On one pitch," says Parrish, "he went from prospect to no chance." After this release, Wilson retired. His front seven teeth are fake. He keeps his two front teeth in a jar at home.

Why? I asked.

"I keep them to remind me how life can change in just a second," he said.

Another couple of teeth are lost somewhere on the field in Lakeland. Wilson never has nightmares about that accident. "But," he said "players from both teams told me that *they* have had nightmares about it. The funny thing is, I've had a recurring dream ever since I was eight years old. It's not about drowning or anything. My dream is always about getting hit in the teeth with a baseball . . . and then my worst nightmare came true."

Nightmare? Red Sox pitcher Bryce Florie was hit in the right eye by a line drive by Ryan Thompson of the Yankees on a Friday night in September 2001. He hasn't pitched in the big leagues since.

"It was like it was in slow motion, I saw the ball except for a split second," Florie said. "I was lying on the ground, blood was pouring out of my eye. I could hear myself screaming, but no one could hear me because there were 35,000 there that night. It felt like the right side of my face was on fire. And I couldn't see. When [trainer] Jimmy Rowe got out there, I asked him, 'Is my eye still there?' I knew it was bad, but I didn't know how bad it was because I couldn't see it. I've seen it on tape about twenty-five times. The first five times I saw it, I just cried. I couldn't believe that was me. I thought, 'Oh my God.'"

Florie was taken straight to the hospital. A doctor, using scissors, with Florie awake and watching, snipped off a part of his eye to relieve the pressure on the optic nerve. "There was a bucket next to me," Florie said. "It was full of blood. I had puked up a bucket full of blood." A week later, he had surgery. "They pushed my nose back over where it was supposed to be," he said. "They put plates in my cheek. I was out for a whole day. When I came to, I could see my mother, but I couldn't see all of her. I could see her forehead, but I couldn't see the middle of her torso. The rest was black. There was a pool of blood in my eye."

Soon after the surgery, Florie's vision was so bad, he tried to tie his shoes in the car and smashed his head on the dashboard. "I would try to drink from a straw," he said. "But I couldn't see well enough to put the straw in my mouth. It was sticking in my cheek, but I couldn't feel it because I had no feeling in my cheek." Two months after surgery, Florie tried throwing a tennis ball up against his house, something he did a million times as a kid, only this time, he missed it consistently. "My brother [Bryan, his twin] and I played catch in the yard," he said. "We bought some cheap balls at Sports Authority, balls that come in little bags. We had to keep the ball in the bag because the bag would slow down the ball. When my brother threw regular ball, I'd miss it, and it would roll down the street."

Less than five months after being hit in the eye, Florie was throwing off a mound. A month after that, he was in spring training with the Red Sox, throwing batting practice from behind a screen. "I was scared, I was nervous, I was as petrified as a man can be, but I was as happy as can be because I had made it back," he said. "I couldn't see the ball. Half of my brain was saying that I was doing the right thing, the other half was saying, 'You dumb ass, what are you doing out here?' When I'd finished my first BP, I went down the left-field line, sat on my ass, and cried like a baby. I had made it back. But when Manny [Ramirez] hit a line drive that hit the screen forehead high, that was when the Red Sox ended my comeback attempt. They didn't think I could get out of the way fast enough."

Two months later, Florie was pitching to a hitter on a back field in Fort Myers, Florida, this time without a screen. "I had a lot of problems, my vision in that eye was twenty-eighty, it used to be twenty-twenty," he said. "I saw the hitter, I saw the bat, but I threw every pitch real far inside or real far outside because I didn't want the hitter to hit the ball. I wanted him to swing and miss. And I didn't want it hit back up the middle. Since being hit, I've been hit twice, both times in the wrist. No big deal. But I flinched all the time. On a ground ball to the shortstop, when I was finished ducking and finished flinching, I was looking right at second base. Baseball players are cruel anyway, but they laughed at me. You can't pitch, especially in the big leagues, if you're going to flinch on every pitch. I had to get over that."

Florie says he has. He is thirty-five, and planning a comeback. Mentally, he says, "I'm still battling it. But I have convinced myself that no matter what happens, it can't be worse than what I went through. But I'm wearing Oakley glasses, just in case. No one could blame me for not going back out there. To get back to the big leagues would be a major accomplishment. If I did that, I might say, 'I did it,' and that would be it. But knowing me, that wouldn't be enough."

It's a miracle that a pitcher hasn't been killed by line drive, especially with the size and strength of today's hitters, and especially in college baseball where players use weapons known as aluminum bats. Herb Score's promising career essentially ended after he was hit by a line drive by Gil McDougal in 1957. Former pitcher Byron McLaughlin has a plate in his right cheek courtesy of a line drive hit by Harold Baines: It was traveling 108 mph when it hit him. Blue Jays reliever Dan Plesac was hit in the right thigh by a line drive by Shawon Dunston in spring training 1987. Remarkably, he finished the inning. "I went to the clubhouse," Plesac said. "There was a white spot from the ball. The next day, my leg was black down to my knee. It stayed black, with the white ball spot, until the All-Star break."

Former pitcher Wally Whitehurst often got hit on the mound, none harder than the shot he took in his right thigh off Kevin Mitchell's bat. I asked Whitehurst if he is still affected by that. "Absolutely," he said, extending his right arm. It was covered with goose bumps. He broke out in a sweat at the thought. This was *four years later*.

Reliever Norm Charlton, then a Phillie, was hit in the forehead by a 100-mph line drive by Steve Finley in 1995. Charlton was bleeding as he walked off the field, but was the first one in the clubhouse the next morning, prepared to pitch. (He didn't.) "I had two black eyes and a huge bump in my forehead, I looked like a unicorn," he said. "A couple days afterward, I had to go buy a TV. I looked so deformed, the salesgirl was afraid to wait on me. She had to leave. The store manager had to finish the sale." Charlton was traded to the Mariners that year. "The video guy there had a tape of that play, but he told me he didn't have it because I know he didn't want me to see it," he said. "I *wanted* to see it. I *enjoyed* seeing it because I knew I was ready to pitch the next day."

How can he explain not being afraid?

"Because," said Charlton. "I'm an idiot."

He's a baseball player.

And, Charlton said, "What are the odds of that happening again?" Less than four hours after saying that, the White Sox's Frank Thomas hit a line drive at Charlton. He got his glove up in time to slow it down, but it hit him between the eyes, breaking his nose. He walked off in a trail of blood, and asked trainer Richie Bancells, "How bad is it? I've got a date."

Pitcher Willie Blair, then with the Tigers, was hit in the jaw by Milwaukee's Julio Franco in 1997. "I heard the sound from the bullpen, and it was sickening," said catcher Brian Johnson. Detroit pitching coach Rick Adair said, "It sounded like a boat oar slapping a slab of meat. It was absolutely horrible. My first reaction: Willie is dead." Adair and manager Buddy Bell went to see Blair in the hospital that night. His jaw was wired shut. "The first thing he said was 'I'll be ready to throw Friday,'" Adair said. He was—five days after suffering a fractured jaw. He returned to the major leagues four weeks after being crushed, and went 13–6 the rest of the season, the best stretch of his career. He changed his delivery—he didn't fly open, he stayed more compact—when he returned, allowing him to land in better fielding position. The mechanical change improved his stuff.

"It was a freak thing. I got over it right away," Blair said. "I never thought about getting hit the next time out. I was anxious to get it out of my mind. After that, I still got hit three or four times. On my first start on rehab assignment, a guy hit one right over my head. The catcher came running out yelling, 'Are you OK, are you OK?' I laughed. I said 'I'm all right. Let's go.' In my first start back, [Jason] Giambi hit me in the right forearm. I fell right on my back. The next time out Matt Lawton hit me in the right wrist, then the stomach, but I got him out. I've been hit a lot of times, but none like when Franco hit me."

Blair laughed. "I never went to see a psychiatrist after that. I didn't want to get all screwed up."

An Infielder's Fear

Denny Hocking was playing second base for the Twins in spring training 1996 when monstrous Jose Canseco hit a rocket one-hopper right at him. "It hit five feet in front of me, I should have got out of the way," Hocking said. "That would have been the smarter, the better career-wise move. But I always play hard. . . . It was still stupid."

The ball hit him in the mouth, destroying it. "I was lying there, it seemed like it took a half an hour, for anyone to arrive," Hocking said. "I was kicking my feet like a fish out of water. I felt with my tongue, and my front two teeth seemed to pointing back toward my throat."

He spent two and a half hours in the dentist's chair. "I'm glad it hit me where it did," Hocking said. "If it had hit me in the temple, I'd be dead. If it had hit me in the eye, I would have lost my vision. If it had hit me in the nose, I might have brain damage. It hit me in a spot where there are specialists who can help."

Three days later, he was out taking ground balls. "Guys asked me, 'Are you stupid?'" Hocking said. "Hey, I'd been playing for fifteen years and I got hit once in the face. Maybe it will be another fifteen years before I get hit again." The first ground ball Hocking took after Canseco's smash took a bad hop and went straight at his face. "I adjusted, and made the play," he said. The first game he played, on rehab assignment two weeks after being hit, he wore a mouth guard, like a football player. "I used it one game and threw it away," he said.

Hocking laughed. "I couldn't chew gum for two years after being hit. Finally, I can chew again."

Torre says, "Everyone has fear of a ground ball, too. That's why you get this"—his head lifts up and his eyes close—"on some ground balls. The way you can really tell is when a player goes from Astro-Turf one day to a grass field the next. Ooooooh. That's when you really see the yips."

Astros manager Phil Garner says, "I flinched more on ground balls than I ever did at the plate. I got front teeth knocked out twice by ground balls. I remember having to fight myself to keep my face down." Parrish has a hiatal hernia from a ground ball that hit him in his chest in the late seventies; he still gets heartburn from certain foods because of that grounder. Parrish also was hit so hard by another one-hopper, it embedded in his leg; it just stuck there, defying gravity. He grabbed it and threw the runner out. "I had the commissioner's name imprinted on my thigh," he said. Former Cubs third baseman Ron Santo was hit in the stomach by a Frank Howard one-hopper in spring training. "Knocked me out cold. I woke up in the hospital," said Santo.

I asked ex-manager Jimy Williams if he was ever smoked by a ground ball in the minor leagues.

He took out false front teeth.

"I lost these during infield before a game," he said. "I played in the game that night."

Catcher Brent Mayne says he has no fear of the ball when he's behind the plate because he's comfortable there, and is covered with equipment. "In 1990, I played third base for a few games," he said. "We were playing the Tigers. They had Cecil Fielder, Rob Deer—big right-handed hitters. Now, I'm facing the other way. I have no equipment on, and I'm thinking, 'I'm going to die right here.' I was terrified." Not as terrified as the Tigers minor-league middle infielder who had to play third base in a game in 1997. A wicked one-hopper came at him, he *turned his back* on the ball and tried to run away. The ball hit him in the middle of the back. "That guy has a future as a scout," says Parrish.

Some players never get over being smashed by a ground ball. Former Mariners DH Edgar Martinez was a terrific defensive third baseman when he signed in the early eighties, but in 1988, a bad-hop grounder hit him in his face. He broke a bone below his eye, and has never looked down a grounder the same since. He played third since, never with the same skill.

"It affected me; it took me awhile to get over that," Martinez said. "If it's in your mind, it affects you. I had to talk myself over it. I did. But if I see a bad infield, it all comes back."

The fear always comes back in some form for an infielder, a hitter, or a pitcher. The key is dealing with it, getting past it. Most major leaguers can. We will monitor the progress of Cubs outfielder Adam Greenberg. In 2005, in his first major league at-bat, he was hit in the head by a pitch by the Marlins' Valerio de los Santos. He went on the disabled list soon after, and didn't return to the major leagues the rest of the season.

Greenberg will defeat any fear, as did J. T. Snow, Kevin Seitzer, and Don Zimmer, as did Denny Hocking and Bryce Florie. Seitzer now runs a batting cage in Kansas City. He teaches kids how to hit, but the first thing he does is teach kids the proper way to get out of the way of a pitch by throwing tennis balls at them. "Little League coaches tell kids that when a ball hits them, it doesn't hurt," said Seitzer. "You know what? It really does hurt."

Hurt? That elegant white pearl can kill you.

7

I Need It Now—Stat!

Todd Hundley hit a pinch-hit, extra-inning grand slam on a Friday night in May 1995. It was a rare feat, and, as always, I had to know how often it had happened, and the last time. I was headed to the right place the next morning: a convention in Dallas for SABR, the Society for American Baseball Research. It's like a *Star Trek* convention for baseball. I am a proud member of SABR, yet I respectfully acknowledge that these people are crazy.

"Who from SABR might know where I can find the all-time list of pinch-hit, extra-inning grand slams?" I asked the very first man I saw at the convention. The man smiled and—I am not making this up—pulled the list from his breast pocket. "I have it right here," he said.

That's where statistics belong, right here: in your breast pocket, in your head committed to memory like your phone number, in your home library, or in the *Lee Sinins Encyclopedia* in your laptop so you don't have to lug the eleven-pound *Total Baseball* with you on a road trip as I did, pathetically, many times. Statistics are, and always have been, an integral part of the game. Sometimes they are deceptive, they lie; sometimes they are overused; but when employed properly, they quantify the value of a player or team, they explain, they define, they settle and create great arguments, and they connect us to the past.

Statistics have more meaning in baseball than other sports. Most everyone knows that 3,000 and 500 and 300 are milestone numbers, and that 60, 73, 714, and 755 are significant home run barriers, if not the most recognizable numbers in all sports. Most everyone knows what a .300 average and a 2.00 ERA mean, roughly how long it has been since Ted Williams hit .400, and the approximate length of Joe DiMaggio's hitting streak.

In football, how many people can guess within 5,000 yards the career passing totals of the great Dan Marino? What is a good quarterback rating, and how do you calculate it? What is a huge number of tackles in a season by a middle linebacker? In basketball, what exactly is a steal, and how can it be considered an important number when they didn't even keep track of it until after Jerry West retired? He would have averaged, I'm told, seven a game. Precisely what is a turnover? And, really, how can blocked shots be an official category in NBA statistics, and yet they weren't even tracked until the careers of Bill Russell and Wilt Chamberlain were over? How many would they have averaged per game? Eight? That would be like not counting a pitcher's strikeout totals until the mid-1970s.

Statistics are so important, so revered, and so preserved in baseball because baseball is the only sport in which players and achievements from fifty years ago, if not a hundred years, are still applicable. That's because the game is played largely the same way it was played when Walter Johnson pitched, and why it's relevant to note that the Big Train had more 1–0 shutouts—38—in his career than Pedro Martinez and Curt Schilling combined have shutouts of any score (36).

The bases are the same distance as 160 years ago; the sixty feet six inches from the pitcher's rubber to home plate hasn't changed since 1893. Not much has changed in the game except that players are bigger and stronger, which would make a significant difference in a sport built on athleticism, but baseball is the ultimate skill sport. And the most skilled, and athletic, players from the early 1900s, such as the greatest shortstop of all time, Honus Wagner, would be great players today. Walter Johnson would be a dominant pitcher. I'm way in the minority on this. Steve Wulf, a great writer, great friend, and great editor, told me in 1993 that "John Olerud is better than Babe Ruth." I say if Ruth had today's advantages—weights, small ballparks, a really hard baseball, etc.—he might have hit 800 homers.

These discussions don't exist in other sports because football and basketball are more athletic than skill sports, and the bigger, stronger, faster guy is almost always going to win. Those games have changed so much more than baseball has. In the 1930s, NFL offensive tackles weighed 170 pounds; now they weigh twice that much. College football didn't use the forward pass as a significant weapon until Knute Rockne's epiphany in 1931. Today's NBA doesn't even resemble the game played in the 1950s when point guards were five feet nine, not six feet nine, and almost no one dunked; now, everyone but Steve Nash dunks. Former Celtic point guard Bob Cousy is one of the greatest players ever, and could have played in today's NBA, but he never shot 40 percent from the field in any season. A semireasonable version of Cousy today, John Stockton, shot over 50 percent for his career.

As the son of a doctor of mathematics whose numbers often had practical application to baseball, I've always been intrigued by baseball statistics. I have often wondered, Why have there been many .333 hitters in a season, but only two players in history have qualified for a batting title with a .334 average? How did Bob Gibson lose nine games in 1968 with a 1.12 ERA? Old Hoss Radbourn made 502 starts and completed 488 from 1881 to 1891, which is astonishing, but I want to know what happened in the fourteen starts he *didn't* complete? How could Herm Winningham play nearly fifteen years professionally and never get hit by a pitch? (As he explained to me, "Hey, I ain't letting that ball hit me. It hurts. The last time I was hit was in college, diving back into first base.") How did Norm Cash hit .361 with 132 RBIs in 1961, and not hit .300 or drive in 100 runs in any other season? How did Stan Musial finish with 3,630 hits—1,815 at home, and 1,815 on the road?

For the answers to these questions, and others, I call the Elias Sports Bureau, the official scorekeepers for the four major professional sports. There are few better feelings than finding an illuminating stat that no one has, but when the six thousand baseball books in my home office aren't enough, I call the Elias. I am proud to say I have called them more times over the last twenty-five years than any man alive; in fact, that would be a good Elias note: "In the last twenty-five years, Tim Kurkjian has called our office 3,451 times, 1,117 more than any baseball writer in America." And, thanks mostly to them, I have started more sentences with "It was the first time in baseball history" than any other baseball writer over the last twenty-five years.

The Elias operates in Manhattan out of a tiny office that barely holds the staff of roughly twenty-five. It has been run for the last fifty years by the irrepressible Seymour Siwoff, who says with a signature laugh, "It's nobody's business how old I am," but, sources say, he was born in 1920. For the last fifty years, he has worked seven days a week, twelve hours a day, and makes the drive every day from the far side of Queens to Midtown, which, in itself, is an Elias note. "The way I look at it," Siwoff said, "I have to go somewhere, so I go to the office."

Elias was in the baseball statistics business in the 1920s, but Siwoff began running the company "sometime in the fifties," he said. He was an accountant, and the Elias was about to fold, until Siwoff offered to run it. "In 1963, I was shaving, and a guy on the radio said

computers were the future, and I thought, 'I'd better do something,'"
he said. "Without the computer, there is no Elias. I remember when
we went to the computer I told my wife, 'They're reinventing the
wheel, I'll never survive this.' But somehow I persevered."

Siwoff went to the Elias "as a high school kid. I've always been
one of those people who saved everything. So we turned papers
into computer data. I wish I'd kept even more papers from the
twenties and thirties. We've done the NFL for forty-five years and
the NBA for thirty-five years, but baseball is my favorite. It's like
your kids, you love them all, but I love baseball the most because I
have loved it the longest. There's a certain romance to the game,
and I've always loved numbers. In 1960, I melded on-base percentage and slugging percentage into something I called a power-
efficiency rating, or PER. Now, we have this thing called OPS—I
did that in 1960! But I'm not like the MIT guys. I tell them, 'I'm
not in your class,' but they say, 'But you have wisdom.' I'm not immersed in numbers: they have to *mean* something. I like the games,
too. That's the difference."

The Elias is home to the Hirdt family, brothers Steve, Peter, and
Tom, and Steve's son, Ken. They are brilliant. As Steve says, "We're
the only family when our mother would scold us and say 'How many
times have I told you boys?' we could tell her how many times."

Steve Hirdt may look like an egghead stat guy, but he's anything but. He's the guy you call for statistics, but, more important,
for perspective on the way the game is being played these days. And
he will make you laugh. When only eleven triples were hit in Baltimore's Memorial Stadium in 1985, Steve wrote in the fabulous *Elias
Baseball Analyst* that it "was harder to hit a triple at Pimlico than at
Memorial Stadium." Steve went to see one of his sons pitch in a
high school baseball game, but arrived at the game with two outs
in the first inning, and his son's team was trailing, 1–0. After the
game, which his son's team won, 7–1, Steve asked his son on the

ride home, "So, how many strikeouts did you have?" His son said, "Six." "How many walks?" "Two," his son said. "How many hits did you give up?" Steve asked. His son said, "None."

"You pitched a no-hitter!" Steve said. "But you gave up a run, how could you pitch a no-hitter?"

The keeper of all stats had watched his son throw a no-hitter, and he didn't even realize it.

The great Randy Robles works at the Elias, also. As a kid in Canada, he had an obsession with numbers. "I'd go to an assembly in school, and I'd *have* to count how many empty seats were in the room, or maybe, how many people were in the room," he said. "It was a real problem. So I turned a negative into a positive. What plagued me as a kid became a strength." He got a college degree in mathematics, and a graduate degree in statistics, and wound up working for the Elias. It was Randy Robles who determined the probability (1 in 1,067) of Manny Ramirez hitting his first nine home runs of a season in nine different innings. He doubled-checked his thinking and his work over the phone with my father, Jeff, a Ph.D. in mathematics. And Jeff's youngest son reported this phenomenon on the air that night on *Baseball Tonight*. I couldn't have been more proud.

What they uncover at the Elias, in such a short time, is remarkable. When Paul O'Neill hit a first-inning home run at Yankee Stadium in 2001, and the Yankees won, 1–0, the Elias reported minutes after the game that it was only the second time the Yankees had ever won a home game, 1–0, on a first-inning home run; Babe Ruth, Mickey Mantle, and Roger Maris never did it, just Phil Rizzuto in 1941. Holy Cow! When the Red Sox won consecutive games in 2005 on walk-off home runs, the Elias told us it was the second time in club history that that had been done; the other time was 1935, and Wes Ferrell—a pitcher!—had hit the walk-off homer in each game, first as a pinch hitter, then as a pitcher. When Craig

Biggio moved from catcher to second base in 1992, he became the second player ever to play 100 games at second base and 100 games behind the plate in his career, joining Tom Daly, who played from 1887 to 1903, and Daly, who had a notoriously weak throwing arm, was known to make the long throw to first base underhanded!

When Brandon Duckworth won his first major-league game in 2001, Ken Hirdt slipped a note on my desk an hour before a *Baseball Tonight* show. It said: "Duckworth is the first player with the first name Brandon to win a major-league game." When Phil Bradley hit 26 homers in 1985, Elias reported that he was the first player in history to have twenty-plus homers following a 300 at-bat season in which he hit no home runs. When Yankee first baseman Cecil Fielder failed to make a 3–6–3 double play in Game 1 of the 1996 World Series, Elias told us that he hadn't made that DP in nearly two years. My favorite Elias note was about Bud Black, who was very close to being the Ultimate .500 Pitcher. So, in 1992, I tracked it every day, waiting and waiting for the day it happened. When it came that day in August, I flew to San Francisco to tell Black that his career record was 92-92 and the five teams for which he had played had a record of 796–796—the Ultimate .500 Pitcher.

"You came 1,500 miles to tell me *that*?" Black said, smiling. "Is this all you have to do with your life?"

But the boys at Elias don't deal solely in numbers, they're about perspective and context. In the 2005 National League Championship Series, the Cardinals had runners at first and third with none out, down by a run in the ninth inning. The runner at third, Albert Pujols, tried to score on a slow chopper to third and was thrown out at the plate. It was a baserunning mistake, no doubt, but how bad? One of the worst ever, or nothing unusual? Peter Hirdt of Elias researched that the last time in a postseason game that a runner had been thrown out at home in that situation—one run down, ninth inning, no outs—was the 1909 World Series, some guy named

Bill Abstein of the Pirates. And it was only the second time in Tony LaRussa's storied career as a manager—over 4,000 games, regular and postseason—that one of his players had been thrown out at the plate in a situation like that.

"Where did you get *that*?" LaRussa asked.

"The Elias Sports Bureau," I said.

"What was the other time?" LaRussa asked, even more intrigued.

"Miguel Cairo," I said. "What does it mean?"

"Maybe it means we've been coaching them right," he said.

A good stat isn't a good stat if it is manufactured, or has no relevance. When former outfielder–first baseman Rusty Staub asked the Elias "to come up with some numbers that will get me in the Hall of Fame," the Elias politely declined. Staub was a very good hitter, but hitting a home run when he was nineteen and another when he was forty, and getting 500 hits for four different franchises, make for an interesting career, but not a Hall of Fame career. There is a difference. When Mets third baseman Howard Johnson tied the National League record in 1991 for most sacrifice flies in a season by a switch-hitter, the Elias wrote it in their *Baseball Analyst*, adding, "My God, we've created a monster!"

Stats have become a monster, in a way. Now we calculate every pickoff throw; one season, Jim Deshaies made 355—"I've got to lead the league in *something*," he said, "but how could I have a hundred more than anyone that season?"—and in another season, Matt Clement made nine. We calculate every pitchout, every squeeze bunt attempt, every time a manager plays the infield in, and every double steal. We diagram to which field every hit goes. We chart who has the best batting average on every count. We chart swings and misses, ground balls to second base, and pop-outs to the infield . . . and yes, the Elias has confirmed, Wade Boggs popped out to an infielder in fair territory only three times during the 1985 season. "Who says there's an unemployment problem in this country?" outfielder Andy Van Slyke said in 1991 when the stat explosion began. "Just take the five percent unemployed and give them a baseball stat to follow."

In the 1970s, the Orioles' Earl Weaver was the only manager who asked for, or had access to, batter-pitcher matchup numbers. He kept them on white index cards; the Orioles won a play-off game against the Angels in 1979 because Weaver's cards told him to pinch-hit John Lowenstein against John Montague. Nowadays, any manager, any fan, can find matchup numbers, any numbers, if he knows where to look. In 2002, Giants manager Dusty Baker asked me at the batting cage, "Did you know that Chipper Jones has driven in a runner from third base with less than two outs seven of the last eight times?" No, Dusty, I didn't. How did you?

I find all these data to be fascinating, and, in almost every case, worth exploring. I read almost anything written by Bill James, and even though I can't fully explain his Win Shares statistic, his passion for the game and its numbers is admirable. One of James's many disciples, Craig Wright, has been a friend for over twenty years. In the middle of a conversation, he'll say, "Tim, did you know there was a fellow in the minor leagues in 1928, who was a pitcher, but played the outfield on days he didn't pitch. He hit four home runs in one game as a pitcher, and they were the only home runs he hit that season!" And I will say "No, Craig, I didn't. And neither does anyone else in the world!" In 1999, there was an unprecedented seven-way race for MVP of the American League. I was considering endorsing Rangers catcher Pudge Rodriguez. I asked Craig to run his numbers, which are far too complicated for me to understand. "Pedro Martinez is the MVP," Wright said. "Out of the seven candidates, I've got Pudge Rodriguez rated seventh."

But there is a danger in the proliferation of statistics. There are stat guys, and major-league general managers, who pay attention only to the numbers and disregard the human element to the game, which is a factor in baseball more than any sport. When they build a case through statistics that Roy White was a better player than Jim Rice, well, sorry, I'm out. The stat guys will tell you that Yankee shortstop Derek Jeter's range factor has dropped dramatically over the last few years, and he is no longer a good defensive player. I watch the games, I know Derek Jeter's range isn't what it used to be, but I can't think of anyone I would rather have handling a ground ball in the ninth inning of Game 7 of the World Series. So please, don't tell me Derek Jeter is a bad defensive shortstop.

Defense is tricky when it comes to stats: They can, at times, tell us nothing, and at other times, they can mislead us. For instance, the Pirates' John Wehner holds the National League record for consecutive games (99) without an error by a third baseman, but he did it over a *nine-year* period, and he did it playing an inning or two in some games. The more meaningful record is consecutive chances accepted without an error.

Rangers center fielder Mickey Rivers had a terrible throwing arm, so everyone ran on him, and because of that he led the league in outfield assists one year. Does that mean he has a good arm? Rafael Palmeiro had to ask a writer, "How do you get an assist?" as he was on the verge of winning a Gold Glove at first base: Raffy, when you throw a ball to a teammate and an out is recorded, and sometimes when it isn't, you get an assist. And yet, former first baseman Steve Garvey won Gold Gloves and set fielding records, but rarely threw the ball to a base because he knew he had a terrible arm and might throw the ball away for an error. On the same bunt play that Garvey would run the ball to first for the safe out, Keith Hernandez, the best defensive first baseman ever, would fire it across the diamond to cut down the lead runner at third base. Bill Buckner was a terrific defensive first baseman early in his career, but in his later years, given the option of running the ball to the bag or flipping it to the pitcher covering first, he flipped it. That meant more assists: He holds the major-league record for most assists in a season by a first baseman, 185, in 1985.

Those who ignore the numbers are doing a greater disservice than those who overuse them. In many cases, the numbers simply don't lie. Left-hander Terry Mulholland's move is so quick to the plate, you can't run on him, but you can run all day on Hideo Nomo. Larry Walker had a career average at Coors Field of .348, but on the road, it was nearly seventy points lower. Some guys can't hit left-handed pitching, some left-handers can't get right-handers out, a ground-ball pitcher is a ground-ball pitcher and some managers will not pitch out on 2–0. It is stupid for a manager or general manager to disregard the numbers just because they were researched by some guy who has never played the game a day in his life.

The key is knowing what's important and what isn't, and that has become harder and harder in recent years with the advent of so many new statistics. There is WHIP, a pitcher's walks and hits divided by innings pitched. There is the popular OPS, a combination of on-base percentage and slugging percentage. On base percentage and slugging percentage always have been the most significant indicators of offensive value, long before today's new breed of general managers, led by Oakland's brainy Billy Beane of *Moneyball* and other fame, made it a fashionable stat. Yet the *Moneyball* philosophy places such a high premium on on-base percentage, we are led to believe that a walk indeed is as good as a hit when, in fact, a walk is never as good as a hit. Just because Rich Becker walked 67 times in 285 at-bats in 2000 doesn't make him a good offensive player, especially considering he was a lifetime .256 hitter, and, according to some teammates, he was more interested in drawing a walk than swinging the bat.

Gene Tenace was a very good offensive player for the A's three-peat champions in the 1970s; he was a walk master who hit a lot of home runs. When he went to the awful Padres in 1977, teammates told him he would have to expand his strike zone and drive in more runs. Tenace couldn't do that. He drew his walks, hit some home runs, and the Pads lost 97 games. Sometimes, it's better to have Don Mattingly, not a big walk guy, swing at that pitch that's six inches outside and rifle it down the left-field line for a two-run double. In 2004, the Mariners asked Ichiro Suzuki to take a few more pitches and draw more walks, which he tried for a month and hit .250. That didn't work, so he went back to his slashing style; he hit over .400 after April and set the major-league record with 262 hits.

Look, I love guys who walk a lot. The three greatest hitters of all time, Babe Ruth, Ted Williams, and Barry Bonds, were walk machines. I hate guys who don't walk. Former Reds infielder Ron Oester's angry explanation of "Hey, if I wanted to walk, I would have been a fucking postman," simply doesn't work. Jeff Kunkel was a rookie shortstop for the Rangers in 1984. He didn't walk for his first 132 at-bats in the big leagues in 1984, and when he finally got his first one, in Oakland, *he asked for the ball!* No stat in the last few years is more disgusting than the second-half numbers of Cubs center fielder Corey Patterson in 2002: 2 walks, 79 strikeouts. Kunkel's career never got started, and Patterson's is in trouble, due to horrible plate discipline. But there are too many guys looking to walk, or at least work a deep count. Before you know it, the count is 3–2, and the hitter hasn't swung the bat. In 2004, the Reds' Adam Dunn struck out a record 196 times. He took 72 called third strikes. Ted Williams never struck out that many times in a season, Dunn had that many *looking.* That simply isn't right.

Our acceptance of strikeouts isn't right, either. That trend began in the mideighties when, among others, Rob Deer, Pete Incaviglia, Jay Buhner, Jim Presley, Cory Snyder, and Bo Jackson came to the big leagues, hit 30 home runs in a season, and struck out 150 times. That's when it became OK to K. In 1991, Toronto shortstop Manny Lee became the first player ever to strike out 100 times without hitting a home run. It's routine now for seventy-five players to strike out 100 times in a season: There weren't seventy-five guys who struck out 100 times in a season from 1900 to 1960 *combined*. Frank Robinson had an excellent 1965 season, but says it was his worst year because it was the only year in which he struck out 100 times. Lou Brock sat out the final game of the 1970 season because he had 99 strikeouts, and didn't want to strike out 100 times again. "I had 99 RBIs going in to that game," said Joe Torre, then a star hitter for the Cardinals. "I said, 'Lou, what are you doing? I need you in there, I've got to get 100 RBIs. You've got to be on base for me.' Then I realized what he was doing." (Torre got his hundredth; Brock did not.)

Brock's guilt doesn't exist today. Instead of shortening up and trying to put the ball in play, hitters are swinging on 0–2 the same way they do on 3–0. Hall of Famer Joe Sewell struck out four times in 608 at-bats in 1925; Deer struck out four times *in a game* a record seventeen times! Bill Buckner never struck out three times in a game in his career; today, it's routine that sixty times a season a player strikes out four times in one game. The Marlins' Preston Wilson once struck out more times—forty—in April, which is a short month, than the great DiMaggio struck out in any season of his career.

Players may not care about their high strikeout totals, but some care greatly about their stats. Bobby Bonilla, then a Pirate, once stood in the shower one night complaining to a teammate how he lost a possible RBI when, get this, *the eventual winning run* scored for the Pirates in the eighth inning on a wild pitch when Bonilla was at the plate. Frank Thomas, a future Hall of Famer, once screamed, "You cost me an RBI, man!" at a teammate when he failed to try to score from third on a relatively shallow fly ball. Maybe it's better to be like former Blue Jay Junior Felix, who, after being hit by a pitch with the bases loaded, asked the first-base coach, "Do I get an RBI for that?" Yes, Junior. And you get one for a bases-loaded walk.

Maybe ignorance is bliss. Oriole outfielder Lee Lacy asked me at the batting cage one night, "Did Nellie Fox hit five hundred home runs?" No, I explained, Nellie Fox hit thirty-five home runs; you must be thinking about Jimmie Foxx. I have written many times that in the year (1941) that Joe DiMaggio hit in fifty-six consecutive games, he struck out thirteen times. A radio guy in Toronto got that one fouled up, and said on the air, "I saw an interesting stat: the year in which Babe Ruth hit sixty home runs, he struck out thirteen times." (Ruth struck out 89 times that year. His high was 93, fourteen fewer than Manny Lee in 1991).

Then there was the sports anchor in Seattle who interviewed Roger Clemens one week after he had set the record for strikeouts in a nine-inning game—20—against the Mariners in 1986. That's twenty of the twenty-seven outs on strikeouts. That's positively Danny Almontian.

"Roger, the last time you faced the Mariners, you struck out *thirty*," the TV guy said.

"Well," Roger said, "it was only twenty."

"Well," the TV man said, "maybe thirty the next time."

Clemens forever will be commended for not following that idiotic line with something like, "Yeah, I'm going to pitch ten innings tomorrow and strike out *everyone!*"

But statistics, despite their trappings, and their deceptions, are blissful. They are fun to play with. Pete Rose told me in the winter of 1984, "Did you know that I've played in more *winning* games than Joe DiMaggio played *games?*" No, Pete, I didn't, but it's no surprise that *you* did. In 1979, the Pirates' Omar Moreno got the nickname Omar the Out Maker because of his defense, but also because he played every day, hit leadoff, rarely walked, and didn't hit for a high average. Twenty-five years later, at my insistence, a friend researched that the most outs ever made by one player in one season was none other than Omar the Out Maker in 1980. And, in 1979, Moreno's teammate, Frank Taveras, who hit behind him, made the second most outs in history.

Stats make for great trivia questions, but clearly the best ones are in baseball. What other sport would supply this scene: A friend greets me at the door of a party with "OK, name the four players who have ten or more letters in their last name, and hit forty home runs in a season?" And, of course, I can't concentrate on anything or anyone at the party until I get Yastrzemski, Petrocelli, Campanella, and Kluszewski. Which, of course, leads to my friend's next question: Name the eleven players in history who have four or fewer letters in their last name, and hit forty homers in a season, and I cannot rest until I get Sosa, Ruth, Foxx, Mays, Bell, Rice, Dunn, Ott, Mize, Cash, and the hardest answer of all time, Wally Post.

Stats are great fun for Fantasy League players also. I don't play Fantasy Baseball, but I fully support all such leagues because they get people of all ages and sexes even more interested in baseball, which is great for me because I write and talk about baseball for a living. My friend Tim Cowlishaw's wife, Lori, became so conversant in baseball through Fantasy Leagues, when it came time to picking middle relievers, she said something along the lines of "If you're not certain what to do, just take a Crim," as in ex-Brewers reliever Chuck Crim, who, obviously, she could not have ever possibly known otherwise.

I read the morning box scores for bigger reasons—identifying trends, as well as identifying who won and lost the games—than seeing whether Scott Podsednik stole a base. And, I don't play Fantasy League because I don't want to be like the elderly man who had, for reasons obviously well beyond winning the thousand-dollar first prize in his Fantasy League, ranked every active player by position, and was wondering if I could examine his lists to be sure that, for instance, Livan Hernandez should be ranked seventy-ninth among starting pitchers.

"When do you want me to go over these lists?" I asked.

"Could you do it now?" he said.

There are people like this all over the country. Some of them work at SABR. Once a month, I receive their newsletter, which I always read with great interest because I realize there are people out there who are even more screwed up than I am. Routinely someone has done this type of research: Jack Chesbro pitched 325⅔ innings, not 324⅔, in 1903. I have spoken at several SABR meetings, and have enjoyed them all, but knowing that these guys and girls have memorized lists of statistics that I have never even seen, I'm extremely careful with my facts and my opinions. At my first speech for SABR sometime in the late '80s, I was asked to name the greatest left-handed pitcher in baseball history, and, without really thinking about it, or without having done the proper research, I named Sandy Koufax. With the reaction I got, it was as if I had named Woody Fryman. I quickly reconsidered and made Lefty Grove my choice. I was back in the club.

Years after my Todd Hundley pinch-hit grand slam experience at the SABR convention, I found out that the man who was carrying around that information in his breast pocket was David Vincent, who would become the author of *The Home Run Encyclopedia*, and the man that some major-league teams and writers go to with questions about homers. In his database, Vincent, a senior system engineer at EDS, has every home run hit in major-league history, complete with, among other things, date, batter, pitcher, and ballpark.

That tedious process began in the early 1990s when a team of twenty-five to thirty people, most of them SABR members, began pulling home run data from newspapers from many years ago. All the data was entered electronically in his database, which Vincent would update daily. In the last five years, electronic feeds allow Vincent to update daily in about five minutes. What he can find, and so quickly, is amazing. In 2003, the Marlins' Derek Lee hit his twenty-eighth homer of the season on his twenty-eighth birthday, the third player ever with such a coincidence.

"The silliest one I've ever done came from Jayson [Stark, of ESPN.com]," Vincent said. "It was the longest combined letters in the names of guys who hit back-to-back home runs. Grudzielanek and Stankiewicz had twenty-three letters, barely edging out Yastrzemski and Conigliaro."

Being *The Home Run Encyclopedia* has brought a certain amount of prestige. "On the other hand," Vincent said, "I have been asked many times, 'How much time do you spend on this?' My uncle asked me ten years ago, 'Do you get any money for this?' I catch a lot of crap for it, but it's OK. My wife thinks I'm crazy . . . but that has nothing to do with baseball."

Signs, Signs, Everywhere a Sign

Rich Donnelly is the third-base coach for the Dodgers. He works in a box and spends his days making strange gyrations, hundreds of them per game, to hitters and base runners. "I figured out there are sixteen parts of my body that I can touch, and I touch all sixteen during a game," he says. He is relaying signs, a skill that demands repetition and balance: They must be simple enough for his players to understand yet complicated enough so as not to be stolen by the opposition. Donnelly starts some mornings by practicing in the bathroom mirror.

"I brush my teeth and ask my wife, 'See if you can find the bunt sign, honey,'" Donnelly said, laughing. "But it's kind of tough because I don't have Dodgers written across my pajamas. Then she'll give me her signs: The hat means take out of the garbage, the nose means clean up the kitchen, and the ear means there are two stalls in the barn that need sweeping. She'll say, 'I know some of your players miss signs, but you won't miss my signs.'"

Giving and stealing signs is baseball's secret game, the one that is played behind the scenes when no one is looking except the other team, which is always looking. It has been an integral part of baseball since the 1800s when Sliding Billy Hamilton was stealing a hundred bases a year, and opponents were trying to figure out when he was going. "If you don't try to steal signs, you're not doing your job," said Hall of Famer Paul Molitor. Thousands of signs per game are being sent, some are real, some fake, and every night, the opposition is trying to steal them because it could mean the difference between winning and losing. "The game moves so quickly for the manager and coaches because we're working our butts off," said Donnelly. "The average fan has no idea what's going on, with signs on every play. To sit in the dugout and watch all of it happen is really cool."

Over the last ten to fifteen years, the art of giving and stealing signs has taken on even greater importance because managers have assumed control of games: They call all pitchouts, pickoff throws, slide steps, and step-offs (a pitcher steps off the mound to check the intent of the runner), and occasionally will even call a pitch if the catcher looks over for help. There are signs exchanged from everywhere, from manager to third-base coach, from third-base coach to the hitter, from the shortstop to the second baseman. And someone is constantly watching. No one watched closer than former Angels manager Gene Mauch. "When I was signaling to the second baseman about who was covering the bag on the steal, Gene would look at my neck and see the veins sticking out, which meant my mouth was open, and from that, he could figure out who was covering the bag," said ex-Orioles shortstop Cal Ripken. "He'd relay that information to the hitter. So, when we played the Angels, I would have to cover my entire neck with my glove so Gene couldn't see the veins."

It is considered by most to be great gamesmanship when a player, coach, or manager steals a sign, but when it's done electronically, it's considered cheating. At Chicago's Comiskey Park for part of the 1980s, there was a twenty-five-watt refrigerator bulb in the scoreboard. A member of the White Sox would watch the television broadcast from the manager's office, and, with the view from the center-field camera, would determine what pitch the catcher was calling. There was a toggle switch in the office. Just flip the switch and the light in the scoreboard would come on, telling the White Sox's hitter if a fastball or an off-speed pitch was coming.

The 1984 Cubs won the National League East partly because, with electronic help similar to what was going on at Comiskey Park, "we knew other team's signs better than they knew them," said Johnny Oates, then a coach for the Cubs. Davey Lopes played on that '84 team. "Sometimes when a pitcher is getting hit, you'll hear someone say, 'It's like the hitter knows what's coming,'" he said. "That's because they *do* know what's coming."

The 1951 Giants came from 13½ games behind in August to win the pennant from the Dodgers. According to a story in *The Wall Street Journal* several years ago, the Giants had a telescope placed in center field at their home park, the Polo Grounds. The person using the telescope would steal the catcher's signs and, using a buzzer system, would relay that information to someone in the Giants bullpen in left-center field. From the bullpen, what pitch was coming would be relayed to the Giants' hitter in the batter's box.

"That's all overrated. There are no secrets in baseball now," says former Rangers manager Buck Showalter. "With all the guys who move from team to team today, you don't think one of them is going to tell his new team that his old team has a hidden camera in the center-field bleachers?"

Protecting the signs is the job of the manager. He sets the signs in spring training, then usually changes them before the start of the season. Sometimes, a manager will change the signs several times during the course of a season, even during a game if he feels a sign has been stolen. "I put a hit-and-run play on, and both of our guys missed it," said former Padres third-base coach Tim Flannery.

"[Cardinals manager Tony] LaRussa pitched out on the play. He looked at me. I thought, 'I think it's time to change the signs.'"

If a team trades a player, the manager probably will change the signs if that player is facing his old team soon after the deal. "We traded Jeffrey Hammonds, and a month later, I asked him, 'Do you remember the signs?'" said Donnelly. "He said, 'Hell no,' and I believed him. After we traded Craig Counsell to Arizona, he ran out to second base and yelled at me, 'You changed the sons a bitches, didn't you?' He knew that I knew that he knew."

Some managers are so determined to keep their signs secret, it gets complicated. Preston Gomez, who managed the Padres and Astros, briefly had a different set of signs for every player on his team. Ex-Phillies manager Danny Ozark had different signs for infielders, outfielders, catchers, and pitchers, which required three sets of signs when he called for a hit-and-run with an infielder on second, a catcher on first, and an outfielder at the plate. When Davey Johnson played in Japan, his manager was certain that his team's clubhouse was bugged by the opposing team, which could listen in on the signs meetings, so all of Johnson's players had the signs written on plastic wristbands in a series of numbers. The manager would call out numbers, the players would look at their wristbands to see what play was on.

The manager sends the sign to the third-base coach, who sends a different sign to the hitter and the runner. When Johnny Oates managed the Rangers, and they played at old Comiskey Park, he would have his coaches build a human fortress around him so he couldn't be seen by White Sox coach Joe Nossek, who is one of the best at stealing signs, a skill he acquired in the 1960s as a reserve outfielder for the White Sox. Ex-Twins manager Tom Kelly did the same against Nossek. "Most people think it's all I do, and that's probably right," Nossek once said. "Even if we don't have the signs, they think I might have them, so it works as a psychological advantage for us." Nossek usually sat in the corner of the dugout near the plate and stared at the manager and third-base coach, and anyone else who might give away a sign. When Nossek steals a sign, he remembers it "because managers get comfortable with signs, and two, three years later, they might go back to them."

Brewers manager Ned Yost often hides in the dugout tunnel to give his signs because he doesn't want to be seen by the enemy. Or he'll have two of his coaches giving signs at the same time so opposing coaches such as the Cardinals' Jose Oquendo don't know where to look. "It's coming from one of us," Yost yelled one night at Oquendo. "Pick one." Angels manager Mike Scioscia, a former catcher, is very good at stealing signs. So is former Phillies coach Gary Varsho, who, like Nossek, didn't play much in his career, so he spent his time on the bench—watching. "He won a game for us as a player in Pittsburgh. He stole their hit-and-run sign; we pitched out and caught their guy stealing to end the game," said Donnelly. Former Brewers coach Rich Dauer stole the signs of six teams in 2005. "Richie would say, 'He [the opposing third-base coach] hasn't touched his chin in about an hour,'" Donnelly said. "Then he would touch his chin, and something would happen."

To prevent a sign being stolen, managers will try the strangest things. Cardinals manager Tony LaRussa would occasionally have his trainer, Barry Weinberg, deliver the sign to the third-base coach. "If he takes out his tongue depressor," Donnelly said, "it's a steal." Gene Mauch did the same thing with his trainer, as have many other managers, including former Pirates manager Jim Leyland. The steal sign was the folding of the arms, but it was cold, so Pirates trainer Kent Biggerstaff folded his arms, the runner went and was thrown out.

"What are you doing?!" Leyland yelled.

"It was cold," Biggerstaff said. "I'm sorry."

Leyland, like LaRussa, is very sneaky. On what appeared to be a certain bunt situation with his pitcher at the plate, Leyland would leap off the bench in apparent anger after the pitcher didn't bunt at the first pitch. He would deke the opponent into believing that the bunt would be on on the next pitch, the infield would charge, and the pitcher would swing away. Few teams squeeze more often and more successfully than the Cardinals. LaRussa's squeeze sign once was an idle conversation with a coach on the bench. It didn't appear that LaRussa was paying attention, then boom! here comes the squeeze. The squeeze didn't work as well for Gary Pettis of the 1990 Rangers. He was on third base and the squeeze was on. But the hitter was walked intentionally, which, obviously, canceled the squeeze. Pettis broke home *during an intentional walk* and was tagged out easily.

"They didn't take the squeeze off," Pettis told manager Bobby Valentine.

"You're going to have to do better than that," Rangers pitcher Charlie Hough said.

Showalter managed in the minor leagues against veteran manager Johnny Lipon. Showalter was sure that he had stolen Lipon's squeeze sign, so he pitched out. Showalter was wrong, there was no play on. The hitter never looked at the third-base coach, and on the next pitch, he squeezed the runner home. "I finally realized that he'd called the squeeze for the following pitch," Showalter said. So, the next time they played Lipon's team, there was a similar situation. Showalter pitched out on the second pitch, not the first, and nailed the runner.

Lipon tipped his cap to Showalter.

"It's about time, young fella," he yelled.

After the manager, the most important person in the delivering of signs is the third-base coach. Donnelly runs the signs meetings in spring training, usually in the privacy of the clubhouse, where, unlike in Japan, the room isn't bugged. "Guys take notes," said Donnelly. "They don't want to forget. Sometimes they forget if they haven't seen the hit-and-run sign for a month. So I'll walk by their lockers and say, 'OK, give me the hit-and-run.'"

A third-base coach usually uses an indicator, which alerts the player that a play is coming. It can be as simple as the touch of the cap, but if there's no touch of the cap, a third-base coach can go through all sorts of gyrations, but no play is on. There is also a wipe-off sign, that is, a sign that negates all the signs that had been flashed to that point. Third-base coaches routinely put signs on and take them off to deceive the opponent. Some teams use the scoreboard as the indicator: If there are none out, the sign being used is the third sign. If there is one out, the first sign is the sign. With two out, the second sign is the sign.

Donnelly, who has been coaching third base in the major leagues for nearly twenty years, says the easiest way to give his signs away is to quicken his cadence, or slow his cadence, alerting the opponent that a play might be on. "So I purposely go real fast or real slow sometimes," he said. "It's such a great feeling; it's a real momentum swing when you steal a sign and get an out. And I'm livid when one of our guys misses a sign; it could be a big momentum swing in the opposite direction. I practice my signs so no one will steal them. I practice when I'm driving; it makes the time go quicker. Someone will pull up next to me at a light and see me doing my signs. I'll roll down the window and say, 'Well, do you have them?' He'll roll down his window and say, 'What the hell are you talking about?'"

Former Padres third-base coach Tim Flannery said, "I would test my signs on eleven-year-old kids in the neighborhood. I'd tell our players that if eleven-year-olds can get them, so should you, but with our guys, I'm never quite sure. When I'm on the airplane, I'll practice the signs with them. I'll give them signs while they're taking showers. They don't like that much."

Signs are missed on occasion. "I've found that the foreign players are better with the signs than American players," said Donnelly. "We had a guy last year from Japan, [pitcher] Toma Ohka. He was great. He never missed a thing." When Leyland managed in the minor leagues, he gave a player named Kirby Farrell the bunt sign three times, and Farrell missed it each time. Finally, Leyland cupped his hands and, from the dugout, yelled, "Bunt!"

Farrell cupped his hands and yelled back: "What?"

Some signs are seen but ignored. In Baltimore in 1985, Rangers DH Cliff Johnson was given the take sign on 3–0. He was so insulted, he gave the third-base coach the middle finger.

Rickey Henderson is the greatest base stealer in baseball history, but he was never very good with signs. One night with the Mets, he reached another career milestone, which he did quite often, and got a standing ovation from the crowd at Shea Stadium. No one loved a standing ovation more than Rickey, who, as always, took off his helmet and tipped it to the crowd. The applause died down, and Rickey looked at third-base coach Cookie Rojas for the sign. Rickey being Rickey, his signs were very simple. "A clapping of the hands was the steal sign," said then-Mets manager Bobby Valentine. "Cookie looked at Rickey and clapped his hands . . . Rickey took off his helmet and tipped it to the third-base coach."

There is an art to stealing signs from the catcher, which isn't easy, and isn't done nearly as much today as say, twenty years ago. The runner leads off second base and sees what fingers the catcher is putting down. But in those situations, the catcher changes his signs: Instead of putting down one finger for a fastball, two for a curveball, etc., the catcher will go through an intricate series of signs. Maybe he'll put down 1-3-1-2-5, and the pitcher is looking for the third number, and the third number was a one, a fastball. Or to be less complicated, it will be tied to the count: If the pitcher is ahead in the count, the sign is the first number that the catcher puts down. Behind in the count, it's the second. Even, it's the third.

Paul Molitor learned about stealing from the catcher from Brewers veterans Larry Hisle and Ted Simmons. "Ted would lead off second and figure out the sequence," Molitor said. "Or I'd come back from second and tell him what I saw. He'd put the information in the computer, Simmons-style [in his head], and he'd determine that the sequence I saw meant slider."

Molitor taught the 1993 Blue Jays his method, and they won a second straight World Championship that year. Molitor would lead off second and tap his helmet to tell the hitter that a fastball was coming. Or he would give location: If he leaned to his left, the pitch was coming to the outside part of the plate; if he leaned to the right, it was coming inside. Molitor became so good at stealing signs, he could steal one when he was on first base if he got a big enough lead, and if the catcher was lazy and didn't close his legs far enough, allowing Molitor to see his fingers. The Angels once stole the signs from Orioles catcher Chris Hoiles because he was putting his fingers too far down in his stance, and they could see them from the bench.

In the midnineties, Royals catcher Brent Mayne was sure that Indians knew every pitch that was coming after they scored eight runs in the first inning. "So I told every pitcher after the inning that there would be no more signs that game," said Mayne. "Just throw whatever you want, and I'll catch it." The Indians only scored two runs the rest of the game. "Mike Krukow was a veteran pitcher with the Giants, I was a young catcher, and I couldn't figure out the signs with men on base," said Diamondbacks manager Bob Melvin. "Finally, I told him, 'Throw whatever you like, I'll catch it.' And it worked out well."

Sometimes, a hitter can steal from the pitcher. Former pitcher Orel Hershiser liked to keep his index right finger out of his glove when he pitched. "But I used to wiggle it when I threw my breaking ball, and the hitter could see it," Hershiser said. "So I had my glove company build me a new glove with a little piece of leather that would cover my finger. That way, I could keep my finger out of my glove, but the hitter couldn't see it wiggle. Sometimes, that stuff doesn't matter. In 1988, (the Mets') Doc Gooden was tipping all his pitches. We knew what was coming, but he was so good, we still couldn't hit him." Roger Clemens uses a new glove, or relatively new glove, for almost every start. He likes a firm glove so the hitter can't see him pressing his fingers against it, and therefore perhaps detecting his grip.

Showalter and Melvin, among others, say that many hitters today don't want to know what's coming. Cal Ripken told me that he didn't want to know. He was an intelligent hitter; he had a good idea what was coming anyway. "And what if they're wrong?" he said.

Tony Gwynn, the greatest hitter since Ted Williams, said the same thing. "I go by what I see," he said. "I don't want anyone else clogging my thinking up there. Guys on our bench will talk about that stuff, I move to the other end of the dugout." Former American League MVP George Bell was one of the best at stealing from the catcher and passing it on to the hitter, but he didn't want anyone telling him what was coming, not after what happened to him: A teammate signaled to him that a breaking ball was coming, but the pitcher threw a fastball. Bell waited for the ball to break, it didn't, and hit him flush in the face.

Today it is rare that a hitter can determine what pitch is coming. "They're more interested in location," said Donnelly. "If you know it's inside, then it has to be a fastball. No one throws a curveball or a slider on the inside part of the plate. Only twice has anyone on our team asked me if I can see the changeup coming, that is, see the changeup grip in the pitcher's glove from the third-base coach's box. I never have. That's really hard to see."

Some players believe that stealing a catcher's signs is cheating, and if you cheat and get caught, there will be retaliation, which could mean a pitch at your head. A hitter will likely get drilled if he peeks at the catcher's signs. "Eric Karros peeked against us," said former Giants pitcher Jeff Brantley. "The next time he peeked, [Giants catcher Kirt] Manwaring was ready. Karros peeked. Kirt gave him the finger." And yet hitters still peek for location. "It happens a lot in day games with sunglasses," says Melvin. That's why you'll see a catcher set up in the middle of the plate, and, as the pitch is coming, move to the inside corner, outside corner, up or down. But some pitchers, including Roger Clemens, find it distracting, and don't like it when a catcher moves his target that late.

Most pitchers also don't like it when the manager calls the pitchouts and the pickoff throws and the slide steps, but that change in strategy began roughly twenty years ago with Giants manager Roger Craig. Now, every team does it in order to control the other team's running game, and because managers sometimes don't trust their players to do it right on their own.

"Check your brains at the door," said Valentine. "We'll take it from there."

Red Sox pitcher Matt Clement isn't very good at throwing to the bases—he sometimes throws a slider—so he made only nine pickoff throws one season. Randy Johnson isn't particularly good at throwing to the bases, either. Former Braves reliever Mark Wohlers had a mental block throwing to bases, pitchouts, etc., so they were rarely called. The Brewers don't like closer Derrick Turnbow to make pickoff throws because he throws too hard.

Every time a runner gets on base, there are signals going from the manager (or a coach) to the catcher, then to the pitcher. Showalter said that in one game, the Phillies knew every time the Rangers had a steal or hit-and-run on. Finally, he looked in their dugout and saw former Ranger catcher Mark Parent, who was stealing every sign. Showalter touched his middle finger to his nose, looked at Parent and smiled, as if to say, "OK, you got me."

Donnelly has been in charge of controlling the running game for several of his teams over the last ten years. It is a great moment, one that most fans never even recognize, when a runner on first base is moving back to the bag when the pitch is coming in. It is a great moment, also hidden from pedestrian eyes, when a pitcher steps off the mound and the reaction of the runner at second discloses that a steal possibility had been thwarted. And after every good and bad moment, Donnelly often congratulates or scolds his players for their work.

"We talk about those things all the time, throughout the game," Donnelly said. "I meet with the pitchers and catchers every day about what we're going to do that night with the signs. Sometimes I'll meet with the pitchers in a bathroom stall. When it comes to signs, I trust no one."

9

I'm Whacked

Mike Toomey, a major-league scout, called me on a Tuesday. "Come on over," he said frantically. "I've got the Cubs-Expos game on DirecTV." When I arrived, Toomey was sitting in a chair that was stationed two feet from the television. His shirt was stained, he had a dip of tobacco under his lip, and his hair was standing straight up. In one hand, he was holding a stopwatch. "I'm timing pitchers to the plate," he said. "I've got Vazquez at 1.2!"

In his other hand, Toomey was holding a radar gun, which he had pointed directly at the TV. "This is the newest gun," he said, "you can get a pitcher's velocity off the TV," which, gullibly, I believed. Toomey apologized for making me look stupid, then looked around at his house, his situation, and his ragged self, shook his head and said, "I'm whacked."

All scouts are whacked. They have to be. They're the guys who, by any means possible, find the players. They're the guys who drive three hundred miles to see a high school pitcher throw two innings in the rain. They're the guys who travel the world—Toomey has scouted in seven countries—looking for players in towns so small, the only way to get there is by Lionel Train. "I took a ferry from

Vermont to Canada to see a game," Toomey said. They're the guys who sit behind the screen behind home plate with big straw hats on their heads, a stopwatch in one hand, a radar gun in the other, and with eyes that don't miss a thing.

They love the game as much as anyone, they are the lifeblood of an organization, they are the guys who help determine what really matters about a player: Can he play? They're the guys who spend two hundred days a year on the road for a yearly salary that doesn't match what Alex Rodriguez makes in two innings, they rarely get credit for their work and when budget cuts are made, it usually begins with scouting. When ex-Reds owner Marge Schott cut her scouting budget, she said, "Oh, scouts don't do anything except go to games."

They do so much more. Scouts found speedy outfielder Jeff Stone running barefooted through a cornfield in Missouri. They found Vladimir Guerrero at a tryout camp in the Dominican Republic; he was sixteen, he arrived on the back of a motorcycle, he was wearing two different shoes, and had to stuff a sock into one of the shoes to make it fit. Expos scout Fred Ferreira signed Guerrero that day and gave the guy who drove the motorcycle $200, and says, "I still don't know if the guy on that bike knows who he brought us that day." Braves scout Paul Snyder found catcher Javy Lopez in Puerto Rico, but so as not to alert other scouts to his interest, he escaped the ballpark by crawling under a set of bleachers.

"I tore up a brand-new shirt. My wife was really angry," Snyder said. "But I got the player."

Scouts found Kenny Rogers in Plant City, Florida, in 1982. He was seventeen years old, a 135-pound, left-handed outfielder-shortstop, but because he is left-handed and had arm strength, the Rangers drafted him as a pitcher in the thirty-fifth round on the recommendation of scout Joe Klein. "When he went to pro ball," Klein said, "he had no idea where he was going, or what pro ball was." In Rogers's first spring training, he threw off the mound for Sid Hudson, the Rangers' minor-league pitching instructor. Rogers was then asked to pitch from the stretch. "I don't know how to do that," Rogers said. Nearly twenty-five years later, Rogers is still pitching in the major leagues, and has one of the game's best pick-off moves.

"The day I saw Joe Beimel pitch in high school," Toomey said of the reliever who had pitched for several big-league teams entering 2007, "the shortstop on his team was a girl."

Whacked? Joe Marchese was a great scout for the Rangers. He was driving on an interstate in Florida many years ago when he picked up a hitchhiker, who asked what Marchese did for a living. "I'm a baseball scout," he said. The hitchhiker said, "Great, I'm a baseball pitcher," Marchese, now thoroughly interested, had to see this kid throw, but had neither a ball or glove. "So Joe pulled off to the side of the road by an orange grove," said Klein, then the general manager of the Rangers. "He climbed a tree and picked thirty oranges and told the kid, 'Throw these at that tree, and we'll see what kind of arm you have.'" The hitchhiker wasn't worth signing, but the point is, scouts are always looking for players, and there's no telling where they might find one, even in an orange grove.

But when you find him, you're not sure what you have, and what he'll turn out to be. There are more mistakes, miscalculations, and great discoveries in baseball than any other sport, given the high degree of difficulty of the game, the mental aspect of the game, and the uncertainty of the aluminum bat, which is so much more potent than a wood bat, it's like scouting basketball players on a 9½-foot hoop. (That's why Toomey carries wooden bats in the trunk of his car at all times.) In basketball, a scout can watch a big-time college player run up the floor about ten times, and basically know if he can play in the NBA. Scouts knew LeBron James would be an immediate star in the NBA after jumping from high school. In football, a 225-pound guy who loves to hit people, and runs a 4.4 in the forty, is going to play in the NFL. And he might make an impact his rookie season. That's why ESPN televises the NFL draft relentlessly for three days—college kids are ready for the next step.

It doesn't work that way in baseball. College baseball isn't nearly as advanced as college basketball or college football, mainly because baseball is far more of a skill sport than an athletic sport, and there isn't enough time to master the necessary skills in baseball by age twenty. Only seventeen players in the forty-year history of the June draft have gone straight from high school or college to the major leagues, but a number of them (John Olerud, Dave Winfield, and Bob Horner are the most notable exceptions) had to go to the minor leagues to learn the game. There is no LeBron James in baseball. The Rangers brought pitcher David Clyde from high school to the major leagues in 1973; he was hopelessly overmatched. He went 4–8 that first year, and 18–33 in parts of five seasons and was gone forever.

"He was the worst athlete I've ever seen in a major-league uniform," said Rangers coach Rich Donnelly. "When he needed to make some adjustments, he was incapable of doing it."

Pitcher Mike Morgan was brought from high school to the major leagues in 1978.

"Whatever finger I put down, that's what you throw, kid," his catcher, Jim Essian, told Morgan.

"You'll only need one finger," Morgan said. "I only throw one pitch, a fastball."

Morgan lost nineteen of his first twenty-one decisions, then was sent back to the minor leagues for two years.

Scouts are expected to evaluate and project players who are eighteen years old, yet in baseball, more than any other sport, players, without explanation, find their game at age thirty, or find it at twenty-five and lose it at twenty-seven, as did Joe Charboneau, who won the American League Rookie of the Year in 1980 when he hit twenty-three home runs, then hit only six the rest of his career. When was the last time an NBA player averaged 12 points a game for his first eight seasons, then scored thirty a game when he turned thirty? Never? That's essentially what Cubs first baseman Derrek Lee did during his spectacular 2005 season. "When you plant a seed, you water, you weed, you make sure it gets sunlight, you know it's going to surface," says Ted Simmons, a former catcher and general manager, and now one of the game's best scouts. "Baseball players aren't the same. You put the seed in the ground, and you can do everything humanly possible to give it a chance to grow, and it might not come up."

That's why few people outside baseball's inner circle pay close attention to Major League Baseball's Amateur Draft. Some number-one picks take five years to get to the major leagues, and some never make it at all. That never happens in the NFL or NBA. Pitcher Brien Taylor was the Yankees' first overall pick in the June 1991 draft. He threw left-handed, he threw 97 mph, his numbers in high school were phenomenal, he was going to be a star someday in New York, but he never pitched a day in the major leagues for a variety of reasons. The annual draft is filled with busts and surprises, far more than in football or basketball. Don Mattingly, a near Hall of Famer, was drafted in the nineteenth round in 1979, behind quarterbacks Dan Marino, John Elway, and Jay Schroeder. Mike Piazza, the greatest hitting catcher of all time, was a sixty-third round selection. Cardinals shortstop David Eckstein was never even drafted; he walked on at the University of Florida.

Why so many misses? In baseball, you can watch a player for three years in the minor leagues and still not know if he's ready for Triple-A. A scout can watch a player for a week and not see him go in the hole to make a throw, or charge a bunt, or cut loose from the outfield. Former Mets general manager Joe McIlvaine was the cross-checker for the Mets, that is, the scout who goes in for one last look at a player whom the team might draft. McIlvaine had one look at Ty Gainey, who was a high school first baseman with power. "The day I saw him," said McIlvaine, "he was intentionally walked four times, so I never saw him swing the bat. His pitcher threw a perfect game, with twenty strikeouts. So, I went to see a player and I never saw him swing the bat, or throw a ball, or field or catch a ball."

It's so easy to miss on a player because some of them are so difficult to evaluate. Really, what was a scout to do with Mike Bertolucci, who pitched for Del Campo High in Fair Oaks, California, in the early 1990s? He threw 131⅓ innings one year, and struck out 130. He threw 77 to 82 mph; he threw a sinker, a curveball, a riser, and a changeup. The only problem was, he threw *underhand*. Imagine writing out that report for the scouting director. (Bertolucci ended up pitching in college, but no pro ball.)

Stranger players than Bertolucci have been spotted at tryout camps. I attended one for the Orioles in 1981 for the standard "I tried out for the Orioles" story for *The Washington Star*. The pitcher I faced that day was brought in from Pennsylvania just for this camp; he threw 90 mph, and as he crossed the foul line on the way to the mound, he stopped and did a back flip. (Great. I had to face a guy throwing that hard, *and* he was crazy). Approximately five hundred "players" showed up that day, but most of them didn't understand that Oriole scout Dick Bowie was hoping to find maybe one who was worth signing to play in Rookie Ball. Yet the clueless guy who took ground balls next to me at third base actually believed he was trying out for the Orioles, and thought if he had a good day, which was impossible, he would be playing third base in the major leagues within a couple weeks. This guy—as God is my witness—was wearing a button-down dress shirt, and had a gold medallion the size of a frozen pizza hanging from his neck. Imagine being a scout and having to look at *that.*

"I went to a tryout camp in 1982. It was awful," said Jack Daugherty, who played first base and the outfield for several big-league seasons with the Rangers. "I took ground balls next to a guy who was wearing cutoff Haggar pants and *black dress shoes.*"

Toomey laughed. "You can't believe some of the things I've seen at tryout camps," he said. "I've seen guys in cutoff jeans and construction boots, guys who just got off work. I've seen fifty-year-old men with beards down to their navel. 'I really think I can do this,' they say. One guy, maybe forty, said he was a pitcher. He told me all the pitches he threw, fastball, slider, curveball, cut fastball—he must have listed ten. I let him throw for a few minutes, which was more than enough. He said, 'But you haven't seen my knuckle-ball yet.'"

Toomey has seen it all in nearly twenty-five years of scouting. He was a terrific college player—most scouts are former players—he managed in the minor leagues, and he grew up in sports as the son of a coach, Frank Toomey, who coached football at Florida State and University of Maryland. Mike Toomey got to see great players in all sports at a young age, which helps him scout players today. At age twenty-nine, he settled on scouting as a career because "I love the game, I love finding the players, I love working with kids, I love being at the ballpark. I love scouting. A good scout has to be a communicator. He has to be organized, resilient, and flexible. He has to be an ambassador for the game. He has to be a grinder who is driven by passion for the game. He has to be a competitor. You have to want to beat the next guy to get that player. But the chase sometimes is as good as the kill. The experiences, the small towns, and the characters you meet. I once took my mother on a scouting trip with me; she loves baseball. We saw parts of five games in one day."

There is nothing more exhilarating to a scout than finding a good-looking player. Sometimes, they are easy to find. Jack Cust, who has played in the big leagues for several teams, was a high school star in Flemington, New Jersey, in the mid-1990s. "I hit every day from age eight to eighteen," Cust said. "I mean every day." He had his own batting practice pitcher, whom he paid. Cust's father arranged private batting practice sessions for scouts who wanted to see his son hit. After Cust played in a high school basketball game one night, he said to Toomey, "Let's go hit." They drove forty-five minutes to a batting cage where they were met by Kerry Baker, Cust's batting practice pitcher. He had a hundred new baseballs. Cust hit for over an hour. He wound up being the number-one pick of the Arizona Diamondbacks in 1997.

Most times, the players are harder to find. It takes a lot of looking. To prepare for the 2002 June draft for the Expos, Toomey was on the road for all but four days in a three-month period. He went to forty-five states, including Hawaii, Alaska, Wyoming, and both Dakotas. He saw more than 150 games, sometimes three in a day. He saw roughly a thousand players.

"I've gotten some interesting directions from people. They weren't exactly MapQuest directions," Toomey said. "I asked one guy how to get to a ballpark. He said, 'The first thing you have to do is get back in your car.' When the trip was finally over, on the last day of the draft, I was sitting in Olympic Stadium [then home of the Expos], looking out at the field, and a black cat ran across the diamond. And there was this pigeon, out on the ledge, that didn't move for at least ten minutes, and it was looking right at me. Black cats and clay pigeons. Sounds like an album. I think it was a sign that it was time to go home."

On other long trips, Toomey said, "I'd have a three A.M. or four A.M. wake-up call every day, I'd have three or four plane reservations a day, and I wouldn't know where I was going until I got up at three in the morning. The Weather Channel is a scout's best friend. You need to see a pitcher in Pennsylvania, but the front is coming through there, so I'll go to Delaware instead. Sometimes you have to call the high school to see if the kid is pitching. The secretary says, 'I don't even know if we have a game today. Hey, Mr. Brown, could you ask Mr. Johnson if Johnny pitching today?' She'll get back on the phone and say, 'Coach says he's tender and can't pitch today.' Things like that happen all the time. Sandy Johnson was our scouting director when I was with the Rangers. He came from Texas to Baltimore to see a kid of mine pitch. But when he arrived, I called him and told him that I'd just heard that the kid was sore, and wasn't going to be able to pitch. Sandy never left the Baltimore airport. He got on a plane to South Carolina. A scout always has a backup game."

Paul Snyder of the Braves flew seven hundred miles to Paint Branch High School in Burtonsville, Maryland, to see outfielder Dwight Maness from William Penn High School in New Castle, Delaware, but the game was rained out. "Paul was disappointed, but I told him, 'Follow me,'" Toomey said. "I knew a kid on the Paint Branch team—Chris Waldron—who had a covered batting cage at his house. I got clearance that it would be OK to go over there. So the team bus from New Castle parked at the Waldron's house. Mrs. Waldron came out with a look on her face like 'What is going on here?' Dwight Maness got off the bus, hit in the cage for fifteen minutes, got back on the bus. Paul Snyder said, 'I've seen all I needed to see.'"

Toomey went to the University of Kansas to see John Mayberry Jr., son of the former major leaguer with the same name. "I only got one day to see him, and I was late. I was coming from another game." Toomey said. "I got to the gate at the ballpark, and I saw Mayberry at the plate. The lady said, 'That will be five dollars, sir.' I told her, 'I'll pay you in a minute, I've got to see this kid.' I ran in. If I had paid right then, I would have missed seeing a mammoth home run."

Toomey went to see a pitcher in rural Honaker, Virginia, many years ago. "The townspeople were all sitting on top of the hill looking down at the game in the hollow," Toomey said. "This fella comes up to me in the third inning and says of the pitcher, 'That's my boy. He's the best boy around these parts and yours.' He says, 'You ever seen a ball that goes like this?' (The ball zigzagged, like a fast-moving insect.) I said, 'No, sir, I've never seen that.' He said, 'I don't know what you city folks call it, but down here, we call that the Monkey Ball.'"

Toomey videotaped that kid. He videotapes many of the players he scouts. He has tapes of Craig Biggio as a catcher at Seton Hall, with a skinny Mo Vaughn in the on-deck circle. He has Delino DeShields *pitching* in high school. He has Mike Mussina pitching on a hill next to a graveyard with about ten people in the stands. "My scout buddies call me Cecil B. DeMille," Toomey said. "They call me Metro Goldwyn Mayer. But I'd rather have a video camera than a radar gun any day. Look at this!" Toomey has a video of a dog that watched every pitch of a game in Honaker. Wherever the ball was hit, the dog ran in that direction, always staying behind the fence. "Watch him!" Toomey said. "Seven innings he did that. He never took his eyes off the ball." Now that's a bird dog scout.

Big players can come from small towns. "I went to a field in Alabama where Bo Jackson played in high school," said Ed Farmer, a former major-league pitcher who scouted for five years for the Orioles. "I asked the area scout, 'What's the longest ball you saw Bo hit here?' He said, 'See that fence? He hit it over that fence. See that track behind it? He hit it over that. See the football field beyond the track? He hit it over that. See the track beyond the football field? He hit it on that track.' I added the distances and came up with seven hundred feet. I asked another scout the same question. Same answer. Two scouts, same story, seven hundred feet."

Small towns? Mullins, West Virginia. "Oh boy," says Toomey.

"That's where the hoot owls make love to the chickens." In the third inning, an older man sat next to Toomey and asked, "Whoya lookin' at?" Toomey said he was looking at the pitcher, a kid named John Campbell. A couple of innings later, the same man edged over next to Toomey and asked, "How hard is he a throwin'?" Toomey said, "Eighty-eight miles an hour. Then this guy turned to the crowd and yelled, 'Eighty-eight miles an hour! He's going to sign John.' Before you know it, the whole town is standing behind me, and this guy is reading my radar gun and screaming, 'It's up to eighty-nine miles an hour. Mr. Toomey's going to sign John. He's going to sign John.'"

Signing a player can be harder than finding a player. Toomey likes to go into the player's house to have dinner with the family. "You learn a lot, the way people are, when you're in their house," Toomey said. "You learn a lot about who makes the decisions in the family, and usually it's the mother. It's a good sign when the father says, 'Mr. Toomey, it has been Johnny's dream his whole life to play pro ball. If you make him a fair offer, he wants to play now.' But there are red flags, also, like when the mom says, 'Johnny has never been away from home, I've done his laundry his whole life, and he really loves Susan.'"

Toomey has the players he's scouting fill out a questionnaire, which asks for, among other things, grade point average, aspirations, expected signing bonus, whether anyone else in the family has played pro ball, etc. "The old cards had a question about church preference, you know, Catholic, Jewish, Methodist," Toomey said. "One kid wrote down under church preference, 'Red brick.' Red brick! Now *that's* what you call a red flag.'"

When a scout sees a player he likes, he has to convince his bosses—the cross-checker or the scouting director or even the general manager—that the player is worth signing. "I never let anyone talk me off a player. A scout must have the courage of his conviction," Toomey said. Jerry Jordan, a scout for the Phillies, really liked a left-handed pitcher from Charleston, West Virginia, named Pice. Jordan had his cross-checker, Dick Lawlor, come to see Pice pitch. But Pice had a bad day; his velocity was down. "It was the funniest thing I've ever seen," Toomey said. "Pice would throw, and Old Jerry would squeeze that radar gun—one of the old ray guns made out of steel—so hard, he was trying to squeeze extra velocity out of the guy, like he could control how hard the pitcher was throwing. All to show his boss that this guy was good enough to sign. But it didn't work. I said, 'Jerry, if you squeeze that gun any tighter, you'll get lead poisoning.'"

Whether or not he signs a player, a scout never forgets a player. "We all have a mental Rolodex," Toomey said. My oldest brother, Andy, was a great player at Catholic University in the early 1970s, but since he was twenty-two years old when he finished college, and was headed to MIT for graduate school, he wasn't drafted. (Teams normally like to draft a high school kid whose only interest is playing baseball, then they turn him over to their instructors to teach him how to play.) Nearly thirty years after my brother had played his last collegiate game, I was wearing a Catholic University golf shirt when I ran into Orioles scout Gary Nickels in spring training. I had known Nickels for fifteen years, but now he looked at me and my shirt, and I saw the gears turning in his head. "Kurkjian? . . . Kurkjian? Your brother played at Catholic U.," Nickels said. "Left-handed hitter, good power, could run and could really throw, right?" he said. A precise scouting report, thirty years later.

Scouts never forget a town, a ballpark, or a field, either.

"Nothing was worse than the Ellipse," Toomey said of the home field for the team he coached, and later scouted, at George Washington University. "The field was located between the White House and the Washington Monument," Toomey said. "Homeless people would routinely be lying in the outfield. Some days I've seen a four-man outfield, some days I've seen a seven-man outfield. There were no benches. People off the street—sometimes congressmen—would walk up and ask, 'Who's pitching today?' I've seen Japanese tourists walk right through a game. We had to stop the game. The ground rules changed every day. They were something like 'Draw an imaginary line from third base to that green car that's parked down there.' Then you had to hope no one moved the green car."

During one game against Catholic University, the CU players had parked illegally, so the game had to be stopped until the players moved their cars. That was not a problem for the GW team: it traveled to all its games in a laundry truck. "Just roll down the back and out came the players," Toomey said. "Once, we were playing at home against Georgetown, but the Georgetown coach said there was no way we'd be able to play the game because there was a cold front in Wyoming. Wyoming! They weren't very good, so we went and picked up their team in our truck, beat them in a doubleheader, then took them back home.

"Imagine scouting *that*."

The more civilized form of scouting is major-league advance scouting. That involves going to major-league ballparks, staying in nice hotels in big cities, and scouting major-league players—no Monkey Balls, or dogs that follow every pitch, or girls playing short-stop. An advance scout is invaluable to a team's success; it's his job to follow his team's next opponent and record almost everything that that team does, including when they hit-and-run, when they bunt, on what counts they like to steal third, who doesn't throw well from the outfield, etc. The White Sox had six advance scouts following the Astros in the 2005 National League Championship Series, which is one reason why the White Sox swept them in the World Series: They knew everything about them. "Randy Johnson doesn't like to field bunts," Toomey said. "Kerry Wood falls off to the first base side violently after every pitch. Those are things that might help you win a ball game." Toomey once scouted the Mets for nearly a month, and found that Todd Zeile took the first pitch 72 times in a stretch of 76 at-bats.

"[Ex-Mets manager] Bobby Valentine was the best manager for an advance guy to work for," Toomey said. "He really cared about what we had to say. And he would say, 'I know [Tom] Glavine pitches away, away, away, away, away, but I need to know *when* he comes inside. I need the count, the inning, the situation, the hitter.' Those are the things you look for. As an advance scout, you take it personally. When you alert the manager to something, and it works out for our team, that's what it's all about. You live and die with that stuff. It really hurts when they don't listen or read what you have to say. I've seen managers take fifty pages from an advance scout and throw it in the trash can."

Such disrespect for scouts comes in other forms. There is no Hall of Fame for scouts. There is no union. They make so little money, it's embarrassing: The men who find the players who eventually make $15 million a year are still making, on average, around $35,000 a year. They have expense accounts and get paid for mileage, yet when Toomey scouted for the Expos, he drove to Harrisburg, Pennsylvania, a trip of 234 miles, but a secretary in the Expos offices said the trip was actually 226 miles: He had to redo the report for a grand total of $2.40.

Forty years ago, back when scouts carried only a stopwatch, a pencil, and a notebook, they were revered in their organization. When they said, "Take this guy in the eighth round," it was done. It doesn't work that way anymore. Some teams have pulled some scouts off the road and have them scout a team on TV to save money. "I had to go to a seminar run by our GM to explain what slugging percentage is, and how to evaluate it," one scout said. "That's for someone else. I'm paid to watch the players." Two-thirds of the teams use a scouting service provided by industry-leader IBM or E Solutions that allows a scouting director to make a computer search, for example, for every amateur left-handed pitcher in the country, under age twenty-one, over six feet four, who throws 90 mph. Yet most, if not all of that data, is provided by the scouts.

"I've never found a player sitting in front of a computer screen, I've got to get in my car and go see them myself," Toomey said. "I don't see the confidence that teams used to have in scouts. So many good scouts are being laid off or replaced. It's a financial thing. Instead of giving a guy two or three states to scout, we're giving him seven, and letting him do the work of two or three guys just to save a buck. Guys with thirty years in the game, great ambassadors of the game, guys who love it, are being let go. We're bringing in guys at entry-level salaries, who don't have a feel for the game, and letting them find the players, then the cross-checker comes in and makes the decision whether the guy can play. That's not scouting. Let's quit the BS. You can take your numbers and your categories and stick 'em up your ass. Do you like the player, and where do you like him? There is no loyalty to scouts. Scouts needed a union. The guys who have dedicated their lives to the game are fading out. The game can't afford to lose them. I miss the old-time scouts."

Julian Morgan was an old-time scout for many teams, including the Mets. "He'd go in the backwoods of Georgia and sign the black players," said Toomey. "He'd go to places where other guys wouldn't go. Julian knew every flea market in Georgia and Florida. He'd go to every flea market and buy old golf clubs, ones with the wooden shafts, and he'd open up the window of his room at the Days Inn in Jacksonville and would line the clubs up and sell them. He'd stay at $18-a-night hotels that didn't even have phones in the room."

Joe Branzell was an old-time scout with the Rangers. "He'd stay at the St. John's Inn along the St. John's River in Polatka [Florida]," Toomey said. "He would hang a clothesline from one tree to another behind his hotel; he would wash his clothes in the sink and hang them on the line. They looked like the American flag flapping in the wind. You'd have to get a tetanus shot before you got in Joe's car. He had pots and pans in the back seat. He would cook in his room, he was always trying to save a buck. All scouts did that."

Ellis Clary was an old-time scout for several teams. "He had a heart attack, and was basically pronounced dead," said Farmer. "He was in the ambulance on the way to the hospital when he came to. He asked, 'Where the hell are we?' The ambulance guy said, 'On the way to the hospital in an ambulance.' Ellis asked, 'Where is the ballpark? Get the mileage from the ballpark to the hospital. I'm going to need that for my expense account.'"

Gene Hassell was an old-time scout for multiple teams. "We were in Lynchburg, Virginia, one night," Toomey said, "and he told me, 'Little man, I'm not feeling very good. Would you stay with me tonight?' "I said, 'Sure.' Right before we went to bed, he put a 38-caliber pistol on the bedside and told me, 'If someone tries to come through that door, shoot their ass.'"

Leon Hamilton was an old-time scout with the Mets. "Legend has it that he went to some old hotel and had a friend distract the clerk while Leon pilfered a whole bunch of receipts for the hotel," according to Toomey. "They say that sometimes he would sleep at home, but he would put in the receipts for that hotel on his expense report. His team finally got suspicious when he was still turning in receipts at the hotel that had burned down three years prior. He got fired for a while, but the team hired him back again. He was a good scout."

All those guys are gone. They don't make scouts like they used to. But there is hope in guys such as Mike Toomey, now the special assistant to the general manager of the Kansas City Royals. At age fifty-four, he's one of the old-time guys now, and he has learned to adjust to the changes in the game, the filing of reports via computer, and the use of the Internet for statistical information. "I always said that I never needed a cell phone," Toomey said. "Now I have three hundred numbers in my cell phone."

Toomey gets angry at the way scouts are treated, but the glint in his eyes isn't gone for long. As he left my house after being interviewed, he was off to Sterling, Virginia—only about an hour away, nothing for a scout—to work with two high school kids. Maybe these kids will be good enough someday to play pro ball. So Toomey put his baseball hat on, put a dip of tobacco under his lip, jumped in his car, which has wooden bats, and all sorts of other workout equipment, in the trunk. He was happy again. He was on the road, looking for players. Soon, he would be off to Venezuela to scout winter ball games. For him, it doesn't matter what country, or what level of play, there's nothing better than being at a game.

"When you look through a screen for a living," Toomey said, "you've got to be a little whacked."

10

There Was a Blimp in Left Field

Indians pitcher Brian Anderson boarded the team bus at 8:00 A.M. for the two-hour drive to Vero Beach, Florida, for a spring training game in 2003. Thirty minutes into the trip, Anderson realized that he had forgotten his hat, his spikes, and his glove back in Winter Haven.

"I was running late that morning because I knew I was going to get to hit in the game, so I was looking for the really important things: batting gloves and a bat," Anderson said. "When we got to Vero, I was in full panic mode. I borrowed a car and went to a mall, but there wasn't one glove in the whole mall, but I found some Adidas spikes. On the way back to the ballpark, I saw a Wal-Mart. I thought, 'Hey, Wal-Mart has everything . . . tires . . . produce . . . it must have a baseball glove.' I found one: $29.95, already broken in. It was a softball glove. A Wilson. It was awful. I borrowed someone's hat and pitched in the game. Of course, I got three comebackers to the mound, and I caught them all because my new glove was as big as a butterfly net; it made [Greg] Maddux's glove look small. That day reminded me of when I was seventeen playing Legion ball. That is spring training to me."

And that's why it's so great; that's why it's my favorite time of year. It makes you feel young again, no matter how old you are, no matter how many times you have been—I've gone to spring training the last twenty-five years. It is a sign that the long, cold winter is nearly over, and that sunshine and summer vacation is on the way. It is a time for optimism, a fresh start, and hope: No one has lost a game, the rookies have so much promise, and the veterans believe it will be their best year. Hope? It was in spring training in 1992 that Jim Palmer attempted to become the only player to play in the major leagues after being elected to the Hall of Fame. It didn't work out, but spring training is the time to make a comeback, to take up switch-hitting, experiment with a knuckleball or switch positions.

It is baseball in its purest form, a time for wind sprints, fundamentals, sliding practice, day games, "B" games, split-squad games and simulated games on a back field when no one is watching. Millionaire players are humanized and humbled in spring training. They aren't getting enormous paychecks every two weeks, and they're getting the same meal money as the rookie in his first big-league camp. No one is exempt from the three-hour bus rides, playing on fields that aren't manicured to major-league standards and facing anonymous Class A pitchers who throw really hard, but have no idea where the ball is going. It is the one time of year that Alex Rodriguez and the twenty-year-old kid are on equal ground. It is the one time of year that a player gets on the bus in uniform, just like in high school.

In some of these little spring training towns, there isn't much to do except play baseball. "Yuma [Arizona] was the best," said former catcher Terry Kennedy of the Padres' spring training site from 1969 to 1993. "We played baseball all day, and cooked out every night. That was it. When we left there, we were ready for the season." The absence of a night light in some spring training sites means fewer chances for the players to get in trouble, but occasionally it happens. Former Orioles pitcher Dennis Martinez, after a night of drinking, crashed his car into a Howard Johnson's restaurant. The next day, teammate Mike Flanagan reminded him, "Dennis, Burger King has a drive-through, McDonald's has a drive-through, Howard Johnson's *doesn't* have a drive-through."

Fundamentals? Pitcher's fielding practice—the dreaded PFP—is done only in spring training, and it is tedious beyond words, but it is important. Just ask the 2006 Tigers. Their pitchers made an error in five straight World Series games. "I made three errors the first month of the [2005] season because I missed spring training and all the fielding drills," said Brewers pitcher Ben Sheets. The Orioles used to run a fielding drill in which the pitchers put their throwing hand behind their back so they wouldn't reflexively try to catch a hard ground ball with their bare hand and perhaps break a finger. Recalcitrant Kevin Brown refused to take part in the drill, calling it "stupid," but in June of 1995, he tried to catch a hard comebacker barehanded; he broke a finger and missed a month.

"We're always inventing drills and conditioning programs in spring training," said Dodgers third-base coach Rich Donnelly, who has been to spring training as a player or a coach for thirty-eight years. "Years ago, we'd do ten jumping jacks, touch our toes twice, then play. Today, these strength and conditioning coaches are always coming up with new stuff: rubber bands, parachutes, cones. I just can't imagine Ted Williams going to spring training and running with a parachute on his back, or Babe Ruth jumping over a bunch of cones."

It is a time to practice bunt plays, rundown plays, and cutoff plays, situations and drills that are very difficult to work on during the season: The repetition done in spring training usually has to last the entire season. In spring training 1971, the Senators were working on a rundown play, but there was confusion about the proper way to run it. A major argument ensued between the players and coaches. "One of our coaches asked [manager] Ted [Williams] to settle the argument," said Senators catcher Rick Stelmaszek. "Ted hated those drills anyway, but he dragged himself out of the dugout and listened to both sides screaming that their way was right. Finally, Ted had had enough. He said, 'Fuck it, let's hit.'"

Spring training is a time of confusion because there are so many players in camp, some of them have to wear a number in the 80s. In 1980, Scott Meyer, a nonroster catcher with the A's, wore number 100 because there were a hundred players in camp. "We were training at the old Scottsdale Stadium, which had one field," said Mickey Morabito, the A's traveling secretary. "We had guys lined up ten deep for drills. There was nowhere to go." Even some managers keep a numerical roster handy so they can keep track of the players. Writers should, too. In spring training 1988, a *Miami Herald* writer asked around the press box for the scheduled pitchers for the White Sox for the next day. I never looked up from my computer and said, jokingly, "Joel Horlen and Gary Peters," who were White Sox pitchers in the 1960s. In 1988, both were fifty years old. The next morning, in the upper-right-hand corner of the front page of the *Herald* sports section were that day's scheduled pitchers for the White Sox: Joel Horlen and Gary Peters.

Spring training is a time for the fans, especially kids. Families take vacations to spring training. Getting a player's autograph is easier then because everything and everyone is more relaxed than during the regular season. Well, except for when the Red Sox and Yankees played for the first time in spring training 2004, their first meeting since Aaron Boone's home run had sent the Yankees to the World Series and the Red Sox home. Tickets were scalped for $500 *for an exhibition game*. Before the game, there was a fight in the parking lot at City of Palms Park in Fort Myers between a Yankee fan and a Red Sox fan . . . both of them women.

Usually, spring training is a happy, friendly time. In 1989, I left tickets for a friend, Ron Petrella, so he could see his beloved Pirates in an exhibition game against the Orioles.

"The tickets weren't there," he told me the next day.

"Oh, no," I said. "What did you do? Did you get in the game?"

"Not quite," Petrella said. "Since they lost my tickets, they gave me an all-access pass for the game, so I went on the field for batting practice. I went in the dugout, and was invited by some of the Pirates to stay there for the game. I high-fived Andy Van Slyke after he hit a homer. I talked to [manager] Jim Leyland during the game. I stuck my head out of the dugout to wave to my wife, and all these people in the stands waved back at me. They thought I was someone important. I think the Pirates thought I was the owner's son."

Spring training is a time for afternoon golf, fishing, NCAA basketball pools, and evenings at the track. It is a time to bend the rules in the name of fun. Singer Charley Pride works out with the Rangers every year. Singer Garth Brooks worked out with the Mets and Padres in separate years; he even played in a few exhibition games. Only in spring training would Barry Bonds dress up as Paula Abdul in the Giants' spoof of *American Idol*.

It is a time to meet and bond with new teammates. In spring training 1999, Rickey Henderson of the Mets was reunited with first baseman John Olerud, who had been his teammate with the Blue Jays six years earlier. As most people know, Olerud wore a helmet instead of a hat in the field for his career because in college he had an aneurysm which required brain surgery, so, to protect his head, he was allowed to wear a helmet in the field. The story surely apactophal, Henderson was talking to Olerud one day, noticed the helmet, and said, "You know, when I played in Toronto, we had a guy who wore a helmet."

"Rickey," said Olerud, "that was *me*."

Bonding? After the 1972 season, the Orioles traded for catcher

Earl Williams. That first spring, Baltimore manager Earl Weaver started Williams in the first four exhibition games so he could learn more about the top four pitchers in the rotation. Williams walked into Weaver's office before the fourth game and shouted, "Don't we have any other fucking catchers on this team?" Williams only lasted two years in Baltimore.

In 2006, the Padres signed power-hitting catcher Mike Piazza, who met his new teammates in spring training. Some had played against him for years, but they didn't realize how strong he was. "We have this hand-squeeze strength test," said Padres manager Bruce Bochy. "A lot of guys can barely do it. Mike did it easily. It was like Herman Munster."

It is a time to meet the hot young prospects. It was in spring training 2006 that we learned that Rangers second baseman Ian Kinsler's father was a former prison warden. It was in spring training 1984 that a writer took Phillies rookie Jeff Stone to lunch, asked if he wanted a shrimp cocktail, and Stone said, "No, thanks, I don't drink." This was the same Jeff Stone who, in his first year of pro ball in Oregon, looked at the night sky and asked a teammate, "Is that the same moon we have at home?" Spring training 1985 was the first for Rangers reliever Mitch Williams. In his first throwing session against hitters, his first pitch *missed the batting cage.* Then Williams hit veteran Alan Bannister with a pitch. The two veterans next in line to hit, Buddy Bell and Larry Parrish, refused to bat against Williams, and were excused from batting practice. "That's OK," Williams later said, "I didn't want to kill a teammate in my first spring in a major-league camp."

Years later, when Williams was established, but only slightly less wild, he got word that one of his teammates was supposedly planning to fake an injury so he wouldn't have to play that season, but would get service time and a major-league salary by staying on the disabled list all year. So, in batting practice, Williams hit the guy in the head with a pitch. "*Now*," Williams screamed, "you're hurt!"

It is a time to see what the winter had done—good or bad—to players' bodies. When Mariners second baseman Bret Boone came to spring training in 2001 buffed beyond belief, former teammate Tony Gwynn looked at him and, startled, said, "What happened to you?" Boone said he had hired a personal trainer and worked out like never before in the winter. "He looks like Tarzan," Seattle manager Lou Piniella said. When the Yankees' Jason Giambi came to camp in 2004 looking thirty pounds lighter after the BALCO steroid scandal had hit, he said he had lost four pounds and claimed he had gotten fit by cutting out junk foods.

It is the most important time of year for some players because it might be their chance to make a major-league team for the first time. It was in spring training 2001 that Albert Pujols came from nowhere to win a starting job with the Cardinals. "Every day he did something that made us keep him on our club," said Cardinals manager Tony LaRussa. For the young player, his ten at-bats in spring training might be the biggest ten he will ever get. For the veteran reliever who is hanging on, trying to win just one more job, the seven innings he'll throw in spring training might mean the difference between another year in the major leagues, and retirement. The hardest job for a manager is giving seventy players a chance to prove themselves in spring training—for he knows that ten at-bats or seven innings of pitching aren't enough for a player to prove himself.

It is an entirely different story for established players with guaranteed contracts and guaranteed spots on the roster. For them, spring training is too long: The position players say they need about two weeks, not six weeks, to get ready; most pitchers say they need at most a month. The spring is nothing more than a time to get in shape, find their swing, and not get hurt. Most players are so wealthy they don't have to work a real job in the off-season, as players did twenty years ago, so they spend the winter working out. "I hired a personal trainer this winter," said Rangers DH Phil Nevin in spring training 2006. "Everyone does. When was the last time you heard about a player coming to camp in terrible shape?" Twenty years ago, hitters took batting practice off a coach for the first two weeks of spring training to get their timing back. "We hit against our real pitchers the first day of camp," said Brewers third baseman Jeff Cirillo in spring training 2006.

It is a time for cuts. Usually three or four times every spring, the manager has to call players into his office and tell them that they didn't make the club. Most players know it's coming, but some don't, some get released, which can result in tears, tirades, and retirements. It also is a time for contract holdouts. Rickey Henderson left camp in spring training 1991, the year after he won the American League MVP, in a salary dispute. Eventually, he came back, and played for his original salary, but Rickey always seemed to have trouble with his contract. He once told Mets general manager Steve Phillips that he wanted a Winnebago, a Madden-like Cruiser, in his contract. Phillips wouldn't give it to him.

"He called me 'GM' because he didn't know my name," Phillips said. "He'd say, 'Hey, GM, Rickey has a black circle around his heart over this contract. Rickey had a black circle around his heart when he was with the Yankees, and you know how that turned out.'" This is the same Rickey Henderson who didn't cash a signing bonus check of $1 million from the Mets for six months because he was "waiting for the interest rate to go up."

It is the only time of year when winning and losing, and the statistics of the game, are largely irrelevant. The Cubs went 7–20 in spring training 1984, and went on to win the National League East that season. The 2002 Orioles went 20–9 in spring training, but lost 95 games during the regular season. There is an unconfirmed story that Yankees right fielder Lou Piniella purposely dropped a fly ball in extra innings of an exhibition game because everyone was tired, and the Yankees wanted to go home more than they wanted to win.

Late in spring training 1984, Rangers outfielder Larry Parrish told his teammates to purposely make outs against Royals starter Paul Splittorff, who was nearing the end of a solid career, but needed a good, final start of spring training to make the team. If Splittorff had pitched well against the Rangers, Parrish figured, they would get to face him in the first month of the regular season, then they could light him up when the games counted.

When Jim Edmonds was with the Angels, he got so many hits one spring, he asked out of the lineup because he feared that he was using up his best swings during a time when they didn't count. And yet, baseball is filled with stories of players who crush the ball in spring training, but not in the regular season. One was former Rangers outfielder Joe Lovitto, one of the great spring training hitters of all time, but once the season began, he said, "It was the same old shit." He finished with a .216 average in four big-league seasons.

It is a time for small towns in Florida and Arizona to come to life the day that pitchers and catchers report in February. Lakeland has been home to Tigertown, and Joker Marchant Stadium, for sixty-one years. The Pirates have trained in Bradenton, Florida, for thirty-eight years. The Marlins used to train in Viera, Florida. "It was so windy there," said former Marlins coach Rich Donnelly, "it was like training on the deck of an aircraft carrier." The Reds trained for ten years in Plant City, Florida. The clubhouse was located about fifty feet from a pond. One day, an enormous alligator emerged and stood motionless for fifteen minutes, then darted back into the water. "They had to go get that rascal," said former Reds pitcher Jeff Brantley. "They sent some divers and got him out of that pond before he could eat one of the players."

Vero Beach has been home to Dodgertown since 1947. There

used to be nothing better than going to Vero even for even one day in spring training. It had a golf course on the premises, an open bar, and a pool table in the pressroom. When the O'Malley family owned the team, they would have special events, such as Christmas in Dodgertown, and all the employees there were made to feel like family. If you were lucky enough to go there on the right day, there was a chance you would see Sandy Koufax, a special spring training instructor, throwing batting practice. He was maybe fifty, but his motion was as fluid as ever, and he still threw hard. It was like going back in time.

My first spring training was in 1982 in Pompano Beach, Florida. I was the new beat writer for the Rangers, and as I drove to the ballpark that first day, I found the location on the map. It read MUNICIPAL STADIUM, HOME OF THE WASHINGTON SENATORS. The Senators had moved to Texas ten years earlier. It was a dump of a spring training site, with seating capacity of about eight hundred, and with only one practice field. The clubhouse was tiny. "I didn't even have a locker," said former Rangers pitcher Jack Lazorko. "My locker was made from chicken wire."

There was no weight room that first year. The players did their running in full uniform through a municipal park that was inhabited by all sorts of people, including those on their lunch break. "It was a joke," said Rangers pitcher Ron Darling. "There were benches halfway through the course. We used to stop there for a rest. The one day that we got timed, we all figured out shortcuts through the park so we would have a much better time."

Beyond the left-field fence at Municipal Stadium was the airstrip where the Goodyear blimp was stationed. "I drove that blimp one day. That was the highlight of my spring training, baseball was secondary to the blimp in Pompano Beach," said Rich Donnelly, then a coach for the Rangers. "We drove it as low as we could go. We drove it over the team hotel once, guys were on the deck drinking, and we were yelling at them from inside the blimp."

There has never been anything like spring training in Pompano Beach with Doug Rader as the manager. One day, he had a picnic in center field for the players. He had the equipment man, Joe Macko, buy a bunch of beach blankets, and had the coaches serve the players hot dogs. One Saturday night, Rader and Donnelly went to evening mass in full uniform and spikes. "I was so embarrassed," Donnelly said. "Doug thought it was great."

One spring, the Rangers were having trouble scoring runs, so on the way to the ballpark, Rader picked up a drunk named Nick on the street. Rader dressed him in a Ranger uniform and brought him out of the dugout to talk to the team about hitting, introducing him as "one of the finest hitting instructors" in baseball. "This poor guy was so hung over—hadn't shaved in weeks, he smelled, he had peed in his pants, he had thrown up on himself," said Donnelly. "He came out with a fungo bat and said, 'OK, you grab this thing, and you swing it like this.' It was ridiculous. But [outfielder] Mickey [Rivers] said, 'That's right. Listen to this guy. He knows what he's talking about.' Everyone cracked up. We cleaned him up, gave him something to eat, dropped him back downtown in a Ranger uniform."

I covered the Orioles for three years at Bobby Maduro Stadium in downtown Miami. My first day there in February 1986, I was cut off by a speeding truck—it had BOMB SQUAD written on the side—at 7:45 A.M. When I arrived at the ballpark, a policeman had his foot on a man's neck and a gun pointed at his head, not fifty feet from the media parking lot. There was one main field, then the famed Little Field, which was just an infield, with a fence ten feet beyond the infield grass. "Just like at Fenway Park," said Orioles pitcher Mike Flanagan. He was traded in 1987 to the Blue Jays, who trained across the state in Dunedin. When asked about the difference between the west coast and east coast of Florida, Flanagan laughed and said, "No armed guards in the parking lot."

Twenty-five years ago, it was standard that teams would train their major-league team in one site, and their minor leaguers in another; sometimes, they were three hours apart. Now, teams have spectacular spring training complexes that house both major- and minor-league players, which is great for continuity. These new complexes have sensational playing fields, seating for nearly ten thousand fans, and clubhouses that are much better and much more spacious than the clubhouses in some of the old-time ballparks in the major leagues.

Spring training has changed so much in the last twenty-five years, but to baseball fans, especially in the Northeast, the four best words in the English language are "Pitchers and catchers report." The pilgrimage to spring training is a special one for fans and players alike, though not like it used to be when players would sometimes drive as many as three thousand miles to camp to get the full effect of going to spring training. Former Marlins center fielder Chuck Carr drove a thousand miles to the club's first spring training in 1993. He stopped at as many pool halls as he could find. "And I took a lot of people's money on the way," he said.

That spring, Carr kept his cue stick next to his glove in his locker, which brings us back to Brian Anderson, the flaky left-hander who forgot his glove and spikes on the trip to Vero.

"I was a Nike guy, so I had to black out the Adidas stripes on my spikes," said Anderson. "I was a Rawlings guy, so I had to black out the Wilson label on my new glove. I had violated every part of my contract. The next spring, this lady comes up to me with a picture of me to sign. I'm halfway through my windup, and it's a perfect shot of my blacked-out shoes and blacked-out glove. That story could only happen in spring training."

11

The Sun Will Rise, the Sun Will Set, and I'll Have Lunch

At the winter meetings in 1975 in Hollywood, Florida, White Sox general manager Roland Hemond noticed an unusual configuration in the lobby of the Diplomat Hotel. There were four tables arranged in a circle, so he suggested to his new owner, Bill Veeck, that the White Sox should set up in the lobby and make deals from there, to which Veeck said, "What are you waiting for?" Hemond put up an OPEN FOR BUSINESS sign and started dealing.

"By midnight," Hemond said, "we had made four trades."

Thirty-one years later, I don't think I even saw half of the thirty general managers in the four days at the winter meetings in Orlando. Most of them didn't even make an appearance in the lobby; they were sequestered in their suites with their cell phones, BlackBerrys, computers, contract books, and reams and reams of reports. About the only time you see a GM is in the interview room, where they are required to go if they make a trade or sign a player, or in the workout room at 6:30 in the morning on the Stairmaster or an exercise bike.

No role in baseball has changed more than that of the GM. Twenty years ago, it was a job for a former player or a seasoned executive, a veteran baseball guy who had worked his way through the ranks of farm director, scouting director, and assistant GM, someone expert in player evaluation and the art of making a trade. In certain years in the 1980s, 75 percent of the GMs were former major-league players. In 2006, only four of the thirty GMs had played in the major leagues; only one third had played professional ball; and some of them hadn't even played baseball in high school. It has become a job for young, extremely bright, sometimes Ivy League–educated guys whose specialties include arcane waiver rules, interpreting a spreadsheet, statistical analysis, and managing massive payrolls.

Working out at 6:30 A.M.? Twenty-five years ago, that's when some general managers were going to bed after a night of drinking and dealing. "It's like they said, 'The GM with the biggest bar in his room made the most trades,'" said Orioles co-GM Jim Duquette. It was the classic "smoke-filled room" environment when deals were made; now the rooms of general managers are filled with bottles of Dasani water, the humming of computers, and the bleating of cell phones.

I like the old way better. I miss Phillies GM Paul Owens. At one winter meetings in the early eighties, Owens, then in his sixties, had had a few too many, and, at 1:30 in the morning, arguing with a colleague about the proper way to do a hook slide, he yanked off his coat and demonstrated the slide across the floor of the hotel lobby. And it was "the Pope," as Owens was called, who once had his PR man wake up the Phillies beat writers at 2:30 A.M. for "a major announcement." The writers went to Owens's room, where he said, "I'm proud to announce that we got Sutter." But it wasn't Bruce Sutter, who was baseball's best closer, it was minor-leaguer Burke Sutter, who did not require a 2:30 A.M. wake-up call.

I miss former White Sox GM Ken Harrelson. I once called him to check on a trade rumor with my team, the Rangers, and Harrelson not only confirmed the talks, but volunteered the names of the players involved—on the record—several days before the deal was made. (Sadly, Harrleson only lasted one year in the job.) That would never, ever happen today. And they don't make GMs like Larry Doughty anymore, either. He is a former Pirates GM who once boasted to his manager and his coaches that he could make a shot from the opposite foul line on a basketball court—that is a 79-foot shot—while sitting on his butt.

I miss Roland Hemond, who, in an attempt to end the Orioles' major-league record for the longest losing streak at the start of a season, wore the suit that he had worn in the celebration for the White Sox winning the American League West title in 1983. It had been on display, under glass, for six years at Comiskey Park, and it had shrunk badly because it had been soaked with champagne. But for good luck, Hemond wore it one day in Minneapolis: The pants highwatered halfway up his legs. But the Orioles lost their nineteenth game in a row.

I miss Hank Peters, GM of the World Champion Orioles in 1983. As he stood on the podium with the championship trophy in his hand, Orioles owner Edward Bennett Williams whispered in his ear, "I'm worried about next year." In 1988, two weeks after his team had allowed a major league record ten home runs in a game in Toronto, Peters invited me into his office. "I call it 'the Barrage,'" he said, mischievously. He showed me a tape of the complete at-bats of each of the ten homers. "We're sending this tape to all the pitchers in our organization to show them the proper way *not* to pitch," he said.

I miss Al Rosen, a former Giants GM. He was one of the first GMs to include salary details when he signed a player "because you guys [the media] are going to find out anyway, and this way, you won't get it wrong." I miss Clyde King, a former Yankee GM who told the funniest stories. When he was a high school basketball player in North Carolina, he says, he confused an opponent one game by wearing two left sneakers, so when his defender looked at King's feet to see which way he was going, he couldn't tell.

I miss Jack McKeon, a former Padres GM who earned the nickname "Trader Jack" because he would walk the halls of the winter meetings, always smoking a cigar, and always looking for a trade to make. I miss Sandy Alderson, formerly of the A's, who once played basketball against some writers in a pickup game in spring training. Alderson, who had served as an officer in Vietnam, was playing a little rough when a writer, who had no idea that Alderson had a military background, said to him, "Whoa, stand down, soldier." The next time down the floor, Alderson elbowed the writer clear across the lane.

I miss former Red Sox GM Lou Gorman. One agent said that Gorman fell asleep during a negotiation on a player's contract. "I had to drop the *Baseball Encyclopedia* on the floor to wake him up," the agent said. "When he woke up, I should have said, 'OK Lou, the deal is done.'" Gorman was good at what he did, but he occasionally did and said funny things. When once describing the potent lineup of the Seattle Mariners, Gorman said, "Well, they have more than just Griffey in the middle of the order, they have others, they have Bailey Howell . . ." He meant Jay Buhner, not the crew-cut small forward of the Boston Celtics in the late sixties. And when Red Sox ace Roger Clemens walked out of camp one year in a contract dispute, Gorman was asked what he was going to do about it. He said, "The sun will rise, the sun will set, and I'll have lunch."

I even miss Howard Fox, a former general manager of the Twins. "We were playing on the West Coast, and the next morning I get a call from Howard, who was on the golf course, and he says, 'How did you guys do last night?'" said former Twins manager Ray Miller. "He didn't even know whether we had won or lost. I told him that we needed a player last night, someone had gotten hurt, and I couldn't find him anywhere. Finally, he said that he'd see what he could do. We needed a shortstop, and an outfielder showed up."

Today's GM isn't playing golf. Today's GM is working harder than ever, has more responsibility than ever, and is under more pressure than ever to win. It is a daily challenge for a GM to keep up with all that's going on with his team, his minor-league system, the disabled list, the waiver wire, etc. Thanks to free agency in the major and minor leagues, and new rules and regulations on player movement, players are coming and going from teams at extraordinary rates, and it's up the GM to know where everyone is going. In 1980, the Braves used eleven pitchers all year. In 2000, the Indians used thirty-four pitchers, a major-league record. Veteran pitcher Chuck Finley and some teammates had a contest to see who could come the closest to naming all thirty-four pitchers: "The best anyone did was twenty-seven, meaning the best we had still forgot seven pitchers who pitched for our team this year," Finley said, laughing. "There was a difference of opinion on one pitcher's name. One guy said was it was Kane Davis. The other said it was Davis Kane." (It was Kane Davis.)

"The GM job is a brutal job now," says ESPN analyst Steve Phillips, a former GM for the Mets.

Why? "Two reasons," says Braves GM John Schuerholz, who is sixty-five years old and has been doing the job for twenty-five years. "First, the impact of the financial decisions we have to make has exploded. Every decision we make now could save our owner millions and millions of dollars. And every decision could cost our owner millions and millions of dollars.

"Secondly, the media. The media has become so enormous over the years, and the GM has to be the point person to respond in a knowledgeable way. We have to communicate for the organization for things that haven't even happened yet. The GM has to be more prepared today than ever. You have to be good at it. It's a very challenging part of the job."

Bright, young, hungry people are needed in every line of work, every business, including baseball. But Schuerholz wonders if some of these young guys are ready for the job of GM. "In my view, they're not seasoned enough," he said. "It's not that they're not smart enough. It's not that they haven't collected baseball cards since they were eight years old. It's not that they haven't gotten a degree online. It's just that you can't replace experience."

John Hart, a GM for nearly fifteen years, resigned from that job with the Rangers in 2005 in part because, among other factors, he could no longer deal with the media. Because of his distant and acrimonious relationship with the press, he didn't feel like he could be the front man, the objective spokesperson for the organization that a GM has to be. He also had grown tired of dealing with millionaire players and their demanding agents, so he quit to become a consultant for $500,000 a year. At the 2005 winter meetings in Dallas, he was dressed in a sweat suit, and was the most relaxed person in the lobby because he's not a GM.

Hart's replacement is Jon Daniels, twenty-nine. Twenty years ago, it was inconceivable to think that a team would name a twenty-nine-year-old as GM, but Daniels is one of several over the last fifteen years to be named as a GM in his late twenties or early thirties. Daniels went to Cornell, one of four GMs who have an Ivy League education: there are as many Ivy League GMs as GMs who played in the major leagues. That's the trend today. Owners have chosen to trust their millions to men with a background in business, finance, economics, and law, not men who can demonstrate the proper way to do a hook slide in the wee hours of the morning.

Jon Daniels may do very well for the Rangers. Like most of the young GMs, he is very intelligent and hardworking, a wizard with numbers and with the Internet. But the danger with most of the young GMs is their lack of a baseball background. After Cornell, Daniels went to work briefly on Wall Street; his only baseball involvement was that as a serious Rotisserie League player. He interned with the Colorado Rockies for several years before being hired by the Rangers as Hart's assistant. When Daniels was named GM, one veteran Ranger player was surprised, saying, "I don't even know what he looks like."

Like Daniels, some other young GMs come from backgrounds that weren't primarily baseball related. Indians GM Mark Shapiro played football at Princeton. Dodgers GM Ned Coletti began his career as a sportswriter, then became the PR director of the Cubs. Rockies GM Dan O'Dowd was a marketing guy with the Orioles. Ex-Dodgers GM Paul DePodesta played wide receiver at Harvard. DePodesta says he finds it interesting that at Harvard he was criticized for being "a jock," but in baseball was criticized for being "a nerd."

Nationals GM Jim Bowden became the Reds GM at age thirty-one, which made him, at the time, the youngest in major-league history. "I wanted to be a GM when I was eight years old," Bowden said. "[Red Sox GM] Dick O'Connell traded Reggie Smith, I didn't like the trade, and that's when I decided I wanted to be a GM. Back when I was a kid, I was playing APBA and Strat-O-Matic, making trades and setting rosters and doing statistical analysis. But kids today have all these cool video games, and they do everything for you."

Bowden went to Rollins College in Florida, where he was a roommate with John Galbreath, a son of the owner of the Pittsburgh Pirates. "I majored in business communications, but I designed it for baseball," Bowden said. "During spring training, I went to the Pirates' facility every day. When I was in college, I was learning how to be a general manager from Pete Peterson and other guys. I did player interviews. It was all planned."

The epitome of the young GM is the Red Sox's Theo Epstein, who, at twenty-eight, became the youngest GM in baseball history, and whose background is more attuned to writing than baseball. His grandfather Philip Epstein co-wrote the screenplay for *Casablanca*. His father, Lesley, is the director of creative writing at Boston University. His sister, Anya, is a screenwriter, most recently for the TV show *Commander in Chief*. His brother-in-law, Danny Futterman, wrote the screenplay for the movie *Capote*. His brother, Paul, is a social worker. Theo loves Pearl Jam, and has played and sung on several CDs. In high school, he was much more of a soccer player than a baseball player.

Epstein, who went to Yale, got his start in baseball in 1992 as a summer intern with the Orioles, who were owned by Yalie Eli Jacobs, and had another Yalie, Calvin Hill, working in the front office. When Orioles president Larry Lucchino and Dr. Charles Steinberg, the Orioles' director of public affairs, went to San Diego, they took Epstein with them. The Padres sent him to law school at the University of San Diego while he was working for the club. When Lucchino and Steinberg went to Boston, they took Epstein with them.

Lucchino named Epstein Red Sox general manager in 2002, and now Epstein is a white knight in Boston, the man who, in 2004, helped deliver the franchise's first World Series championship in eighty-six years. He resigned in 2005 partly because of a strained relationship with Lucchino and partly because he'd lost all semblance of a private life. Brutal job? Who leaves the dream setup of being the GM of the team you grew up worshiping? What thirty-two-year-old turns down a three-year, $2.5-million contract? Three months later, Epstein returned to the job, much to the delight of all of New England. He is a fascinating guy—he didn't get his driver's license until he was twenty-three—and is fascinated by many things. His success in baseball has made him somewhat arrogant; it has given him an air of being better than everyone. He has become more guarded and less accessible to the media. And yet he remains a fun, self-deprecating guy, especially about his singing voice. When the Red Sox passed on drafting catcher Aaron Greenblatt from Brookline High School, which Epstein attended, Epstein explained, "I would have had every Jewish mother from Brookline on me for twenty years."

With most of the young GMs who never played the game after high school, there is a real question about how well they really know and understand the game. Computer printouts and abstruse statistics are great, for they really are barometers to a player's effectiveness, but there is no substitute for a GM being able to look at a baseball player and evaluate whether he can play. Epstein certainly can't do that as well as White Sox general manager Kenny Williams, who played in the major leagues. But Epstein surrounds himself with veteran baseball men who can evaluate players. If the numbers and the contract particulars suggest that a player can help the Red Sox, Epstein will target that player; then he dispatches a veteran scout to see if the guy can play.

Not all the young GMs work that way. Some of them are so immersed in numbers, they don't factor in the human qualities of a player. Some of them get so caught up in the running of the team, they think they know it all. This really causes a problem for veteran baseball guys who work for them. "I hate my GM," a veteran manager once told me. "I want to beat the hell out of him." A veteran scout told me that his young GM was so annoying and so immature, "I want to hit him. But I know that would kill him."

Billy Beane, of the book *MoneyBall,* is probably the best known general manager in the game today. He can crunch the numbers, he can see where the game is going with the best of the Ivy League GMs, but being a former major-league player, he can also look at a player and tell you if he can play. That's what separates Beane from others. He was portrayed in *Moneyball* as arrogant, hot-tempered, and competitive, among other things. I have seen all that behavior, including in pickup basketball, where he is really competitive. But there is no denying his brilliance, ingenuity, vision, and courage.

Beane has established a philosophy for his team, including eschewing the stolen base because the risk of advancing ninety feet far outweighs the reward. "You guys were last in the league in steals with twenty-nine," I told Beane one spring. He said, "Great. I wish we'd had fewer."

Beane told me in 2005, "If you're sitting in your box watching a game and you say, 'We need to rebuild,' it's too late." Beane always is looking ahead, even when he doesn't want to, but knows he has to. Following the 2004 season in which the A's won 91 games and barely missed a fifth straight trip to the play-offs, Beane traded pitchers Mark Mulder and Tim Hudson. They were his favorite guys on the team—he had drafted them—but they were going to make too much money, and the small-market A's were not going to be able to afford them, so Beane traded them at their peak value. In baseball history, only two other pitchers as young as Mulder or Hudson, with winning percentages as high as theirs, had ever been traded, and Beane matched that total in three weeks. The A's still won 88 games in 2005, and nearly made the play-offs. In 2006, they made it to the American League Championship Series.

Beane has been fearless about not only trading away star players, but giving young players a chance to play in the major leagues. "I'll take talent over experience any day," he said. That's how Hudson, Mulder, Barry Zito, Bobby Crosby, and many other A's got their start: Their GM showed faith in them by throwing them into the middle of a pennant race.

Under Beane's tutelage, J. P. Ricciardi became the general manager of the Blue Jays and DePodesta of the Dodgers. A's assistant GM David Forst, who went to Harvard, will be a GM someday. One of Epstein's guys, Josh Byrnes, is the GM of the Diamondbacks. Two others, young Ben Cherington and Jed Hoyer of the Red Sox, may also be GMs someday.

Meet the new boss, *not* the same as the old boss. The trend of hiring young, slick, bright guys as general managers will continue. There will be no more who wear two left shoes, who wear ridiculously shrunken suits for good luck, shoot a basketball from his butt from three-quarters court, fall asleep during a contract negotiation, mistake Jay Buhner for Bailey Howell, or ask his manager the next day, "How did you guys do last night?" And, regrettably, we'll never see another OPEN FOR BUSINESS sign in the lobby of the winter meetings.

12

It's Ambidextrous, Not Amphibious

Cardinals pitcher Mark Mulder hit line drive after line drive during batting practice before Game 3 of the 2005 National League Championship Series. His swing is left-handed and it is especially gorgeous for a pitcher. Mulder throws left-handed, but after his BP was over, he autographed some baseballs. He signed them with his right hand. What is that?

"I write right-handed," Mulder said. "Everything I do below my waist, I do right-handed. Don't ask me to explain because I don't know why. I play golf right-handed. I bowl right-handed. If I played hockey, I would shoot right-handed because it's down here. I shoot pool right-handed. I can play tennis with either hand. I played in a charity softball game and I had to pitch, and I had to pitch underhanded, so I pitched right-handed. But since I throw left-handed, I had to switch my glove to my other hand so if a ball was hit back to me, I could catch, then throw it with my left hand . . . I know, I'm completely screwed up."

You think? One of the best left-handed pitchers in the game cannot pitch a softball left-handed because it is an underhand motion?

"That's the most peculiar form of ambidexterity I've ever heard of," said Ted Simmons, one of the greatest switch-hitters ever.

Peculiar? Mark Mulder is way beyond that. Peculiar is former pitcher Dave Stieb, who throws and bats right-handed, but shoots a basketball left-handed. And former outfielder Jim Dwyer, who bats left-handed, but carries left-handed and right-handed clubs in his golf bag because he hits some shots better right-handed than left-handed. And former outfielder Andy Van Slyke, who throws and plays golf right-handed, writes, bats, and plays hockey left-handed. "I tried to hit a golf ball left-handed, and I whiffed," he said. "It confuses me, especially the hockey and golf thing. Why left-handed one way and the other way right-handed? It's a left-brain, right-brain thing, but for me, it's a no-brain thing."

There are a lot of screwed-up players in baseball, and, in that regard, screwed-up is good. It means that both hands work well. It means that the hand that goes inside the glove is dexterous, so chances are it will help the player defensively, if not in all ways. I learned this the first time I met the great Brooks Robinson, who won sixteen Gold Gloves at third base. He was at a luncheon in 1981, and he ate with his left hand. Later that day, I saw him signing autographs with his left hand. How could this be? How much more right-handed can you get than a right-handed-hitting third baseman? "I noticed it the first day I met him," said Davey Johnson, who played second base for the Orioles when Robinson was the third baseman. "I looked at Brooks and thought to myself, 'He's the best defensive third baseman of all time, and he writes with his left hand.' So I wrote with my left hand for a year hoping that it would make me a better defensive second baseman. It didn't work."

I've talked to hundreds of players about forms of ambidexterity, and I've found very few who are completely right-handed or left-handed. More often, there is someone such as the Astros' Craig Biggio, who bats and throws right-handed, yet writes and eats left-handed. Ex-outfielder Al Oliver throws and hits left-handed, but plays racquetball right-handed. Former outfielder Lance Johnson bats and throws left-handed, but writes right-handed. So did Babe Ruth, the greatest player ever. Tom House, a former major-league pitcher, throws and bats left-handed, he knocks in a nail and swings a sledgehammer left-handed, but writes, eats, plays Ping-Pong and tennis right-handed. He kicks right-footed, but when doing squats, his left leg is his dominant leg. For movement requiring power, he uses his left hand or foot; for movement requiring finesse, he uses his right.

Why is this? And why are great athletes, at least it seems to me, more like this than nonathletes?

"They have a genetic predisposition," said House, who has a degree in kinesiology. "Kids that are gifted athletes have more nerve endings for the brain to program. When the brain says go, more is being accessed. The genetically blessed have more nerves in more muscles, and their brains work very well with the nervous system. Their freeway system has a lot more outlets than nonathletes. And if there's enough repetition of a skill or an exercise at an early age, the athletes can flip-flop—left to right, right to left—much more easily."

Mets closer Billy Wagner was born right-handed, he does everything right-handed, but he broke his right arm as a young boy, switched to throwing a baseball left-handed, and now throws 100 mph left-handed. That is extraordinary. Left-hander Tommy John, who won 288 games in the big leagues, was born right-handed, but had to switch after a childhood accident. "When he switched," one general manager told me, "that's when he started to stutter."

John stutters, but, he said, the rest "is not true."

I have a friend, who is in his fifties and not particularly athletic, who says if he decided to start throwing left-handed, he would be an accomplished thrower within a month. That is preposterous. He could practice for twenty years and wouldn't look athletic throwing a baseball with his left hand. But if a ball is put in the opposite hand of a child who is genetically predisposed to athletics, the child could learn to throw with the opposite hand a lot easier than my fifty-year-old friend. Rich Donnelly, the Dodgers third baseman, does everything right-handed except hit a baseball, twist the bottle off a cap, and clap. Since his oldest son Bubba was five years old, every Tuesday at the Donnelly house was "left-handed day," so Bubba had to do everything—eat, write, shoot a basketball, etc.—left-handed. That training—he had a great left hand—helped him to play basketball at Robert Morris University.

"That's how my father did it with me," Donnelly said. "Every Tuesday, I brought lunch to school because I didn't want to use a fork because I didn't want to embarrass myself. . . . When I used a fork, by the time I got the food in my mouth, it was two o'clock. I bet if you asked all right-handed nonathletes to eat with their left hand, they would starve. But with athletes, maybe 90 percent of them had 'left-handed Tuesdays' that we don't know about."

Some baseball players are ambidextrous, or, as former infielder Jim Morrison once called it, "amphibious," which he defined as "being able to throw underwater." There have been four ambidextrous pitchers in baseball history, the first being Tony Mullane, who actually pitched right-handed and left-handed in one game in 1882. In *The Baseball Encyclopedia*, Mullane is listed as "Bats, Both. Throws, Both." Jackie Price, the unusual shortstop from the 1940s, learned to throw a pitch right-handed and left-handed at the same time—a fastball with one, a curveball with the other.

"I could pitch in a game left-handed, I know it. I can throw 80 mph at least," right-hander Greg Harris told me in spring training 1985. He was special case, he was also a switch-hitter, and could play golf left-handed or right-handed. He showed me the special glove he had made, one that, with an adjustment, would go from a right-handed glove to a left-handed glove. So, in 1995, in a meaningless game in September, Expos manager Felipe Alou allowed Harris to pitch an inning throwing right-handed and left-handed. Paul Richards, a former major-league catcher, threw with both hands. Hall of Famer George Brett, a right-handed thrower, used to throw batting practice left-handed. Indians catcher Victor Martinez says he throws 75 mph left-handed "with a curveball and a slider."

And then there is the curious case of Travis Lee, the first baseman for the Tampa Bay Devil Rays, and Tom Foley, the Devil Rays' third-base coach. Lee throws a baseball left-handed, but in high school he was a *right-handed* quarterback. Foley throws right-handed, but in high school he played quarterback and threw *left-handed*. How can this be? Throwing a football and throwing a baseball use basically the same motion, yet in the same clubhouse, two guys throw a baseball with the opposite hand they use to throw a football. This is not a first for Foley. When he played for the Pirates, teammate Steve Cooke pitched left-handed, but was a right-handed quarterback in high school.

"I do everything right-handed; the only thing I do left-handed is play baseball," Lee said. "I don't know why. I asked my parents and they told me when I was a kid, I just picked up a left-hander's glove and started throwing." But when Lee picked up a football, he threw it right-handed. "I can throw a baseball with my right hand, but I can't throw a football left-handed—all I throw are wounded ducks," Lee said. "In high school, guys would say, 'Roll to your right and throw right-handed; roll to you left and throw left-handed.' But I couldn't do that."

Lee says he "just doesn't feel comfortable" with the glove on his left hand. "In a perfect world," he said, "I'd catch the ball, take my glove off, switch hands, and throw with my right."

Foley is the opposite. "I'm left-handed, but I bowl and shoot pool right-handed—I have no idea why," he said. "My dad was right-handed. He gave me a right-hander's glove, so I threw right-handed." Foley can throw a baseball left-handed, also. Can he throw a football right-handed? "I had to after I separated my shoulder in high school," he said. "I sat out two weeks, then our other quarterback got hurt, so I had to play, and I played right-handed. I completed four out of seven passes. There were some strange looks on the sidelines."

Foley smiled. "It's weird. If I lost my left hand, I'd be dead. I can't wipe my ass right-handed."

Lee and Foley confuse me, as does Rickey Henderson, on many levels, I must say. He bats right-handed, but throws left-handed. Only four nonpitchers in major-league history have played 1,000 games—roughly ten seasons—batting right-handed and throwing left-handed: Henderson, Cleon Jones, Hal Chase, and Hick Carpenter, who played in the nineteenth century. Former outfielder Mark Carreon is one of only another three who played 500 games that way. Why are these guys so rare, and yet there are hundreds of players who bat left-handed and throw right-handed, à la Joe Morgan, George Brett, and Carl Yastrzemski? Is it just that there are a lot more right-handed people in the world than there are left-handers?

"It means I'm using both sides of my brain, which is good . . . I think," said Carreon, who shares his right-left distinction with former Yale first baseman George Herbert Walker Bush and Eddie Gaedel, the midget who batted once for the 1951 Browns. There are usually only two or three players per year who bat right-handed and throw left-handed, yet there are usually around thirty pitchers who are that way, including Randy Johnson. Why so many pitchers, and so few position players? Pitcher Terry Mulholland, who is a terrible hitter, says, "I know I'm a left-handed hitter, but I bat right-handed because I'm the youngest of five boys, and my dad wasn't about to teach the last one how to hit left-handed."

And then there are switch-hitters. The first great switch-hitter in baseball was shortstop George Davis, a Hall of Famer who drove in 136 runs in 1897. By 1927, 6.2 percent of all nonpitchers were switch-hitters. Frankie Frisch, a Hall of Fame second baseman, had a .316 lifetime average, the highest among switch-hitters. But by 1952, the major leagues had only eight switch-hitters, 2.5 percent of all nonpitchers. Then Mickey Mantle reached his prime. "My father made me a switch-hitter when I was eleven because my father loved Mickey Mantle," said infielder Carlos Baerga. "I'm sure a lot of fathers did what mine did."

Mantle's influence wasn't as important as the birth of Astro-Turf and the return of the speed game. The 1987 St. Louis Cardinals, who won the NL pennant, regularly used six switch-hitters. They beat the ball into the turf and ran really fast. By 1992, the major leagues had 99 switch-hitters, 17.2 percent of all nonpitchers. It had fallen to 16 percent in 2005, partly because of the return to natural grass fields and the accent on power, not speed.

Most switch-hitters are natural right-handed hitters who moved to the other side of the box for two main reasons: (*a*) so they wouldn't have to see the breaking ball that's coming at them: it's frightening, and it's hard to hit; and (b) to get a step and a half closer to first base, which could result in more infield hits. White Sox manager Ozzie Guillen was such a terrible right-handed hitter when he signed at age sixteen, the Padres made him into a switch-hitter. He became so much better left-handed, he stayed that way, and dropped right-handed.

"If you try to do it when you're twenty-two, it's too late," says infielder Jose Valentin, a natural left-handed hitter who gave up switch-hitting after six years in the major leagues, then went back to switch-hitting. "In Little League, you're seeing a fastball and an occasional curveball. In pro ball, you see everything."

Giants second baseman Ray Durham was made into a switch-hitter in pro ball in 1991. "I was so bad at first, there would be days where I wouldn't get the ball out of the infield, or wouldn't even hit the ball," he said. "I thought, 'There's no way this is ever going to work.' But after all the sweat, all the blood on my hands, now I'm actually better from the left side. I've hit left-handed twice against [left-hander] Andy Pettitte. How do you figure that?"

Former second baseman Harold Reynolds was made a switch-hitter in his first year of pro ball at age nineteen. "And I hit .590 in high school!" he said. "But I had hit left-handed a lot playing Wiffle ball as a kid, so I tried it. My first year, I hit twelve home runs; eleven of them I hit left-handed. But I'm ambidextrous. When I was a kid, I could throw a football forty yards with my left hand. And in H-O-R-S-E, I would always use my left hand to win. But I had some bad days switching-hitting early on. And I remember Omar Vizquel trying to switch-hit early. He was terrible. I remember watching Ozzie Smith when I was fourteen. He was terrible. But we all started lifting weights; we got stronger and became better. I'd come home from pro ball and my best friend, Mickey Riley, would throw to me. He could throw with either hand and could shoot a basketball with either hand. The key with switch-hitting is to hit exactly the same way left-handed as right-handed. But that's so hard to do, to find your identity from each side. Look at Carl Everett: From one side, he's right on top of the plate; from the other, he's way off the plate. The only two switch-hitters I've ever seen who were the same from each side were two of the best, Eddie Murray and Ted Simmons."

Murray learned to switch-hit as a kid in his backyard, swinging at, among other things, coffee-can lids thrown by his brothers. So when his AA manager, Jim Schaffer, told Murray to try switch-hitting, he tried it *that night*, and got a couple of hits. Simmons, a natural left-handed hitter, began switch-hitting at age nine at the urging of his father, a left-handed hitter, and his brothers, who were right-handed hitters, and were fourteen and seven years older than him. "I've seen guys make the switch when they were in the big leagues—Tito Fuentes, Larry Bowa, Don Kessinger," said Simmons. "But, obviously, the earlier you start switch-hitting, the better." Jose Cruz Jr. didn't attempt switch-hitting until his freshman year in college, but hit over .300 from the left side that first year.

"I started in high school," said Phillies shortstop Jimmy Rollins. "I'm a natural right-handed hitter, but I took so many swings left-handed, by my junior year, I was a better hitter left-handed. I remember crying to my dad, 'Dad, I can't hit right-handed any more.'"

First baseman Tony Clark, who is six feet seven, learned to switch-hit when he was eleven years old. "We went to the park every day and played, and since I was so much bigger than everyone else, my friends made me hit left-handed," he said. "I hit left-handed with my right hand on top [cross-handed) until I was twelve. Then I asked my dad, who was my coach, if I could hit left-handed in a game. He put my hands the right way, and I singled up the middle."

J. T. Snow is a natural left-handed hitter, but he was hit in the back by a pitch when he was ten years old—"It didn't feel very good," he said—so, on the advice of his father, he became a switch-hitter. But by 1999, he was struggling badly from the right side—his weaker side—and was getting so few at-bats from that side, he went back to hitting left-handed.

Snow throws left-handed, but of all the switch-hitting non-pitchers in history, only 4.5 percent throw with their left hand—notables include Wes Parker and Lance Berkman. Why? Is the answer as simple as most people in the world are right-handed? Is it as simple as the fact that many switch-hitters are middle infielders, and therefore have to throw right-handed?

Nothing is simple when trying to explain the forms of ambidexterity. Most of the players who are the way they are can't explain it, but they're happy to be that way because it is one reason they are major leaguers. Simmons and House can explain it, but it gets cloudy for me when we're talking about right-brain, left-brain function, synapses, and kinetic awareness.

"I have the greatest example ever of ambidexterity, this is way more impressive than any switch-hitter, or anyone who can throw with both hands," said Simmons. "I know a woman, she's a soccer player and a schoolteacher. She can write on the blackboard with her left hand, and write on the desk—that's two different planes— with her right hand *at the same time*. I asked her, 'Can you write in cursive with each hand?' She said, 'Of course I can.' Try that some-day. That is the most amazing thing I've ever seen."

It's even more amazing than what Mark Mulder does. But not as peculiar.

13

Angel, My Man

A man, probably in his midsixties, was my driver the day I interviewed at ESPN in 1997. He greeted me inside the Bradley International Airport in Hartford, Connecticut, and breathlessly told me, "I just dropped off one of my favorite people in the world, Robin Roberts."

Well, baseball dope that I am, hopeless seamhead that I've always been, said, "Wow, he was great. Hall of Famer, one of the Whiz Kids, won 286 games, helped start the Players Association."

My driver looked at me and said, "*Who* are you talking about?"

"Robin Roberts," I said. "The baseball pitcher."

He said, "No, no, I'm talking about *the* Robin Roberts."

And so I began to understand the stunning power of television. Robin Roberts is an anchorwoman on ESPN, and is one of the cohosts on ABC's *Good Morning America*. She is beautiful, charming, seamless on television, and was once a terrific college basketball player. At the time, I was astonished that any male in his sixties would associate her, not the Hall of Fame pitcher, with the name Robin Roberts. Not anymore.

ESPN is everywhere in America, twenty-four hours a day.

Highlight shows are generically called *SportsCenter,* as facial tissue is called Kleenex. When I hear the name "Boomer," I no longer think first of former Red Sox first baseman George Scott or pitcher David Wells, I think of ESPN's Chris Berman, with whom I covered the Hall of Fame induction ceremony one year in Cooperstown in 95-degree weather. "This is a three-shirt day," he said, carrying two identical light-blue shirts, which he would need after he sweated through the light-blue shirt he was wearing. When I hear Dan Patrick's home run call—a simple "Gone!"—I know it is the same one he used when he played Strat-O-Matic in between shows at CNN. When I hear "web gem," which has become the buzz phrase around baseball for a great defensive play, I think of the former lead producer of *Baseball Tonight,* Judd Burch, who thought of the concept of recognizing defense while driving to work.

"I'm thinking of putting 'web gems' on my license plate," he said.

Baseball Tonight is a nightly staple for baseball fans across America, including George W. Bush, president of the United States. ESPN tried (unsuccessfully) to broadcast a *Baseball Tonight* show from the White House after learning that it was one of his favorite shows, to which a White House aide said, "It's not *one* of his favorite shows; it's his *favorite* show." When Judd Burch announced during a show meeting that *Baseball Tonight* is the favorite show of the most powerful man in the free world, Tommy Edwards, a director on the show, said, with complete seriousness, "That's nothing. When I told the people at National Car Rental that I was a director on *Baseball Tonight,* they upgraded me from an economy car to a midsize for free."

The president is not alone. *Baseball Tonight* won an Emmy for Best Studio Show in 2002. Every major- and minor-league clubhouse in America tunes in every night. When *BBTN* aired an hourlong *Web Gems Special* one year, a number of players from the

Minnesota Twins gathered at a teammate's house to watch it. Players have called the ESPN studio to complain that their play wasn't a web gem that night. *BBTN* is where many ex-players aspire to work. Steve Phillips was the general manager of the New York Mets when he told his PR man while watching *BBTN*, "That's what I want to do someday." Now he's a regular on all things baseball on ESPN. Two freshmen at my daughter Kelly's high school told me, "We watch *Baseball Tonight* every night. It's the best show on TV."

"You stay up until eleven o'clock on school nights?" I asked.

"No," they said. "We watch the midnight show, too."

Former *BBTN* analyst Harold Reynolds played for eleven years in the major leagues, and made two All-Star teams, but says he is "way more recognizable" from being on ESPN than he was as a player. Then again, he played in Seattle. "I went jogging in Seattle in my Mariners sweatshirt one day," Reynolds said, "and this older lady stopped me and said, 'Oh, so you're in the Marines.'" After two appearances on *Baseball Tonight*, I was more recognizable than I'd been in twelve years at a newspaper and eight years at *Sports Illustrated*. Now I am occasionally recognized in airports, in stores, and on the street. Or I'll get that curious look from people who have seen me, but aren't certain where.

"Where do I know you from?" a man asked me one day at the mall. "Do you work at Applebee's?"

The people who work on the show—from the twenty-two-year-old production assistant who cuts highlights to show host John Buccigross, who takes his children on a baseball trip to different ballparks almost every summer, to sixty-one-year-old icon Peter Gammons, who knows more about baseball than any man alive—do so for the love of the game. That's the reason I do it, certainly not for the right to wear more makeup than Tammy Faye Bakker, to walk the halls talking to myself like Jim Ignitowski, or to spend a fortune in clothing so that when I sit next to Harold Reynolds on the set, I don't look like Danny DeVito sitting next to Denzel Washington. You have to love the game to put in the sixteen-hour days, which can include three appearances on *ESPN News*, three *SportsCenters*, two *Baseball Tonight* shows, and two radio shows. You finish work at 1:00 A.M. unless there's a seventeen-inning game on the West Coast, then you might stay until 4:30 A.M. That can be challenging when you need to be back on TV by nine o'clock the next morning . . . *Makeup!*

The days are long, but they're not hard—really, how hard can it be watching baseball games? The preparation for the 10:00 P.M. *Baseball Tonight* begins with a 4:30 meeting, by which time Peter Gammons has called half the general managers in the major leagues, as well as a few managers and scouts. The meetings include between fifteen and twenty people—all with a specific duty on each show—and last from thirty to ninety minutes, depending on the subject matter, intensity, and silliness. Sometimes they're comical, if John Kruk starts telling R-rated stories about the maniacal 1993 Phillies. "Just put a camera in the meeting room," said *BBTN* producer Ed Schimmel, "and put it on TV, and it will be the best show we've ever done." Schimmel arrived late for one meeting, which never happens, so when asked where he was, he said, "Oh, my wife's car caught on fire," then, without pause, he said something like, "What about that pitching matchup tonight in Florida?"

Not all the meetings are fun and games. In 2002, Mets pitcher Shawn Estes attempted to hit Yankees pitcher Roger Clemens with a pitch in retaliation for Clemens hitting Mets catcher Mike Piazza in the head two years earlier. Everyone knew the Mets would take their revenge on Clemens, but Estes, who was the last pitcher capable of doing the job properly, didn't hit Clemens; he threw behind him. Clemens, who has drilled many a hitter in retaliation, smiled in disgust at Estes as if to say, "Is that the best you can do?" We discussed that situation in the 4:30 P.M. meeting. Analyst Rob

Dibble, who had hit his share of hitters, was livid with Estes for not drilling Clemens. F-bombs were flying from Dibble throughout the meeting. Analyst Jeff Brantley, another ex-pitcher who wasn't afraid to knock down a hitter, was almost as mad. Minutes before we were to go on the air that night, host Brian Kenny—a former boxer, former store detective, the son of a cop—told Dibble, "Now just make sure you say on TV what you said today in the meeting."

"Don't worry," Dibble said. "I will."

"No, you won't," Kenny said.

Dibble, his manhood now questioned, had that look in his eye, that frightening look that I saw many times when he pitched. No one challenged Rob Dibble without some sort of fight. Dibble lashed out at Estes with a riff that was so hateful, all that was missing were the F-bombs. Kenny then came to me for my take on the situation. "I'm afraid to speak," I said.

Scared? The 10:00 p.m. *BBTN* is a tightrope; it's a high-wire act with no net; it's live, as are almost all *BBTN* shows, and there are no teleprompters. "It's the hardest job in the building to host," said one of the former hosts, Bill Pidto. "Everything on *SportsCenter* is scripted. Not on *Baseball Tonight*." Because of its starting time, some games are ending, and others are starting, while we're on live TV. The analysts on the set are, like the viewer, seeing some of the highlights for the first time. The analysts had better be prepared for anything, such as identifying a rookie who was just called up, or commenting on a no-hitter that was completed during a show, as was Hideo Nomo's no-no in 2001.

That's the most fun part for me, being on the show when something spectacular happens, which requires perspective. It really helps that the ESPN research department, led by baseball experts Jeff Bennett and Mark Simon, is located next to the *BBTN* pod. And that four, sometimes five, nights a week, a member of the Elias Sports Bureau is stationed in the research department. I was doing the show the night in 2002 when the Mariners' Mike Cameron became the fourteenth player in history to hit four home runs in one game. It was amazing to watch everyone work on such a historic night: We determined, and very quickly, that Cameron and teammate Bret Boone joined Von Hayes as the only players in history to hit two home runs in the first inning of a game, and that Cameron became the first player ever to hit four home runs in the first five innings of a game, meaning he had more homers in five innings than the Pirates had in their last thirteen games.

That's what makes *BBTN* so great for me, that sense of teamwork. At a newspaper or a magazine, it's usually just you and the editor. At *BBTN*, fifteen to twenty people share in the success if the show is good. It's exhilarating for a young production assistant to find the perfect piece of tape to support analyst Jeff Brantley's demonstration on the change in Tom Glavine's pitching motion. When the *BBTN* crew busses to the ballpark for a Sunday morning show during the World Series, it reminds me of my days on the high school baseball and basketball team: If the show is good, it's like riding home after a big win.

Harold Reynolds, who has done more shows as a baseball analyst than anyone at ESPN, was often the leader of that teamwork. There is no better, friendlier person than Harold Reynolds. That guy you see laughing and smiling every night on TV—he has the whitest teeth of any person I've ever met—is who he really is. He's the guy next door, except he has a closet full of $3,000 suits. In my early years on *BBTN*, Harold would sometimes call me at 10:00 A.M. on the day of a show and say, "Let's go hit." So, like two seventh-graders cutting school, we would go to the batting cage, then hit golf balls, then get ice cream.

Reynolds's greatest strength is his touch with people. When Darryl Strawberry, then of the Yankees, was in the hospital, Reynolds persuaded the Yankees players—at least twenty of them—to come out on to the field after a game and present Strawberry with a get-well card, TV style. No one else could have persuaded the Yankees to do that. When he and I left Pac Bell Park late one night after a World Series game in 2002, he playfully asked a couple of policemen if they could give us a ride back to our hotel, which they gladly did, and put the flashers on so we could move quicker through traffic.

"How long have you known them?" I asked.

"I just met them," Harold said.

There's nothing better than preparing for a show by going to what we call the War Room, which includes twenty television monitors, and watching about twelve games at one time, all the while talking baseball with Harold Reynolds. "Which runner came in the hardest to second base to break up a double play?" I once asked him. He smiled and said, "Bo Jackson, no doubt. When he got on first base, I would yell over to him, 'Remember Bo, this ain't football.'"

Reynolds's primary partner was John Kruk, who also is the same in real life as he is on TV: hilarious, acerbic, and irreverent. He's also a great student of the game. "I bet our Phillies team in 1993 didn't turn a 5–4–3 double play all year," he once told me. The marvelous Ken Hirdt of the Elias Sports Bureau looked it up: They turned two all year, none after May 7. Kruk told me that former teammate Dave Hollins was so intense "he wouldn't talk to anyone on the other team. He wouldn't even talk to guys on his own team some days. One day, [Padres pitcher] Doug Brocail, who was his roommate in the minor leagues, came up and put his arm around Dave at the cage, as if to say, 'Hey, we both made it.' Doug was the best man at Dave's wedding. Hollins started screaming at him because he was on the other team." For Kruk, the team always came first. One night on the air, he was angry that pitcher Derek Lowe, who had been traded to the Dodgers, put on a Red Sox jersey for a twenty-minute pregame ceremony in which the Red Sox were presented their 2004 World Series rings. Lowe had won three clinching games for Boston. "When I was traded by the Phillies," Kruk said. "I gave away all my Phillies stuff, or I threw it away. They weren't my team anymore. Why would I want their stuff?"

Bobby Valentine did *BBTN* for only one year, which was unfortunate for me, because I learned so much from him. He sees everything. We would be watching games and he'd say, "Watch Mike Piazza catch. He never drops a pitch. I've never seen a catcher who catches more balls than Mike." On ex-Mets shortstop Rey Ordoñez, Valentine said, "No one ever went back on a pop-up better than Rey. He wasn't a good hitter. He went to a batting cage during the season and met some guy who gave him a hitting lesson. Now that guy is his hitting coach." We would watch Kevin Brown pitch and Valentine would say, "Look, his foot isn't on the rubber during his windup. That's a balk. He balks every time, and no one calls it."

"Do you like Kevin Brown?" I asked him.

"The only conversation I ever had with him, we were sitting on the runway at an airport," said Valentine, who managed Brown with the Rangers. Brown had been an engineering major at Georgia Tech. "I asked him, 'How does this plane take off?' So he told me. It was fascinating. But I can't remember another conversation with him about anything."

Former analyst Buck Showalter is so observant, so funny, and tells the best stories. When he managed in Arizona, he had a rule that no player was to throw anything at a coach; that is, after a hitter made the third out, he was not allowed to throw his helmet for the first-base coach to pick up: Coaches were worthy of far more respect than that. Showalter learned that when he managed the Yankees. Graig Nettles, a great Yankee, was the first-base coach. Outfielder Mel Hall, who wasn't a good Yankee, threw his helmet at Nettles after making an out. Nettles picked up Hall's helmet, went to the dugout, took out a bat, smashed it into a thousand pieces, and said, "Mel, here's your fucking helmet."

Everything Showalter does, especially in baseball, has to be done precisely. "My dad and I used to line the field before my games as a kid," he told me. "Every line was perfectly straight. If I wasn't a manager, I would be a groundskeeper." So, when it came time to demonstrate the take-out slide on the *BBTN* set, Showalter went to the camera operators before the shot and told them, "I'm only going to do this once, so don't miss it." Dressed in a three-piece suit, Showalter executed a real take-out slide, and knocked Harold Reynolds, the second baseman in the demonstration, to the floor. He should have known that Showalter wouldn't have done it any other way. They both laughed mightily on the air.

In ex-knuckleball pitcher Tom Candiotti's only night on *BBTN*, he told the story of playing knuckleballer Hoyt Wilhelm in Billy Crystal's terrific movie *61*. "I had just been released, and I was really mad about not being picked up by anyone," Candiotti said. "So when Billy asked me to play the part, he told me he wanted it to be as real as possible, so throw the hardest, best knuckler, I could. So I did. Barry Pepper (who played Roger Maris in the movie) swung and missed about fifty pitches in a row. He had no chance. Billy came to the mound and told me, 'OK, maybe not your *best* knuckler.' So I threw some much slower, and he hit a few, and then I hit him with a pitch. The whole crew came running out, like he was dead. I said, 'Hey, it was only fifty mph. Let's go.'"

The analysts are only as good as the *BBTN* host. They're all good—John Buccigross, Rece Davis, Scott Reiss—but no one steers the ship better than Ravech, who is as calm and savvy a TV guy as there is. He can read a highlight, see out of the corner of his eye that an analyst wants to say something; he lets the analyst speak, then seamlessly goes back to reading the highlight. For every show, we have a rundown, which is like a map—it details when and where in the show we'll talk about certain subjects. One night in 1998, my first year on *BBTN*, a woman's basketball game that we followed ended fifty minutes early, and we had to do a fifty-minute *BBTN* with no rundown, no preparation time, and no ideas.

"Good luck," Judd Burch, said in our ears seconds before the show, "you're going to need it." It turned out to be a great show because Ravech guided it, and never once panicked.

The producer runs each show from the control room and communicates with the host and analysts through an earpiece called an IFB; Orioles general manager Mike Flanagan, who did TV for several years, called it an "IUD, for safety in broadcasting." It can be distracting to be talking on live TV about one subject, and have a producer talking in your ear about something else, but you learn to deal with it. No one is better in your ear than Gus Ramsey, a *BBTN* producer, and perhaps the cleverest guy at ESPN. He has provided so many great lines to so many anchors, he's the guy who said of ex–Trail Blazers center Arvidis Sabonis, "He's not my Vidis, he's not your Vidis, he's Arvidis." He's the guy who told me in my ear one night, "[Mets reliever] Dan Wheeler has inherited nine base runners this season, and all nine have scored." It was Gus Ramsey on a midnight *BBTN* show who, when reliever Rudy Seanez entered the game, told Ravech to announce it as "This is Seanez," in reference to "This is CNN," which Ravech gladly did.

No one runs a better show than Judd Burch. And no one loves the game—especially the Phillies—more than Judd Burch. He was headed for umpiring school when ESPN called to offer him a job twelve years ago, but he still is the umpire expert. (There is an expert on everything at ESPN.) I've been covering baseball for twenty-five years and I don't know all the umpires, or that they even wore numbers on their uniforms: Burch knows the number of every umpire, he knows every umpire by sight, and he can imitate every umpire's strike and out calls.

"Do Ed Vargo," ESPN analyst Larry Bowa begged Burch.

Burch did Ed Vargo's strike call.

"Oh my God," Bowa said. "That's perfect."

Burch must have impersonated ten umpires. All were perfect.

Burch will talk in the ear of the analysts as a close play unfolds, and because we might not be sure who made the call, he will tell us, for instance, "Accurately called by Jerry Meals." When *Baseball Tonight* goes on the road, the analysts talk to the players in the clubhouse; Burch visits the umpires' room. "Guess who I just met today?" Burch once told me.

Who?

"Angel Hernandez," he said, excitedly.

The only thing Burch loves more than the umpires is the Phillies. We play a game in the newsroom at ESPN: Give Judd Burch the date of any Phillies game in recent years, and see if he can tell you the score, and any pertinent details, of the game. "OK, Judd, May 17, 2005," said Gus Ramsey, challenging Burch on a Phillies game of a year and a half earlier. Burch thought for twenty seconds and said, "Charlie Reliford worked the plate. The Phillies scored two in the bottom of the first. They beat the Cardinals, 7–5." Exactly right on all counts. When former Philly John Kruk came to ESPN several years ago, Burch began re-living old Phillies games in which Kruk played. Occasionally, Burch would correct Kruk on his facts.

"You're not married, are you?" Kruk said.

"No," said Burch.

Burch goes to at least forty Phillies games per year, and has made trips around the country to see them play. If he isn't at the game, he watches them on TV or on his computer. He misses maybe one Phillies game per year, some years he misses none, but I was with him on the Sunday before the All-Star game in Chicago in 2003 when he was unable to watch the Phillies game because he was working off-site and had no access to a TV or his computer. He was getting play-by-play over the phone for what was a dramatic ninth inning.

"Who were you talking to?" I asked.

"My mother. Who else?" he said.

After every Phillies win, Burch celebrates by listening to the song "Oh Happy Day." When he's working on *BBTN*—I am not making this up—he leaves the office and goes to his car to listen to the song, then comes back to work. After David Bell's ninth-inning home run had given the Phillies a stunning victory over the Reds in 2005, Burch looked at me.

"I'm going to need a moment," he said, then left the room.

So when you hear Ravech, or any *SportsCenter* anchor say "Oh Happy Day" after a Phillies' victory, it is a tribute to Judd Burch. It is one of many inside jokes on *Baseball Tonight*, mostly due to the fun-loving nature of Ravech and Buccigross and the other hosts. *Baseball Tonight*, Ravech says, "is one big inside joke." He occasionally refers to Cardinals third baseman Scott Rolen as "Careful," as in, "Careful picks up a ground ball and guns it to first." Rolen was Burch's favorite Phillies' player, but several years ago, he made a mental mistake in a game, so Ravech suggested in a *BBTN* meeting that we should be critical of Rolen, to which Burch said, "Careful." One of Ravech's home run calls used to be "Kung Pow" because Burch, when he wasn't working, enjoyed watching the Phillies on his computer and ordering Chinese food, his favorite being Kung Pao Chicken.

When Jim Thome does something dramatic, Ravech often says, "Hats off to Jim Thome," because when Thome would come to an ESPN studio to be interviewed, he always asked for a hat as a souvenir. When Joe Mays strikes out a hitter, Ravech says, "No one serves it up like Joe," referring to a cafeteria worker at ESPN named Joe who discounts food orders for Ravech. And when Nationals catcher Brian Schneider makes a good play, Ravech sometimes will say, "The boy has become a man," a reference to the bar mitzvah of

Brian Schneider, the son of Jeff Schneider, who was then the coordinating producer of *BBTN*.

When Ravech says of a real hard thrower, "It's going 101, but seems like 98," that's in reference to Schneider's once getting a speeding ticket for going 101 mph, then telling Ravech, "It seemed like I was only going 98." When Valentine was on the show, and a pitcher was throwing gas, Ravech would say, "A mighty wind just blew by," which was a reference to Valentine, who farted so often during shows, Ravech nicknamed him "Mighty Wind."

"We're amusing ourselves. We're the only ones who get some of this stuff," said Ravech. "The show is like a soap opera. You have to tune in every night to know what's going on. If someone on our show has a flat tire that day, or ran out of gas, it'll be on the show that night."

For at least two years, Ravech routinely referred to Royals shortstop Angel Berroa as "My Man." One night on *Baseball Tonight*, Harold Reynolds explained, with great regret, that America didn't even know the names of half of the players on the young, surging Royals. "We'll start at shortstop with . . . with . . ." Reynolds forgot Angel Berroa's name on the air. In his panic, he said, "You know . . . My Man." Looking for help and not getting it from any of the other three guys on the set, Reynolds continued to do the highlight on the anonymous Royals. "Here My Man makes a play in the hole," he said. "And here is My Man at the plate." Reynolds went the entire highlight without using Angel Berroa's name. Since then, Berroa has always been known on *Baseball Tonight* as My Man.

"See," Valentine said after the highlight, "even *we* don't know who these guys are."

To make sure we know who these guys are, *BBTN* takes the show on the road occasionally, and, more than occasionally, the analysts do reports from the field. I cover spring training, the postseason, and selected other stories from the assorted ballparks, including the Hall of Fame induction weekend from Cooperstown. In 1999, I interviewed Hank Aaron and Willie Mays together, then, five minutes later, I interviewed Ted Williams, my father's baseball hero. Talk about a privilege. The interview was taped, it was supposed to be two minutes, three questions, that's it. Ted was great answering the first two. But the third question was about Nolan Ryan, who was being inducted that day, but Ted wanted to talk about Randy Johnson, who wasn't being inducted that day. The great Williams started talking and didn't stop; he was well past two minutes when my producer started giving me the slashed throat sign, meaning to cut him off. What was I to do? Cut off the game's greatest living hitter? Be rude to my father's baseball hero on TV? So I let him go. When he was finally done after five and a half minutes, I thanked him, and threw it back to the studio. Through the magic of videotape, we ran the interview, the first two questions only.

I've had a lot of memorable days in the field, including the day that I interviewed Randy Johnson, and we were both standing up: six feet ten and four feet ten, which had to be the largest disparity in height between adult males in a baseball interview. My friends still laugh about that. I interviewed the massive, tattooed Giambi brothers in their muscle shirts during what could have been the height of the steroid use era in the major leagues: Standing between them, I looked like Gilbert Gottfried interviewing two WWF wrestlers. I interviewed John Rocker minutes after the Braves beat the Mets in a play-off game at Shea Stadium. We were twenty feet from the stands, people were screaming unthinkable expletives at him. "I *love* this," Rocker said.

All of this TV work has been tremendous fun, and has brought me some measure of fame. I was at the gala for the All-Star game in Seattle in 2001 when one of the waiters recognized me because, like me, he was an Armenian. We were talking when another waiter, who was also Armenian walked by.

"Come here, you have to have meet this guy," one waiter said to the other. "He's Armenian, and he covers baseball on ESPN . . . Meet Armen Keteyian."

I bet that never happened to Robin Roberts.

14

Why Can't There Be a
Left-handed Catcher?

I am a baseball snob. I'm *not* some pedantic little twit who thinks
he knows everything about the game, and wants things changed to
meet his specifications, but some things about baseball bother me,
as those on the PGA Tour are bothered when they're called golfers;
they're *players*, and they really hate it when golf is used as a verb, as
in "I golf a lot."

My complaints are less substantial. The catcher and first baseman wear a mitt. A mitt doesn't have fingers; everyone else on the
field wears a glove, which has fingers. It's hitter, not batter, as in
"He's a good hitter." A manager is a manager, not a coach, an annoyance shared by Mariners manager Mike Hargrove, who has a
sign—DON'T CALL ME COACH—on the desk in his office. A pop-out
is to the infield, a fly-out is to the outfield, a hitter doesn't fly out to
shortstop or pop out to center field. You don't play pitcher or play
catcher, you pitch or you catch. The term "beaned" refers only to
someone who has been hit in the head with a pitch. A "grand slam
home run" is redundant, as is the "last four victories in a row," and
the ridiculously redundant "last four straight in a row."

I'm troubled by any baseball movie in which the star has no

baseball skill, which includes all actors who've played Babe Ruth. It's bothersome when the star can't throw a baseball because if you can't throw, you've never played the game, and if you've never played the game, what are you doing in a baseball movie? Kevin Costner can throw a baseball. So can Charlie Sheen. LeVar Burton, Ray Milland, and Tim Robbins cannot. And really, in *The Natural,* did Bump Bailey have to *die* to make room in the lineup for Roy Hobbs? Couldn't he have pulled an oblique muscle like every other big leaguer?

There are parts of the game that fascinate me, and I have to know the answers. Granted, most people don't care about the questions I ask, but those people haven't cut out every box score for the last seventeen years, and they don't have wayward facts—Tommy Leach led the NL in 1902 in home runs with six, and all were inside-the-park homers—rolling around in their heads every day of their lives. So, here are twenty-five things that bother me, confuse me, intrigue me and make me wonder, and, make others wonder why I don't get a hobby.

1. Why are Gold Gloves often awarded to three center fielders, not a left fielder, center fielder, and right fielder? They are three different positions, why not a Gold Glove for each one? Corner outfielders deserve more respect; they aren't easy positions to play, because of the angle the ball comes off the bat, and the foul territory that must be covered, including the perilous job of running over a bullpen mound to catch a fly ball. "Left field is the hardest outfield position to play, no question," says former Rangers manager Buck Showalter. Ex-Mets manager Bobby Valentine says that center field is the easiest outfield position to play if you have speed, which, of course, is a big if. But giving

three center fielders a Gold Glove is like picking four short-stops for the Gold Glove in the infield. And it's Gold Glove, not Golden Gloves. That is for boxers.

2. Why doesn't someone get charged with an error when, say, the second baseman and shortstop can't decide who should catch a routine pop-up, and it drops untouched? The major-league rule book states that mental errors should not be scored as errors, but it is time to change that rule. The pitcher did his job; he got the hitter to hit an easy pop-up. There is no reason to punish the pitcher because the short-stop and second baseman couldn't decide who should catch it. If the official scorer can't decide who gets the error, find out who was supposed to make the play, then give him the error. If that can't be determined, then give them both an error. Or make a team error. That's not a hit.

3. Why do people insist that "a tie goes to the runner"? It has never been written in any rule book that a tie goes to the runner. No umpire on any legitimate level has ever gone by that premise. That's for Little League, not the major leagues, and yet, dozens of big-league players have used "tie goes to the runner" as an argument on their behalf.

4. Why does a fielder get an assist on a play when no putout is made? Routine ground ball to the second baseman, he throws to first, the first baseman drops it, the first baseman gets an error, the second baseman gets an assist. Baseball is the only major sport where you get credit for an assist when a play is not completed. Should John Stockton have gotten an assist when he made a perfect pass and Karl Malone missed the shot?

5. Why do players slide headfirst into first base when they can run through the bag? "Because it is faster," says former

second baseman Roberto Alomar, who was the best in the game at it. "I don't slow down when I slide into first. Other guys do. They shouldn't slide headfirst into first if they have to slow down. Why do infielders dive for a ball? Because they can extend further when they do. They wouldn't make the play if they didn't dive. Sliding headfirst is a good play if you know what you're doing. What do sprinters do when they get to the tape? They learn forward." Right. They don't dive. Plus, when you slide into first base, the umpire is often looking and listening for a foot hitting the base. When you slide, he doesn't hear that, he might get confused and call a player out when he's safe. I suggest running through the bag. It's faster.

6. Why are the greatest throwing outfielders of all time all right-handed? Roberto Clemente, Carl Furillo, Reggie Smith, Dwight Evans, Ellis Valentine, Ichiro, and many more, and they're all right-handed. Who is the best-throwing left-handed outfielder of all time? Does anyone immediately come to mind? Babe Ruth? Ken Griffey Jr.? You can think of fifty right-handers before you get to a lefty. Is the answer as simple as left-handers with great arms are put on the mound? Perhaps. But Yankees outfielder Paul O'Neill, who throws left-handed, offered an interesting explanation. Most great right-handed-throwing outfielders throw straight over the top. With that motion, the ball goes straighter, truer, and holds its line. But, says O'Neill, most left-handed-throwing outfielders throw closer to three-quarters: left-handers have natural movement on their throws, and a tailing action at the end. It doesn't hold its line as well. "I thought I threw straight over the top," said O'Neill. "But when I looked at myself throw, I don't throw from straight over the top. My arm angle has dropped."

7. Why can a pitcher who's on the pitching rubber fake a throw to third base or to second base, but can't fake a throw to first base, or it's a balk? To two bases it's not a balk, to one base it is. The fake-throw-to-third-then-throw-to-first move should be a balk. A balk is, by definition, "deceiving the runner." What's more deceiving than that?

8. Why do so many people still believe that had Bill Buckner cleanly fielded Mookie Wilson's ground ball in Game 6 of the 1986 World Series, the Red Sox would have won the World Series? It was a hideous error, no doubt one of the worst in baseball history, but the score was *tied* at the time. If Buckner had fielded it, and flipped it to first in time to get the speedy Wilson, the game would have continued.

9. Why don't knuckleball pitchers get more respect? They're seen as freaks who throw a track pitch rather than major league pitchers who throw a pitch that is really hard to throw, and to hit. I covered Charlie Hough for four years in Texas. He was their best pitcher all those years, but he was old and a knuckleballer, so manager Doug Rader used to say, "We expect every start to be Charlie's last. Someday, he's going to just calcify on the mound, and we're going to have to carry him off."

10. Why do people call them RBI instead of RBIs? It's same idea as POWs. Who calls them POW?

11. Why is it so ridiculous to have a left-handed catcher? "It isn't," says Mike Squires, a brilliant defensive first baseman who caught a few games in an emergency in the major leagues in the 1980s. "The only downside is throwing to second or third on a steal; there are more right-handed hitters to get in your way. That's a small thing. It's the only thing."

12. What's so preposterous about having a pitcher who doubles as a DH? OK, the risk of injury is a major concern, but some pitchers are pretty durable, and some of them can really hit. If you didn't know that the Rockies' Jason Jennings, the Astros' Brandon Backe, or the Marlins' Dontrelle Willis (and several others) were pitchers, you would think, from the look of their swing, that they were everyday players. If a pitcher worked at it enough, he might be able to DH on days that he didn't pitch. Willis pinch-hit nearly twenty times in 2004–05. In 2005, he batted seventh in the order one game because he was a better hitter than the two everyday players who hit behind him. Don't tell me there isn't enough time to work with a pitcher on his hitting. Some pitchers take BP every day. If we have a two-way player in the NFL, we can have a pitcher-DH.

13. What's the fascination with hitting for the cycle? Look, I like cycles, they're cool, they're fun, but they're a statistical oddity, that's it. How great an achievement can it be when Babe Ruth, Willie Mays, and Hank Aaron never hit for a cycle? What would you rather do, hit two home runs and two doubles in a game, or hit for the cycle? We make far too big a deal out of cycles. When Jeff Frye of the Blue Jays several years ago needed a single for the cycle and purposely stopped at first base instead of running to second for what would have been an easy double, that was it for me and cycles.

14. Why is the word "uncorked" used only when referring to champagne and wild pitches?

15. How could Eric Karros finish his career with more steals than Joe DiMaggio (59–30)? OK, we understand that DiMaggio played on great, slugging teams that didn't run

because they didn't have to, and in that era, teams didn't run, period: in 1950, DiMaggio's brother Dom led the league in steals with fifteen. But Joe D. still is among the most graceful runners of all time, and Eric Karros . . . is not. When told late in his career that he had more stolen bases than DiMaggio, Karros's eyes lit up. "Really?" he said.

16. Why is it that a base runner doesn't take more criticism for being thrown out trying to advance on a throw to the plate? Example, two out, runner at second. Batter singles. Runner scores. The throw to the plate is cut off by the first baseman. The batter-runner tries to advance to second on the throw home and is thrown out by ten feet at second. Everyone shakes his hand for knocking in a run. Hey, he made an out on the bases. His excuse is that he was trying to draw a throw so the runner could score, but usually that isn't enough of an excuse. How is that any different than being thrown out trying to stretch a single into a double? It's an out, and it could have been avoided if the batter-runner had watched the cutoff play.

17. Why do so many teams guard the line in almost all close, late-inning situations? The idea is to prevent a double down the line, but when a closer comes in the ninth throwing 98 mph, and the guy at the plate is incapable of pulling the ball against someone throwing that hard, why guard the line and leave that big hole between third and shortstop?

18. Why aren't pitchers allowed to catch pop-ups? It's a ridiculous tradition that it's better to have one of the infielders go sprawling across the mound to catch a routine pop-up while the pitcher runs away from the play like the ball is filled with poisonous gas. Ex-Met pitcher Sid

Fernandez said he went eight years into his career before he caught a pop-up. Most pitchers (but not Sid) are good athletes. Many of them played shortstop in high school when they weren't pitching. John Smoltz, Greg Maddux, Mike Mussina, Mike Hampton, these guys are as good athletes as almost anyone on the field. Let's quit babying these pitchers and let them catch the ball. It's not that hard.

19. Why is it an unwritten rule that you can't break up a pitcher's no-hitter with a bunt late in the game? This is preposterous. OK, if the score is 12–0 with two outs in the ninth inning, maybe dropping a bunt isn't the manliest thing to do in a no-hitter. But in 2001, Arizona's Curt Schilling had a perfect game going in the eighth when Padres catcher Ben Davis bunted for a hit with the score, 2–0. Schilling, who had paralyzing stuff that Davis could barely see, let alone hit, finished with a three-hitter. Arizona manager Bob Brenly, always a smart, reasonable voice, called Davis's play "chickenshit." It wasn't. Ask most managers, including Phil Garner, and they'll tell you there was nothing wrong with what Davis did. Davis and the Padres were in a pennant race, they were trying to win the game. Since when is an opponents' personal achievement more important than winning a game? And what's wrong with asking a pitcher to field his position?

20. When is a lead so big that you're no longer allowed to steal a base without "rubbing it in"? A team, I am told, has to be comfortably ahead. Please define "comfortably." In this era of uncontrollable offense, what is it? Five runs, six, seven? What about at Coors Field, where every game is always close given the thin air and the potential for a big inning? Is it ten runs? Granted, stealing a base when

your team is ahead 15–0 is excessive. But one year, Colorado's Tom Goodwin stole a base when his team was ahead, 9–1, at Coors, then got two pitches thrown over his head for what the opposition thought was rubbing it in. The Rockies won that game, 12–10.

21. Why is the "defensive indifference" rule so poorly defined. The intent of that rule is to not give a stolen base to a guy who steals when his team is ahead 17–0. But I covered a game in Oakland when Orioles manager Frank Robinson decided that his pitcher and his catcher had no chance of throwing out the great Rickey Henderson, so they let him steal second and third base without a throw in the first inning. The first inning! Henderson scored in that inning, and the A's won the game 2–1. His run turned out to be very important, and yet Henderson was not credited with a steal either time because the official scorer ruled "defensive indifference." Henderson was punished by the scorer basically because he was too good. That's not the spirit of the rule. (Henderson was eventually credited with two steals.)

22. Why does a pitcher, after giving up a tremendously long home run on a pitch right down the middle, sometimes knock down the next hitter with a pitch? It makes no sense. You make a terrible pitch, the hitter does his job, so you act like a ten-year-old bully and hit the next batter. What is that?

23. Why do we rank teams by the highest batting average, not the most runs scored? The idea of the game is to score the most runs, not hit for a high average. Runs scored was the first individual statistic kept in baseball history, yet it is rarely mentioned when we reel off a player's offensive achievements. One of the most underplayed stories of

the last ten years was Rickey Henderson breaking Ty Cobb's career record for runs scored.

24. Why do some play-by-play announcers insist on not "jinxing" the pitcher by telling the fans that he has a no-hitter going? They're supposed to be telling us what's going on in the game. What's more important than telling us about a no-hitter? If you're driving in your car, listening on the radio, the play-by-play man has an obligation to tell you what's going on in the game. If a pitcher has a no-hitter going, you'll stay tuned. If the announcer doesn't tell you, the casual fan may switch channels.

25. Why do some people believe that Babe Ruth was a big, fat load who clowned his way through the major leagues, who ran the bases backward, and would have no chance of playing today? Babe Ruth is the greatest player of all time, and would be a great player if he played today. Period. He dominated his era like no player in history; he was the best left-handed pitcher in the American League, then decided to become a hitter, and became the best hitter ever. When he hit his 138th home run, he became the all-time leader, meaning his final 586 only added to his record. When he got to 700 home runs, no one in baseball had 350. He played in his prime at six foot two, 215 pounds, a big man in any era, a huge man in the 1920s. He was an above average defensive outfielder and he ran a lot better than he was given credit for: He finished with 136 career triples, more than any player active in 2005, and 130 more than the career total of Mark McGwire.

15

Just Grab That Bat as Tight as You Can, Son

Jim Fregosi played eighteen years, and managed fifteen years, in the major leagues. Several years ago, when his son was ten, Fregosi went to one of his youth league practices and offered to help. Not to be the coach, just to be a special instructor who would assist in any way possible.

"We won't be needing your help," the youth league coach said. "We know what we're doing."

Oh, really.

I am worried about our kids in baseball. I am worried that not enough of them are playing the game. We are losing them to soccer (I like soccer, my daughter, Kelly, can really play) and lacrosse and other sports that provide more action, more success, and less heartache. In soccer, you can put a fat, unathletic ten-year-old at fullback and tell him to kick the ball away from the goal; he does that a few times, and he's had a good day. But in baseball, a ten-year-old plays right field, goes 0 for 2 with two strikeouts, gets hit by a pitch, drops the only fly ball hit to him, and goes home thinking that he's terrible and that baseball is no fun.

"In basketball, you can have an awful game, but you might

make a great pass or a dunk, and you take something positive away from it," said Buddy Bell, a major-league third baseman for eighteen years. "But in baseball, you can go a whole week without doing anything well."

I drive past a field or a park on a gorgeous day and I don't see kids playing baseball like we did. I see them playing an organized game, with a coach screaming and instructing on every play, telling them when to swing even as the pitch is coming. What I don't see is a pickup game with ten or twelve kids, not enough for a full game, but enough for the games that we played every day as kids, with ghost runners, pitcher's hand, and right field closed.

That's where a young player develops creativity, which is essential in the game. That's how Omar Vizquel became such a great defensive shortstop, playing pretend games on the fields, streets, and alleys in Venezuela, throwing balls up against the wall and catching them barehanded. That's why the Latin American population in the major leagues grows every year: Those kids are playing, inventing, and reacting, rather than being told what to do every second, as are so many American kids. Too many American kids are playing Nintendo, which will serve them somehow in life, I'm convinced, but not as baseball players.

"Baseball isn't like it was when we were young when we'd go in the backyard and throw to one another and pitch to one another," said Royals special assistant to the general manager Mike Toomey, fifty-five, who has been teaching kids to play the game for nearly thirty years. "You couldn't hit the ball into Mrs. McGillicuddy's yard over there; that's off base. We were innovative. We didn't have all these distractions, computer games, and cars. We had more of a passion for the game. We were throwing all the time; that's how we developed arm strength. I would take fifty balls with me and we'd throw to each other, in cold weather, because we loved the game.

"Now, kids go to fancy indoor facilities and hit off pitching machines, they may play once a week, and they can't understand why they aren't getting better. I watch a kids' practice and there's one kid hitting, one pitching, and thirteen standing around. It's sad to even watch kids play catch today. It's like a snowball fight. They're chasing after the ball rather than playing catch, and it's because they don't play catch anymore. Their mechanics are poor, they don't know how to grip the ball, they don't build arm strength. The instincts aren't there, because there's no more backyard baseball. I never had formal instruction other than my father, who was a great teacher. A lot of times, we figured it out on our own. We played Wiffle ball as kids. One kid had a field in his backyard. He lined the field. If I saw a kid in the backyard doing those things today, I think I'd fall over."

I am worried that our kids are getting too much coaching. Look, any adult who is taking the time out of his or her day to coach a baseball team deserves our admiration. And some youth coaches are really good. But too many others need to go to a few coaching clinics first. Teaching a kid the wrong way to do something is more harmful than not teaching him at all. "I've seen dads who tell their kids, 'Just grab that bat as tight as you can, son,'" Toomey said. "What we teach is to grip the bat like it's a small bird. You have to hold it tight enough so the bird doesn't fly away, but loose enough so you don't hurt the bird."

Please, coaches, let's use some common sense. Please, let's not throw batting practice too hard to the seven-year-old who has never swung a bat before. Let him hit off a tee first, or throw underhand to him, until he begins to understand the fundamentals of the swing. Let's not hit some rocket ground ball on a skinned infield to a kid who has never caught a ground ball in his life, the kid with the blue, plastic glove. Let's roll a few balls to him first to get him the feel of catching a ground ball. "Are you sure you're left-handed?" I asked an eight-year-old kid who couldn't throw a ball ten feet. He shook his head and said, apologetically, "No, I'm right-handed, but my dad bought me this glove, so I have to use it."

And really, does everything have to be about winning and losing when you're talking about eight-year-olds playing baseball? You've got to be kidding. "Here in San Diego," said Tom House, a former major-league pitcher who speaks to thousands of young baseball players a year about physical and emotional development, "We have a coach whose ten-year-old kids drink Red Bull on the bench. Do you know what that can do to a kid?"

I worry about our youth league umpires. They are a part of the development of young players; they are not supposed to belittle a kid who has difficulty playing the hardest game in the world to play. "You have to stand in there. You can't keep bailing out like a baby," one clueless umpire told a youth leaguer who was facing a wild, hard-throwing kid who was twice his size. "Now get back in there and hit like a man." The kid was nine!

My brother Matt who was a very good college baseball player at Catholic University, has coached his son's baseball team for ten years. He takes the kids who aren't good enough to play for the better teams, but want to play. In one game, a thirteen-year-old was hit in the head with a pitch. The kid went down hard, and was sobbing in the dirt for five minutes. He insisted on staying in the game, and started to walk to first base on the hit batsman. But the umpire—in what had to be the worst call ever made by any umpire on any level—told him, "You don't get first base. The helmet is a piece of equipment, and you don't get first when you're hit in a piece of equipment." The umpire put him back at the plate.

I am worried about the safety of the kids. Baseball is a dangerous game, but to understand that, you have to have played it on a legitimate level. Many coaches haven't. The baseball is as hard as a rock. Many of the infields are all dirt, concrete hard, and covered with stones and pebbles—a major leaguer would never take a ground ball on such a field. The aluminum bats are weapons. And yet I've seen coaches admonish a seven-year-old for not getting in front of a bullet ground ball that he has no chance of catching. I tell the kid, "Don't get in front of it!" or at least field it to the side, or backhand it, until he learns to protect himself. The first time a seven-year-old takes a ground ball off the lips, or gets hit in the head by a pitch, he's not coming back to baseball. He's going to play something safer.

"Do you know my story?" Astros manager Phil Garner said.

Garner was the home plate umpire in a Little League game many years ago in Houston when a ten-year-old boy named Ty McLaughlin was hit in the heart with a pitch. His heart was at rest when he was struck; he had three massive heart attacks and died at home plate. Garner named one of sons after Ty McLaughlin. "I know the dangers," Garner said.

It is such a hazardous sport, ex-Mets manager Bobby Valentine says that all kids should be required to wear face masks on their helmets, and chest protector to protect their heart. "That way," he said, "kids wouldn't be as afraid of the ball, and my wife could enjoy the game."

Brewers manager Ned Yost wore a flak jacket—it's called the Flakjak—under his jersey when he was a coach for the Braves. "I didn't wear it for protection. I wore it to show kids that it's OK to wear it," he said. Yost's three sons all have worn one, and they are all good players. "One kid got hit right in the chest with a pitch; he went straight down," Yost said. "The coach came running over. The kid's father came sprinting out of the stands. The kid got up and started laughing. He thought he was hurt badly, then he realized he had the Flakjak on. To know that your kids are protected out there is a great feeling."

The first thing a coach should do is teach a kid the proper technique for getting out of the way of a pitch—to turn the front shoulder away from the ball, not into it, thereby protecting the face.

Former major leaguer Kevin Seitzer, who was beaned badly three times in major leagues, runs a hitting school in Kansas City with former catcher Mike Macfarlane. They toss tennis balls at kids to teach them how to avoid getting hit by a pitch. "When a kid gets hit by a baseball, his father tells him, 'It doesn't hurt,' well, it really *does* hurt," says Seitzer. "Let the kid drill the father with a pitch and see how it feels. When I see a kid with fear, I try everything I can to help him deal with it."

White Sox announcer Ken Harrelson, a former major leaguer, said, "We're losing a thousand kids a year to fear because they're afraid. They think big leaguers aren't afraid, therefore they'll never be big leaguers. The opposite is true. All big leaguers have fear. We talk about fear of the ball on the air three or four times a year. A father once came up to me and said, 'I want to thank you for saving my son's career.' His kid, who was fourteen, had gotten hit in the head. Driving home, he told his father that he was afraid and didn't want to play anymore. That night, they came home and watched the Sox on TV. We [announcers] were talking about fear, and how big leaguers are afraid. He and his dad talked. The kid is playing again."

I am worried that today's kids are learning only how to hit and not how to play. Today's game is a power game—chicks do indeed love the long ball, and the sexiest part of the game is monstrous home runs, which make the player a lot of money. There is a generation of kids out there who spend all day at the batting cage (or the cage that they have in the backyard) pumping token after token in the pitching machine and swinging as many times as they can, as hard as they can. It's baseball, which is great, and it's better than their running the streets, but we have created a generation of designated hitters rather than all-round players.

"Look at the ads in the back of the periodicals. You can buy batting cages, screens, drills, things to put on your bat . . . we sure aren't making any glove men," says Mets assistant GM Sandy Johnson. "We're not getting runners. No one is playing catch. That's gone, too."

Outfielder Jack Cust was the number-one pick of the Diamondbacks in 1998. He has bounced around with several major-league teams, without much success, but still has great power potential. His story is an inspiring one. He hit every day from age eight to eighteen. His father, Jack, a former player, a marvelous guy and a real estate man, found places for his son to hit every day: When a beautician closed down in a strip mall, Jack Cust threw up some nets, set up a JUGS pitching machine, and had his three sons hit there until a new business arrived.

But young Jack Cust, despite the efforts of his teams and his father, doesn't have a defensive position that he plays well enough to stay in the big leagues. And he doesn't run well. He made it to the big leagues, which deserves praise, but being a hitter isn't enough.

I am worried that some major leaguers aren't setting the right example for kids. When you see a youth league pitcher pound his chest after a strikeout, where do you think he gets that? When a ten-year-old strolls around the bases after hitting a home run, raising the roof as he rounds second, he learned that from watching major-league hitters. And we at ESPN are as guilty as anyone for glorifying this behavior by showing it fifty times every night.

Our kids today don't understand the history of the game partly because the major leaguers of today don't understand the history of the game, the players who came before them. That is somewhat understandable, given that they were playing the game instead of studying it, or as George Brett said, "I had better things to do than figure out what John McGraw hit in 1906." When Don Mattingly, one of the best guys the game has ever produced, joined the Yankees, he said he had never heard of Lou Gehrig. As a kid, he thought Babe Ruth was a cartoon character. Outfielder Marquis

Grissom, another terrific guy, when asked about the impact of Jackie Robinson, called him "Frankie" Robinson.

"I just watched Home Run Derby on TV," former Pirates shortstop Jay Bell, a bright guy, said many years ago of the old-time series on ESPN that pitted great sluggers of the past in a home run hitting contest. "Some guy from the Yankees hit a whole bunch of homers."

"Who was it?" a teammate asked. "Mickey Mantle?"

Bell thought about it and said, "Yeah, that was his name."

Mickey Mantle? That was his name?

In the mideighties, a teenager dejectedly left a card-signing one day because he had waited for two hours to get Pete Rose's autograph, but was still in line when the signing ended.

"Did you get anyone else's?" asked Dan Shaughnessy of *The Boston Globe.*

"Yeah," the kid said disgustedly, trying to decipher the signature. "I got Stan . . . Meesial . . . Mooossal . . . Maisel . . . whatever."

"That's Stan Musial," Shaughnessy told him. "He got 3,600 hits."

Our kids don't understand the game as they should because they don't watch enough baseball, or, more accurately, they can't watch. With television networks dictating starting times (because it's all about ratings and money), World Series games are all played at night, usually beginning after eight o'clock EST, and sometimes ending after midnight. Who can stay up for that? My children, who are fourteen and twelve, have seen one World Series game from start to finish. It was something special and memorable when my sixth-grade teacher stopped teaching at one o'clock and let us watch the 1967 World Series on TV in the classroom. Will we ever see another World Series game played in daylight? We can only hope.

But I have hope for our kids because of people such as Cal Ripken and Scott Bradley, a former major-league catcher and now the baseball coach at Princeton University. They are two guys who get it; they understand the needs of young baseball players. In Ripken Baseball, which is a rival to Little League Baseball, Ripken has gone to an intermediate field—one with the bases 70 feet apart and a pitching mound that's 50 feet from the plate—so a twelve-year-old doesn't have to make the colossal jump from the 46-foot pitching distance and 60-foot basepaths to the sixty-feet-six-inches pitching distance and the 90-foot basepaths. By going to a 50–70 setup for a year, kids can make a gradual step, then make another gradual step the next year, helping prevent those arching throws from shortstop to first base.

Ripken Baseball has fenced fields like at the Little League World Series, but Ripken Baseball parks are different because the fences aren't 200 feet around the field; they are 250 feet to center field, which gives the field an alley effect, like a big-league park, and teaches kids to make relay throws to cutoffs and allows kids to go from first to third on a single.

We are finally considering the safety of our kids in certain leagues and towns. Some leagues require that all hitters wear a face mask on the helmet. At Bradley's summer baseball camp at Princeton, the kids work at times with a ball, made by Easton, called an "IncrediBall," which is slightly lighter and softer than a baseball. "It slows down the game just enough to make it easier on kids," Bradley said. "And it doesn't sting as much if it hits you."

The glove companies are starting to make gloves that are softer and better serve the purposes of a kid. "I've seen kids whose dad buys them a $50 or $60 glove, and it's way too big for him, so he can't use it," Bradley said. "Or it's not broken in, and the kid doesn't know how to break it in, so it's stiff as a board. I let some of the kids use a soft, old glove of mine. Or I'll tell them to go to a garage sale and look for an old, beat-up glove."

Many leagues play coach-pitch until a certain age, which is

marvelous as long as there's a coach who can throw strikes. Bradley knows of one league in which a coach is the pitcher, a coach is the catcher, and a coach is the first baseman. "That way, every ball is put in play," Bradley said. "With a dad catching, the catcher isn't always walking back to the backstop to pick up the ball. And if the shortstop can throw it all the way to first, the dad can catch it for an out. So instead of being in the third inning after two hours, they can play nine innings in an hour and a half, and everyone gets six or seven at-bats. But parents scream 'Kids need to learn to pitch.' You learn to pitch by practicing how to pitch."

Many leagues are playing fall schedules, which Bradley likes. "For some reason, maybe because it's played in the fall, people don't care so much about winning," said Bradley. "That's really good. In fall leagues, the coaches let kids move around and play several positions in a game. They let kids try switch-hitting. Every other time of the year, it's so important for everyone to win the league championship. But kids are learning more in fall ball."

The game needs more clear thinkers such as Bradley, who isn't afraid to go against tradition. "So many coaches are teaching kids to 'get in front of that ground ball, block that ball, knock it down,'" he said. "I played with Omar Vizquel. I asked him why so many Hispanic players are better fielders than we have in America, why they're so good at fielding a ball on the side, or on the run. He said, 'It's easy. No one ever told me to block the ball or knock it down. I was taught to *catch* the ball. I learned to catch the ball to the side, or backhand the ball. You have to be able to backhand a ball sometimes.'"

Bradley teaches kids how to catch a ball one-handed. "I tell the kids, 'Your parents are going to cringe when they hear this, but you need to learn how to catch one-handed,'" Bradley said. "It's a one-handed game. Everyone yells, 'Two hands, two hands,' which is good when you're right under the ball. But you're not always going to be right under it. You have to catch a ball on the run sometimes, and you need to do that with one hand. If I see a kid who catches with one hand, I know that he's used to having a glove on his hand."

Bradley smiled. "The other slogan that should be outlawed in youth baseball, and the coach should be suspended for using it, is 'Good eye,'" he said. "I've seen kids who play an entire season and swing the bat one or two times. They're up there taking strikes; they're not learning to swing the bat. But if the pitcher walks four guys in a row, the team scores a run, and the coach is happy, because he might win the game. I'm not saying that you should be up there swinging at everything, but you're not getting any better by walking. If the count is 3–0, I would let kids hit, because it might be the only strike they see."

We can save baseball for our kids. It is worth saving. They are worth saving.

"We've got to make baseball less boring for kids," Bradley said. "At our camp, we run pass patterns to teach the kids how to catch a ball on the run. They love it. Instead of standing around in the outfield, we sometimes let the kids run around the bases, and slide into home plate. They love that, too. We need to keep the kids in baseball until they're fourteen years old, when they can start to play a decent brand of baseball. But we're losing the kids at seven, eight, and nine to soccer and lacrosse because there's more action. We're getting there, but we have got to have our kids leaving the baseball field saying, 'Wow, that was fun.'"

I'm not as worried anymore.

16

I Love Ketchup

Lunch with the commissioner, huh? Bud Selig and I dined in July 1994 to discuss the impending players' strike that would cancel the World Series and nearly ruin the game. We went to a drive-through place near Selig's office in Milwaukee. The commissioner ordered the usual: two hot dogs, a frozen custard, and a Diet Coke. We ate in his Lexus. He balanced the hot dogs, one on each thigh, and marinated them with ketchup.

"I *love* ketchup," he said.

This is the commissioner of the greatest game ever invented? *This* is the leader of a multibillion-dollar industry? This is the man who is guiding baseball into a new stratosphere, a game that is growing daily and expanding globally? This is the guy who is trusted to solve the serious problems in the game? This is the man who is delegated to stand up to the combative leaders at the Players Association and represent the game when Congress demands answers about steroids and antitrust? This seems like a job for a big, imposing, extraordinary man, maybe Clint Eastwood, who, by the way, said in the movie *Dirty Harry*, "no one, but no one, eats ketchup on a hot dog."

Bud Selig certainly doesn't look the part of commissioner. He isn't a charismatic, dynamic leader with commanding presence; he doesn't look like a man who can steer the game into the future. He doesn't always make decisions with firm resolve; he seeks consensus, which isn't easy with thirty millionaire owners, most of whom are in it for profit, not love of the game. Selig comes across at times as a used-car salesman, that's how he made his money, and sometimes you get the feeling he's telling you what you want to hear.

That is one look at Bud Selig. This is the other: He is a small-town, midwest guy who loves the game, cares about the game, and always has. He's not some pretentious suit that eats $400 lunches at fancy New York restaurants and has no time for anyone not on his level. When a sportswriter's son wrote a passionate letter to the commissioner about baseball, the twelve-year-old boy sat next to Selig in his private box for a game. When Selig owned the Brewers, he routinely would visit the press box and fraternize with the writers, something I've never seen another owner do in twenty-five years of covering baseball. "The Orioles always beat us. They had these obscure catchers who got big hits—John Stefero, Dave Criscione," Selig would tell me. "Where did those guys come from?" He wasn't doing so to befriend the media so it would embrace him if he ever became commissioner; he did so because that's who he is: a nice man who loves being at the ballpark. He is a guy with whom you would be comfortable having a beer and a hot dog. Just bring the ketchup.

His legacy as commissioner is checkered. He was in charge when the 1994 season ended on September 14 with a players' strike, which canceled the World Series for the first time since 1904. He has been in charge during baseball's Steroid Era, which has stained this period and the achievements of some players forever. He has been in charge as the disparity between the largest team payroll and smallest payroll has gone from $17 million to $170 million.

But Selig also was the commissioner in 2002 when baseball, for the first time in its contentious labor history, reached a collective bargaining agreement without a work stoppage. He was the commissioner when baseball reached a drug agreement that, ten years ago, would have had zero chance of being accepted by the Players Association. He was the commissioner who somehow talked George Steinbrenner and other big-market owners into revenue sharing, that is, giving some of their money to the smaller-market teams. He was the commissioner when baseball set attendance records in 2004 and 2005, due partly to some of his innovations, including the wild card system and interleague play.

Over the last twenty-five years, the changes in the game have been monumental. We now have lights at Wrigley Field, enormous Coke bottles atop the Green Monster at Fenway Park, and stadium music that accompanies virtually every hitter to the plate—thank goodness for players such as Rangers third baseman Hank Blalock, who, when asked by the marketing guys what song he would like played, said, "No song. I'm not a DJ, I'm a baseball player."

We now have corporate ownership of teams and corporate sponsors—what is the name of the Rangers' ballpark this week?—and, sadly, the end of family-run organizations. Dodgertown hasn't been the same since Peter O'Malley sold the team. We have had re-alignment, but, thankfully, when the teams were moved around, they didn't get to the end and realize, as some feared, that they forgot to put the Kansas City Royals in either league.

We now have twelve-man pitching staffs (Earl Weaver once broke camp with eight pitchers), 100-pitch limits, and we haven't had a pitcher throw 300 innings in a season since Steve Carlton in 1980. The All-Star game now counts for home field advantage in the World Series, and we have the All-Star Home Run Derby, which some will say happens every night in baseball as many of to-day's players swing as hard as they can on every pitch in case they hit it, and often don't. We have specialization of players, especially pitchers, that is so acute that Lee Smith, the all-time leader in saves, entered a game with a runner in scoring position and nobody out only one time during a three-year period in the mid-1990s.

We have a strike zone that is the size of a license plate, or, as former Yankee pitching great Lefty Gomez described it, "From the top of the belt buckle to the bottom of the belt buckle." And now, in roughly half the ballparks, we have a QuesTec system that tracks how well or how poorly an umpire called balls and strikes. We have what we call the K zone on TV, which shows, via a suspended camera, the path of the ball from pitcher to catcher. "Someday," one umpire said, "HAL the Computer is going to be calling balls and strikes."

We have seen the birth of Fantasy Baseball. *ESPN The Magazine*, for which I work, published a forty-four-page special section in spring training 2006 just for Fantasy players such as a friend of mine who, when I was covering the Orioles in 1989, was telling me all about Orioles pitcher Jeff Ballard. Finally, I had to invoke the old "I think I know more about this than you do." We have seen the death of the doubleheader, meaning the death of some of the best-worst clichés of all time, the twin bill, the double dip, and the nightcap.

Much of this change has occurred during Selig's fifteen-year reign as commissioner, and not all of it has been necessarily good. There are two sides to so many facets of the game, and two sides to the man who runs it. The future of the game is bright, yet it is covered with questions, some of them formidable. Where the game is going all depends on your outlook.

The games are arguably better than they've ever been. Look at the postseason baseball that we've seen the last fifteen years. Was the 1991 World Series—Twins over the Braves in seven games— the greatest World Series ever? Or was the 2001 World Series even better when the Diamondbacks, in their fourth year of existence, beat the dynastic Yankees and nonpareil closer, Mariano Rivera, in the ninth inning of the seventh game? There was Atlanta's Francisco Cabrera's two-out, two-run single that beat the Pirates in 1992, Joe Carter's home run in 1993, the Yankee comeback against the Braves in 1996, the Angels' stunning comeback victory over the Giants in Game 6 in 2002, and the collapses in 2003 by the accursed franchises, the Red Sox and Cubs. But, alas, the Red Sox won the World Series in 2004 for the first time in eighty-six years, and became the first team in baseball history to come back from a 3–0 deficit to win a postseason series—against the hated Yankees, no less. And the White Sox followed in 2005 with their first World Championship in eighty-eight years.

The players are better than ever. There are future Hall of Fame players wherever you look: By my unofficial count, the 2006 season featured seventeen active players, who, if they never played another game, would be Hall of Famers. And there are another twenty who are headed to Cooperstown with a few more good years. We are watching one of the three greatest hitters in baseball history (Barry Bonds), three of the ten greatest pitchers (Roger Clemens, Greg Maddux, and Randy Johnson), the greatest closer (Mariano Rivera), the greatest hitting catcher (Mike Piazza), and Alex Rodriguez, who is on his way to being the greatest something. And someday we'll feel privileged to say that we saw Albert Pujols play.

I'm not sure we appreciate what we're watching. "We're not allowed to be as good as the old-timers; that's how baseball works," said Astros first baseman Jeff Bagwell, a future Hall of Famer. In 1994, when baseball's offensive explosion began, Yogi Berra told Bagwell, "The ball is juiced." Bagwell, who loves Yogi, asked him, "Yogi, how many home runs did you hit?" Yogi told him—358. Bagwell looked at me. "Yogi is this tall," he said, jokingly, measuring a man who is five feet tall, "and he's telling me that the ball is juiced."

But as great as the players are, are they playing the game the way it's supposed to be played? Has the staggering amount of money they make changed the way they think about, and do, their job? "They're better than we were," said ex-Oriole Ken Singleton, who finished a commendable career in 1984. "They're bigger, stronger, and faster than we were. But they're not as fundamentally sound, and they aren't students of the game like we were."

In 2004, Phillies catcher Mike Lieberthal asked manager Larry Bowa, "Who is pitching tonight?"

Bowa, shocked by such a question from his catcher only hours before a game, said, "Clemens."

"No," Lieberthal said, "I mean for *us*."

Teams don't take infield before a game, which is one reason why we're seeing fewer and fewer great throwing outfielders: They rarely, if ever, practice cutting loose and throwing to a base. Twenty years ago, teams took infield before every game. "I *had* to take infield before every game. I didn't feel right if I didn't take it," said Bowa, once a brilliant defensive shortstop for the Phillies. "If it rained before a game, and the tarp was on the field, and we didn't have infield, I would *have* to go to the indoor cage and play pepper just to get the feeling of catching a ball and throwing it before a game."

We need more players like Braves third baseman Chipper Jones, a future Hall of Famer. He was the number-one overall pick in the June 1990 draft. His father was his agent. The contract negotiations, which can be interminable and acrimonious when a player hires an agent, lasted about thirty minutes. Larry Jones took his son upstairs after the Braves made their first and only offer. "You can get a lot more than that," Father said to Son. Chipper said, "I know. But I want to play *now*." Jones had faith in his ability. He knew that playing was more important, and that the big money would come later, which it has.

We need more players like Nolan Ryan, who was spectacularly talented and competitive on the field, but so well respected and so well liked off the field because of the dignity with which he carried himself. Many years ago, someone took count of how many team-mates had named a son Nolan or Ryan after the great pitcher. It was close to twenty. Blue Jays infielder Rance Mulliniks, when asked what the game would be like if everyone was like Ryan, said, "Everyone would like each other, and no one would get a hit."

We need more young players like Tampa Bay outfielder Jonny Gomes, who not only can hit, but plays with a joy that isn't found in enough players today. Maybe it's because he even made it to the major leagues. For a brief period in high school, he lived in a car because of some bad luck in his family life. His senior year in high school, he lost a coin flip with his best friend, who got to sit in the front seat: The car was involved in an accident, and the friend in the front seat, who could have been Gomes, was killed. And then, at age twenty, Gomes suffered a heart attack. "If I hadn't been young and athletic," he said, "I'd be dead."

We need more players like A's closer, Huston Street. He looks like he's fourteen years old; he was mistaken for the ball boy not once, but twice, by an opposing player during batting practice in 2005. Finally, Street told the opponent, "I'm one of the players." When he was a rookie in 2005, Street patiently waited before a spring training game for the right time to speak to his baseball hero, the Dodgers' Greg Maddux, whom he had seen pitch on TV many times. After picking Maddux's brain, Street immediately called his father—James, a former quarterback at the University of Texas—to tell him of his talk with Maddux. "He's like a computer," Street said. How marvelous: a young player with respect for the game.

We need more players like Mets third baseman David Wright, the son of a policeman. He understands the game, and the reverence that players should have for it, better than perhaps any young player I've ever met. "The first time I faced Randy Johnson, I was in the box thinking, 'Oh my gosh, I'm facing Randy Johnson,'" Wright said. He wasn't awed to face him, he was honored: There is a distinction. "In the middle of January [2006], we all [many Mets players] went out to dinner in New York," Wright said. "[Catcher] Paul [Lo Duca] and [first baseman] Carlos [Delgado] were talking baseball, and we were discussing pitch counts. If you weren't ready to go, you sure were after that night."

It's easy not to like some of today's players. The average salary is nearly $3 million a year, and Alex Rodriguez makes $20 million a year. Some players, such as Barry Bonds, are spoiled, petulant, and insolent; they care only about themselves, and about nothing around them. Some are indefensible, but it's not easy being a star today given the intrusive nature of the media, when a player make a misstep, it's in every newspaper, on every Web site, every radio show, and all over ESPN. Their riches and fame are so spectacular, people want to see them fall.

"Would you like to be Cal Ripken?" I asked his teammate and friend Brady Anderson in 1995.

"Are you kidding?" Anderson said. "Not for one day."

During the 1995 season, I followed Cal Ripken for a week to see what his daily life was like for a story I wrote for *Sports Illustrated*. One day, I drove to and from the ballpark with him to see what baseball's Iron Man did in his idle moments in his car. We left Oriole Park at Camden Yards at 1.00 A.M. after a game, and afterward he had signed autographs for nearly ninety minutes in ninety-degree heat. We were stopped at a traffic light outside the ballpark. A man came running up to Ripken's truck and knocked on the window.

"Cal," he said, "I know what you're doing wrong at the plate. You've got your hands too high."

And then this idiot, in the middle of the street at one in the morning, showed Ripken how to hit. Ripken listened patiently, thanked the man for the hitting lesson, then drove off when the light turned.

"Has that ever happened?" I asked.

"That happens all the time," Ripken said.

Ripken was named *SI*'s Sportsman of the Year in 1995. It was announced at a private lunch with *SI*'s editors in a private back room at a restaurant in Baltimore. In the middle of lunch, a middle-aged man burst into the room unannounced, carrying all sorts of Ripken memorabilia, including hats, pictures, etc. "Cal," the man said, "I just bought these at the gift store. Could you sign these now?" Ripken politely told the man that he would, but not now, he was eating, but to leave his name and address, he'd get the stuff to him.

"Has that ever happened?" I asked Ripken.

"That happens all the time," he said.

After the 1995 season in which Ripken broke Lou Gehrig's record for consecutive games played, he took his family to secluded Sea Island, Georgia, for a vacation. He was in the grocery store with his family when people recognized him and followed him around the store, asking for his autograph. He finally had to tell them that he was on vacation with his family and that he couldn't stop and sign, otherwise he would be in there all day and his family was almost ready to leave. In the meantime, Ripken's son, Ryan, then age four, had gotten a chocolate donut all over his face. A woman shopper tore open a roll of paper towels and wiped Ryan's face, then asked Ripken if she could keep the paper towel as a souvenir.

"Why?" Ripken asked.

"Because it's your son, and I wiped his face with this towel," she said.

(Being too recognizable wasn't a problem for future Hall of Farmer Roberto Alomar when I spent a day with him in Puerto Rico in the winter of 1996. We were standing outside a Friday's restaurant after having had lunch. A woman approached Alomar, who was wearing a sweat suit, handed him a set of keys, and said, "Can you get my car?" She thought he was the valet! Alomar, who had just signed a huge contract with the Orioles, looked at me, smiled, and whispered, "I could *buy* this restaurant. I could buy the whole chain.")

Ripken made history, and history is made more than ever today, which is good for the game. Over the last twenty-five years, the single-season home run record has been broken twice, we have crowned an all-time leader in stolen bases, runs scored, and walks (the remarkable, underrated Rickey Henderson, a freak, the greatest leadoff man ever), in strikeouts (Nolan Ryan), in hits in a season (Ichiro), we have added eight members to the 300-win club, eight players to the 500-home run fraternity, and eleven men to the 3,000-hit club.

But how should we celebrate all these records and all these men in this Steroid Era? How many of them have come about their achievements unfairly? It is a question that will torment the game, and challenge writers such as myself who vote for the Hall of Fame, for many years to come. We finally have some information about Barry Bonds to evaluate thanks to the book *Game of Shadows,* which claims to have proof of Bonds's rampant use of steroids and human growth hormones for a five-year period starting in 1999. According to the book, Bonds became envious of the attention received by Mark McGwire during the 1998 season, in which he set the single-season home run record with 70. So, Bonds bulked up illegally, broke McGwire's record, and became the greatest slugger that most of us have even seen.

It is a very complicated situation. Bonds is one of the three greatest hitters of all time, with Babe Ruth and Ted Williams. When Bonds allegedly began doing steroids after the 1998 season, he already had Hall of Fame credentials: three MVPs, 400 home runs and 400 stolen bases (no one had ever done that), and six

Gold Gloves. Then he put together five offensive seasons that no one has seen since the days of Ruth. The game wasn't policing steroid use at the time. Everyone in baseball looked the other way. A lot of players were doing steroids; if the claims are true, Bonds just did it better than everyone else. His undeniably remarkable feats gave baseball what it wanted, long home runs and dramatic chases of some of the most remarkable players and records in the game's history. How can you not vote for him for the Hall of Fame?

On the other hand, if the book is true, how *can* you vote for him? If Bonds did use steroids, he is a blatant cheater and a liar who might have perjured himself in his grand jury testimony in the BALCO case. Did he cheat out of jealousy of McGwire and, on some level, out of greed? Could he have hit 73 home runs without the aid of steroids? How much damage has Bonds's steroid scandal done to the game? Have he and others stained the game to the point where the numbers are so tainted, they no longer have meaning in a sport in which they've always had meaning?

It is not right to take away Bonds's records. Baseball has never taken away anyone's records, not Pete Rose's, Joe Jackson's, or of anyone involved in the 1919 Black Sox betting scandal, and they shouldn't start with Bonds. But Bonds's candidacy for the Hall of Fame is another matter, and it is indeed in doubt. I'm glad I don't have to officially vote until five years after he retires because I'll need that much time to examine this confusing case. As for McGwire, in the absence of proof of his alleged steroid use, I'm voting for him for the Hall, but I'm guessing that he won't get 75 percent of the vote and make it to Cooperstown in his first year eligible. He blew it the day he testified before Congress and repeatedly said, "I'm not here to talk about the past." He got some terrible advice from someone. He would have been better off saying, assuming this was true, "I did andro. It is a steroid. It was legal. I got it over the counter. It made me bigger and stronger because I lifted weights like a madman for years. I did it because I couldn't stay healthy, and I couldn't help my team when I was hurt. When andro became illegal, I stopped doing it. You shouldn't do it. It's wrong. I'm sorry."

As for Roger Maris, his legacy will remain safe no matter how many players hit 60 home runs in a season. He was the first to hit 61; he broke the record set by the greatest, most legendary player of all time, Babe Ruth. Maris held the single greatest record in sports for thirty-seven years. His story, his place in history, will never be lost or forgotten. And any player who hit 60 homers in a season, or 500 for a career, while on steroids will never be fully embraced, whether or not they make it to the Hall of Fame. For the rest of their career and lives, people will say, "Oh, he was great, but he was a cheater." And that is punishment indeed.

The players are most responsible for steroid use, but they were not alone in their guilt. Where was the commissioner as this scandal was going on? Where were the owners? Where were the general managers as they were signing free agent players for millions of dollars? Didn't they know that some of those players used steroids? And where was the Players Association? Where was the media? We all missed the story. The genie is out of the bottle. It's too late to correct all that went wrong; all we can do is to look ahead and make sure it doesn't happen again. But given the competitiveness of athletes, another designer drug will come along that will make players bigger, stronger, faster, and better. The players will try the newest drug because they are always looking for an edge. That has been going on with athletes for a thousand years, and likely will never stop.

And neither will baseball's expansion. It is a global game, with over 30 percent of the players coming from Latin America. Several players come to the major leagues from Japan every year. Bobby Valentine, who manages in Japan, told me, "Every everyday player in Japan is good enough to play in the major leagues." I asked him if utility man Joe McEwing, who has had a decent career, would start for every team in Japan, Valentine said McEwing "would never start for the Tokyo Giants. The Japanese players are very good."

The World Baseball Classic—sort of a World Cup for baseball—debuted in 2006 to mostly rave reviews. It showed that baseball is played very well outside the United States. Globalization will grow the game to the point that, in the foreseeable future, major-league baseball will have a franchise in Mexico or Japan. But in this expansion, are we forgetting about the African American players? The RBI (Reviving Baseball In Inner Cities) Program, which builds baseball programs in inner cities, is great, but is it enough? During the 2005 season, only 9 percent of major-league players were black. Former ESPN analyst Harold Reynolds said that he has been to the College World Series in Omaha and not seen more than a few black players.

The cable TV explosion in baseball also has grown the game. Long gone are the days when the NBC Saturday *Game of the Week* was the only game on TV. Now you can watch twelve games a night, which I often do from my house. But are there too many games on TV? Is it good for the game that the Yankees, and now the Mets, have their own cable channels? The revenue the Yankees draw from the YES Network is far greater than the gross revenues of the Tampa Bay Devil Rays, which is one reason why the Yankee payroll was roughly $170 million higher than Tampa Bay's in 2005. And that's not healthy.

College baseball has grown greatly in popularity and skill level; more college kids are going high in the draft and making a quicker impact in the major leagues. But is the aluminum bat hurting the college game, and pro careers? "I call them 'electric bats,'" said former major-leaguer Larry Parrish. "Just plug them in and start hitting." Years ago, outfielder Luis Polonia, who is five feet seven and 155 pounds, used an aluminum bat during batting practice in spring training. I asked him what he would do if he used an aluminum bat for an entire season. Polonia said "I'd hit .400. And I'd hit forty home runs." I asked ex-Oriole pitcher Dave Schmidt twenty years ago what he would do if aluminum bats were allowed in the major leagues. "I would retire," he said. "Or I would get to pitch from fifty feet . . . with a screen in front of me." College baseball has done well changing the specifications of aluminum bats, making them less potent, but wouldn't it be a better game with wooden bats?

Minor League Baseball has grown greatly in popularity, attendance records were broken in 2005. Cities across America have built beautiful minor-league ballparks that are comfortable for the fan, more kid-friendly than major league parks, and more afford-able. Still, there is a colossal difference between the playing conditions in the minor leagues—fields, lights, salary, meal money, travel, and accommodations—compared to the major leagues.

"In Triple-A, you're one step away from being the best in the world, and you have to be a fry-cook in the off-season," said Casey Candaele, a former major-league infielder who spent a lot of time in the minor leagues. "But as long as you can deal with not having hot running water all the time and having greasy food every day, it's a lot of fun." Former Ranger Jack Daugherty played on a Helena, Montana, independent class A team in the late '80s. "I was making $600 a month. I slept in a clothes hamper in the clubhouse," he said. "What a team. We had every imaginable derelict there, even a kleptomaniac. He stole all of my stuff. I had to send home for the glove that I used as a kid."

That was a long time ago, and conditions have gotten much better. Still, why do you think there was such rampant use of steroids in the minor leagues the last few years? Because once you've been to the major leagues, where everything is first-class, a player doesn't ever want to go back to the minor leagues, and he'll do anything he can to stay in the big leagues.

Don Fehr and Gene Orza, who run the Players Association, are brilliant men whose singular function is to protect the players, which they do very well. But are they doing what is best for the game? Are these astronomical salaries ruining the competitive aspect of the game? The union leaders agreed to rewrite the drug policy in baseball twice in the last year, an inconceivable concession ten years ago, but were they too late in acting, and did they only act because they were forced by congressional pressure? It appears, however, that the players have regained some control of their own union. That became clear during the 2002 labor negotiations when well-respected players such as Tom Glavine led the charge not to strike, saving the game from what might have been a long and debilitating work stoppage. In October 2006, the players and owners ratified a five-year agreement two months before the deadline.

The ballparks in baseball are better than ever. Baltimore's Camden Yards in 1992 began a renaissance of retro ballparks, beautiful places that have revitalized downtown areas. If you haven't been to Camden Yards, or AT&T Park in San Francisco, or Safeco Field in Seattle, you must go. But most of these new parks (not AT&T) are publicly funded. Should taxpayers have to pay for these parks so some owner can get even richer? Should it be so expensive for a family of four to go to a major-league game?

And then there is Pete Rose. To some, he is all that is good about baseball, a man who, mostly through grit and determination, got more hits than anyone in baseball history. "Pete Rose *is* baseball," former commissioner Peter Ueberroth once said. To others, he is all that is bad about baseball. He is the personification of the arrogant player who believes he is bigger than the game. He won't be inducted in the Hall of Fame as long as Selig is the commissioner, and maybe ever, because he has acknowledged betting on baseball. "If Pete had killed a man, it would have been less of an infraction," Mel Didier, a scout, once told me. "You weren't around in the aftermath of the Black Sox scandal. I was. The game nearly died because of gambling." When I said on ESPN in January 2005 that I would vote for Rose for the Hall of Fame if he were put on the writer's ballot, Hall of Famer Frank Robinson yelled at me like he never has before, screaming, "How could you say that? He broke the cardinal rule: You don't bet on baseball."

The Rose issue is a complicated one, as are others that will arise in the years ahead. None of these problems will be easy to solve, but baseball has never been easy, and yet the game has always survived. It has withstood two world wars, numerous work stoppages, and scandals of all kinds. It has survived because it's the best game, a game with such great texture, history, and tradition, a game that never disappoints you once you fully invest in it.

In another twenty-five years, it will still be the best game. We will have teams in Las Vegas, in Mexico, and maybe one in Japan. "But those road trips from New York to Kobe are going to be tiring," said Dodgers coach Rich Donnelly. In twenty-five years, no one will be close to Nolan Ryan's strikeout record, Rickey Henderson's record for stolen bases, or Cal Ripken's record for consecutive games played, but there will be forty members of the 500-home run club, not twenty, and Alex Rodriguez will be the all-time home run king with 800, which won't make us forget Hank Aaron or Babe Ruth; it will make us appreciate them even more. In twenty-five years, David Wright will be going into the Hall of Fame as the greatest position player in the history of the Mets, Huston Street will have 300 saves, and Jonny Gomes . . . well, he'll be alive, and smiling. In twenty-five years, we will be arguing whether Albert Pujols or Lou Gehrig is the greatest first baseman of all time, and whether Roger Clemens is better than Walter Johnson. And you know where I will always stand on that one.

A lot will change in the next twenty-five years, but nothing will change, which is why the game is so great. You will have to get twenty-seven outs to win, the defense will have the ball, the pitcher's plate will be sixty feet, six inches from home plate, as it has been since 1893, and the bases will be ninety feet apart, as Alexander Cartwright paced them off—how did he know?—in 1845.

Is this is a great game, or what?

17

Why Waste the 90 Seconds on
the Front Page?

In September 2007, at a fancy Italian restaurant in Washington, D.C., I had my biannual lunch with George Will and Charles Krauthammer. They are two of the smartest men on earth, they write and speak eloquently about important topics such as war, gay marriage, and the President of the United States. And there at lunch, doing all the talking, was me, a baseball nerd who is intrigued by Mitt Romney only because of his first name, a seam-head who, at one point in my life, thought Iraq was the past tense of Iran.

I feel good after these lunches because I realize how much these erudite men love baseball, and how, like me, it consumes them daily.

"When I check into a hotel room—say it's 1456—I will remember it as Ernie Banks's number, and Joe DiMaggio's hitting streak," George Will said. They seem to enjoy listening to my stories of how small Tony Gwynn's hands are, and how big Prince Fielder's arms are.

"Biggest ever," said ex-teammate Rich Donnelly. "His arms are so big, you could put a tattoo of the United States on one bicep, and still have room for Argentina." I'm thankful that at these lunches, we never discuss anything but baseball because if we did, I would feel like Fred Flintstone.

"I spend ninety seconds reading the front page of the paper in the morning," Krauthammer said. "Then I go right to the box scores." To which Will said, "Why waste the ninety seconds?"

There were many reasons to read the box scores in 2007. It was a sensational season, it again confirmed all that I believe: baseball is the best game, it is the hardest game to play, it is an extremely dangerous game, and yet the funniest game, and it is the game with the richest history and tradition. Three players in 2007 hit their 500th home run (a first of any season in history), Sammy Sosa hit no. 600 and Barry Bonds broke Hank Aaron's home run record—a hundred days later, Bonds was indicted for allegedly lying to the grand jury. The season also provided a 300-game winner, a 3,000-hit man, and the first 500-save reliever ever.

Baseball's greatest beauty, its unpredictability, was never clearer than in 2007. The Yankees were 21–29 in late May, they were in deep trouble, yet the New York team that DIDN'T make the playoffs was the Mets, the first team in history to blow a seven-game lead with seventeen to play. The four National League teams that made the playoffs in 2006 didn't in 2007. They were replaced by the Phillies, who started out 3–10 and nearly fired their manager, the Diamondbacks, who had the best record in the league despite being outscored, the Cubs, who had finished last in the Central Division in 2006, and the Rockies, who wrote one of the greatest stories in baseball history, winning 21 of 22 games after September 1, including sweeps of the Phillies and Diamondbacks in the postseason.

The Rockies had never won fourteen out of fifteen during any fifteen-game stretch in their fifteen-year history, then won fourteen out of fifteen to finish the regular season. The last one came in an unforgettable one-game playoff against the Padres in which the Rockies—also for the first time in their history—won an extra inning game that they trailed by three or more runs, scoring four runs in the 13th off the all-time saves leader, the Padres' Trevor Hoffman.

Unpredictable? The Red Sox's Clay Buckholz, the White Sox's Mark Buehrle, and the Tigers' Justin Verlander threw no-hitters; Buckholz's came in his second major-league start, which means it took him two starts to do what the Padres and Mets had not done in 11,504 combined starts: throw a no-hitter. The Red Sox tied a major-league record with four consecutive home runs; in that game, the Yankees' Chase Wright became the second pitcher ever to give up four straight homers, the first since Paul Foytack in 1963. One of the homers off Foytack was hit by Tito Francona, father of Red Sox manager Terry Francona. The first team ever to hit four home runs in succession was the 1961 Braves. The guy who grounded out to end that streak was Joe Torre, who was Chase Wright's manager.

Unpredictable? The Dodgers became the first team ever to get consecutive home runs from the 7–8–9 hitters, with one of them being a pitcher, in this case, Hong Chi-Kuo. Rockies shortstop Troy Tulowitzki became the first rookie to pull an unassisted triple play, and the first player ever to hit a triple in a game in which he pulled an unassisted triple play. The Diamondbacks' Micah Owings became the first pitcher in fifty years to get four hits, hit two home runs, score four runs and drive in six runs in a game, and later became the first pitcher since Whitey Ford in 1953 to have two, four-hit games in a season.

Unpredictable? The Nationals' Ryan Zimmerman became the first player since World War II to strike out four times in a game in which he made three errors. Jake Peavy forgot to go from the stretch after walking Ryan Church on April 30. With Peavy in the windup, Church stole second and scored on a single. The Padres lost, 3–2. The Eyre brothers, Scott and Willie, gave up walk-off hits on the same day: Scott to the Mets and Willie to the Devil Rays. The Astros' Jason Jennings became the first pitcher since 1900 to allow eleven earned runs in the first inning. Keep in mind that in 1968, during an eighteen-start period that included 165 innings and 12 shutouts, the great Bob Gibson allowed only 11 earned runs.

And then there was Rangers 30, Orioles 3. It was the most runs scored in a major-league game in 110 years, it was more runs than the Rangers had scored in their last eight games and more than the Orioles had allowed in their last nine. The 8–9 hitters for the Rangers drove in seven runs each, which surely was a first in major-league history given that the last two teammates to drive in seven runs in the same game were Mickey Mantle and Elston Howard of the 1962 Yankees. The Orioles used only four pitchers; they became the first team in major-league history to have all four pitchers in a game allow at least six runs.

"After three innings, I was thinking, '(Orioles pitcher Daniel) Cabrera is going to throw a shutout,'" said Eric Nadel, the Rangers' radio play-by-play guy. "He's usually really good or really bad. I figured he was really good . . . the next thing I know, we have 30 runs. No team has ever scored that many runs under today's rules—remember, when the Chicago Colts scored that many in 1897, a foul ball wasn't considered a strike. It was amazing. The eighth and ninth inning (when the Rangers scored 16 runs) was a giant blob of ink on my score sheet. The Hall of Fame asked for it. Now I have a free pass to Cooperstown. In the ninth inning, my partner (Victor Rojas) was screaming in the background when I was calling the 30th run scored. It sounded like Ron Santo was my partner."

No one had ever seen a game like it; chances are, no one will ever see it again. I live fifty miles from where the game took place, but I missed it, which I'll regret forever. I had watched the first three innings on TV, then I had to go to a high school orientation for my son, Jeff, who was entering his freshman year. When I got out of the car, the Orioles were leading, 3–0. I turned off my cell phone for two hours. The second I turned it back on, it rang.

"Did you hear what happened in Baltimore?" asked Ed Schimmel, the producer of *Baseball Tonight*. His voice was stern and shaken, I thought someone had died. "The Rangers scored 30 runs," he said. "We're going to need you on the air in about fifteen minutes."

Baseball Tonight host Karl Ravech called at 9 P.M. to do a live TV segment over the phone. I ran through every amazing number I could find, my voice apparently cracking so badly in my excitement that John Kruk, who was sitting next to Ravech on the set, couldn't stop laughing. After my apocalyptic one-minute riff, Ravech thanked me for joining them.

"Is that it? One question! That's all you're going to ask me?" I screamed, hysterically, into the phone on live TV. "Wes Littleton got the save! The Rangers won by 27 runs, and Wes Littleton got the save!" By then, Kruk was incapable of speech, he was laughing so hard.

It was that kind of year, fascinating in every way, from the remarkable achievements on the field, to, as always, the people off the field who are obsessed by the game, including the family of four that spent the summer going to all thirty major league ballparks, then capped it with the Hall of Fame induction ceremony.

"Praise the Lord," said the father, a Baptist minister, who said the baseball odyssey "brought our family even closer together."

Praise ESPN research honcho Jeff Bennett. He told me that he can describe every Topps baseball card for a seven-year period.

"My wheelhouse is 1979 to 1985, I have trouble with some cards in 1981 because it was a strike year, but other than that, I can pretty much nail every one," Bennett said. "OK," I said, "describe Robin Yount's card in 1982?"

Without hesitation, Bennett said, "He's in the on-deck circle looking over his left shoulder at the third-base coach, like he's getting a last-minute sign. He had two cards that year, the other is an action card of him leaving the batter's box." "OK, Paul Molitor in 1981?" "He's sitting in the dugout, looking up at a reporter," Bennett said. "I don't even like the Brewers, but I remember their cards. I know all the Red Sox's cards. That's easy."

Praise ESPN producer Judd Burch, the umpire savant who organized an Umpire Fantasy League. Burch is an exceedingly bright, but bizarre, fellow who knows every major-league umpire by sight, can imitate their strike, ball, and out call, and would much rather meet umpire Hunter Wendelstedt than Astros outfielder Hunter Pence.

"Someone asked me recently about a Phillies' game from 2001," said Burch, who can recite the details of virtually every Phillies' game played in the last fifteen years. "I got the umpire rotation right."

So Burch invented this Umpire Fantasy League in which twelve ESPN employees, including *SportsCenter* anchors John Buccigross, John Anderson, and Neil Everett, each picked out of a hat the uniform numbers (who knew they had numbers?) of four umpires.

"It started as a six-man league, but there was such interest, we expanded to twelve," Burch said. "I knew when I chose uniform number 88 that I had Greg Gibson. Number 53, I knew I had Doug Eddings." Whatever team of umpires had the most ejections during the season, won. I was an expansion team. I didn't make my picks until the second week of the season.

"I'll take Larry Young," I said.

"He's *mine!*" Burch yelled.

The anchors in the league would routinely report on *SportsCenter* after an ejection, saying something like, "For those of you in an Umpire Fantasy League, credit Jerry Meals with the ejection." *Baseball Tonight* host Steve Berthiaume's team was lagging early, at which point he frustratingly said one night on *Baseball Tonight*,

"Dale Scott, whenever you feel like ejecting someone, I'm waiting." And that night, Scott ejected someone.

Burch's team, named Normally Good, won the league, twenty-two ejections to nineteen, passing Anderson's Blue Man Group the last week of the season. "Anderson was led by Joe West and Angel Hernandez, but my big run came from a push by Phil Cuzzi the last week of the season in Milwaukee," Burch said. "It's my understanding that it's the first Umpire Fantasy League ever. I played because I refused to play in a player Fantasy League because that might require me to root against a member of the Phillies. I couldn't do that."

It also was Burch who invented a new home run call for *Sports-Center* anchors: Fill Thine Horn with Oil, and Go.

"It's from the Bible, Samuel 16:1," Burch said. "It has nothing to do with baseball, but growing up, my brothers and I liked the way it sounded. (Anchor) Scott Van Pelt started using it when Jim Thome hit a home run for the Phillies. Now it's used when any Phillie hits a big home run. John Anderson started using it. Then Steve Berthiaume asked me, 'Can I say it, too?' I told him, 'It's in the Bible, someone came up with it before you.' When Chase Utley hit a walk-off homer off September 4, 2006, Scott Van Pelt said on the air: Fill Thine Horn with Oil, and Go *Home*.' My brother is a policeman in Wilmington (Del.). He tried to explain to his coworkers what this home run call business is all about. It's very hard to explain. They all just end up laughing."

Praise Rob Tracy of the Elias Sports Bureau. I told him that Jim Palmer never gave up a grand slam in nearly four thousand innings in his career because he occasionally walked a hitter purposely with the bases loaded rather than risk a slam. So, Rob found the twelve hitters that Palmer had walked with the bases loaded. I read those twelve names—Carlos May was one, for god sakes—to Palmer, saying that this list of players had something to do with his career.

"Oh," he said, "those are the guys I walked with the bases loaded."

Praise Dave Campbell of *ESPN Radio*. He told me the nickname for one of my favorite players, Mickey Rivers, a wonderful guy, but not the smartest guy, a guy who in 1982, as a veteran major-league player, asked to borrow money from me when I was twenty-four years old and making $16,000 a year. Campbell told me that Graig Nettles, a former teammate of Rivers with the Yankees, nicknamed Rivers "Chance," not because Rivers loved to gamble, but because "he was the least likely guy to be named chancellor of a university."

Praise the hilarious Steve Rushin, a former *Sports Illustrated* writer, who I visited this summer at his home in Connecticut. One of the guys who built a deck on his house and finished his basement has been playing Strat-O-Matic baseball in his own league since the late 1960s, only he doesn't buy the real cards, he makes his own, using fictitious players.

"His name is Steve, and the real cards weren't nuanced enough, so he made his own, and he has them laminated like a Waffle House menu," Rushin said. "I've had two-hour conversations with him about this. He left his cement mixer running when he was talking to me about it one day. He didn't bring the cards because he knew you were coming that day. He carries them in his truck, I guess in case he wants to go over strategy on his lunch break. He told me about the best player in his league, Katuby Leister, whom I called Ka-toooby Leister, and he said, 'please don't mispronounce his name, it's "Katuby.' I mispronounced his name? I'm supposed to know this? This is all made up. It isn't real.

"He's got his family and in-laws in his league. He said when he was a kid, he made up names like Ben Dover, but he says now that he's older, he takes better care of the names. He'll say, 'you know, the year that Three-Penny Franklin had in 1974, no one will ever top that,' like the American public is supposed to know who the hell Three-Penny Franklin is." (Funny things always happen around Steve Rushin. In 2001, on Halloween, he and I went to his gym—the Reebok Club, $30 guest fee, by the way—in New York to shoot some hoops. As we were just about ready to leave, two guys came in and challenged us to a game of two-on-two: one of the guys was Adam Sandler, who was dressed in sweatpants with a hole in one knee. We torched them because Sandler's friend was indescribably bad, but Sandler wasn't, and was amazingly competitive. After the game, I immediately called home to tell my children, Kelly, then ten, and Jeffrey, then eight, about what I'd done that day.

"What, you interviewed Derek Jeter?" Jeffrey asked.

"No," I said, "I played two-on-two with Happy Gilmore."

Dad had reached a whole new level with his kids with that news.)

Praise the Delaware State police woman who didn't berate me after ticketing me for speeding (seventy-two mph in a fifty) with my daughter, Kelly, and her friend, Vicky Lisle, in the backseat on the drive to ESPN, and with me on my cell phone *doing a live radio show* in Providence. All of this was on tape, which *Baseball Tonight* host, the mischievous Karl Ravech, found out about, and insisted that we play the humiliating exchange between the police woman, the radio show hosts, and me that night on *Baseball Tonight*.

Praise Orel Hershiser, one of my colleagues on *Baseball Tonight*. In a preshow meeting one afternoon, I asked him if he prepared for a start differently on the road than he did at home. He said, "The one part of my routine that was completely different was how I ate. I never told anyone what restaurant I was going to when I was on the road, especially if we were in the play-offs. I didn't want to know where I was eating in case anyone would try to poison my food. Maybe some chef in New York would know I was eating in his place the night before a big start, and might put something in my food. I wasn't taking any chances."

He wasn't kidding.

"When I was on the road with my wife," he said, "I would order one dish, and she would order another. Then, when the food arrived, we would switch, just in case mine was poisoned."

Praise Hall of Fame pitcher Phil Niekro, a knuckleballer. He won his three hundredth game on the final day of the 1985 season with an 8–0 shutout against the Blue Jays. And he did it throwing only one knuckleball. Here's the story he told me recently.

"The Blue Jays won the division the day before, so they were all hung over," Niekro said. "The night before, my brother, Joe, and I decided that he would relieve me in the game so he could be on the same lineup card for my three hundredth. In the ninth inning, Joe came to the mound and told me that he wasn't coming in because if I got one more out, I'd be the oldest pitcher ever to throw a shutout. So I stayed in. The Blue Jays had runners at second and third. Jeff Burroughs, who was a teammate of mine in Atlanta, was at the plate. We were deciding whether to walk him to load the bases. Burroughs looked at me, pointed to himself, and said, 'Pitch to me.' He swung at a knuckleball that was three feet outside for the final out."

Praise Cal Ripken and Tony Gwynn, two of the best players, and guys, ever. They were inducted in the Hall of Fame in July, an estimated seventy-five thousand people came to Cooperstown, more than twice as many as had ever attended an induction ceremony.

"Guess who we saw at midnight signing autographs in the middle of Main Street?" asked Gus Ramsey, a producer for *Baseball Tonight*. "Cal Ripken. People were chanting his name, so he signed. Then people on the other side of the street started chanting. So he went to their side."

Ripken's touch with people is extraordinary. There is a third-grade teacher in Arlington, Massachusetts, named Teresa Coffman. On the first day of class, she spelled out the rules for the year to her students. "There are only two reasons for you to ever yell in this classroom," she told them. "First, if there is a fire. Second, if you see Cal Ripken walk past this classroom."

Tony Gwynn had a similar effect on people, especially those from San Diego. I spoke to several fans in Cooperstown who openly wept about the impact that he has had on their lives. And it was more than just their marveling at him as a hitter, although there was plenty to marvel about, including this: for a five-year period, 1994–1998, Tony Gwynn hit .337 when he had two strikes. The average major-league hitter hits just under .200 when he has two strikes. Gwynn hit .337. During that five-year period, no other hitter in the game hit as high as Gwynn using *all their strikes* as Gwynn did with two strikes.

Gwynn wasn't nearly as relaxed as Ripken appeared to be on the morning of the induction, which can be excruciatingly difficult on the nerves for some players. At 11:30 A.M., two hours before Tony Gwynn was to make his speech in Cooperstown, his son, Tony Gwynn, Jr., a major-league player, came down to the hotel lobby to meet with his family.

"Dad needs a beer," Tony Jr. said.

Keep in mind, Tony Gwynn doesn't drink.

But thankfully, he made it through the speech.

Praise the Astros' Craig Biggio, who someday will join Ripken and Gwynn in the Hall of Fame. Biggio, who retired after the 2007 season, exemplified all that's right about the game, an overachiever who succeeded by showing up every day ready to play. To appreciate Biggio, look beyond his greatest accomplishment: the twenty-seventh player to reach 3,000 hits. Biggio had the sixth most doubles ever, more than Hank Aaron. He had more extra base hits than Al Kaline, Willie McCovey, Willie Stargell, and Mickey Mantle. He is one of five players with more than 250 homers and more than 400 steals, joining Barry and Bobby Bonds, Rickey Henderson, and

Joe Morgan. Biggio is fifteenth all-time in runs scored, more than Ted Williams. Biggio played in more winning games than Frank Robinson.

And yet one must go even deeper to comprehend his value. He has been hit by a pitch more times than anyone since 1900. In 1997, he did not ground into a double play. He is one of only two players in history to play a full season behind the plate, and a full season at second base, and is the only player to also play a full season in center field. He won four consecutive Gold Gloves at second base. He did all this playing for one team in his career.

The thought of getting 3,000 hits is inconceivable to most players, especially young guys in the big leagues for the first time. The 2007 season was filled with really good rookie players, including the Rockies' Tulowitzki and Milwaukee third baseman Ryan Braun, who had the highest slugging percentage (.634) of any rookie in major-league history. But the 2007 season proved—as baseball always does—how difficult the game is to play. "I could play the outfield, and I could run," said Bob Dernier, an ex-major leaguer, now a minor league instructor for the Cubs. "But every at-bat for me in the big leagues was a fist fight."

What a perfect description. And it was a fist fight all year for many young players, including Royals third baseman Alex Gordon, who finished with a .247 average and 15 home runs, but he struggled mightily early. That is how baseball works, that is why the game is so great: even the best, most gifted players can have a nightly fist fight at the plate.

Hall of Fame third baseman George Brett knows what Gordon went through. In 1973, as a twenty-year-old playing his first season in the big leagues, Brett went 5-for-40 with no RBIs and no walks.

"I'd get to the ballpark, look at the lineup card, and when my name *wasn't* in it, I was thankful," Brett said. "If the game got close late, and (manager) Jack McKeon would walk down the bench looking for a hitter, I'd try to *hide*. I didn't want to play. The more I was exposed, the worse it would be."

Hall of Famer Ryne Sandberg knows what they're talking about. Sandberg was hitless in his first 24-at-bats, and had one hit in his first 32-at-bats, for the Cubs.

"I thought I was way over my head," he said. "I didn't sleep at night. As soon as I got up in the morning, I wanted to go to the park so I could get a hit and get out of the slump. When I finally got a hit, (Cardinals first baseman) Keith Hernandez, who had a ton of hits, told me, "Hey kid, that's the first of many.' And I thought, 'Yeah, right.' I was thinking if I'd get my second hit."

Bad slumps were unimportant when put into perspective by the real tragedy of 2007: death. In chapter 6 of this book, I wrote about the fear of the ball, the dangers of the game, and I wrote that it was a miracle that only one player had ever died from being struck by a ball, adding "the second one could come at any time." And then, it happened. Only July 23, Mike Coolbaugh, thirty-five, the first-base coach for the Tulsa Drillers, a former major leaguer, was killed when hit in the neck with a line drive by one of his hitters. He fell straight to the ground, never regained consciousness, and basically died right on the field.

"People have no understanding of how hard the ball is hit at you," said Rich Donnelly, who has coached third base in the big leagues for twenty years. "You have to be ready for anything on every pitch. You can be quick as a cat, and you'll have no chance. It's a helpless feeling down there. When there's a runner on second base, the third-base coach has to move much closer to the plate to get a look at the runner at second. So now he's about seventy feet from home plate. I don't know about speeds, but I've read studies that the ball leaves the pitcher's hand at ninety-five mph, but it's going two hundred mph when it gets to the pitcher. And it's the same speed when it gets to the coaches' box. Every third- and first-base coach in the major and minor leagues knows what I'm talking about. It is terrifying."

Donnelly is a great athlete. He is sixty. He remains a fabulous racquetball player. He wins age-group tournaments nationally, and beats guys half his age. But every time he stands in the third-base coaches' box, he reminds himself that he must be ready for a rocket line drive.

"I've been hit three times really, really hard," Donnelly said. "I remember the places, the dates, and the time—that's how scary they were. The worst one was Greg Norton. I remember the pitcher and the pitch: Doug Davis threw a slow curveball. A lot of time, it's a slow curveball. The ball hit me in the back of the head, just to the right of my skull, on the fat part of my neck. If I hadn't turned my head in time, I might be done: it would have hit me right in the face. Buddy Bell (then the manager of the Rockies) was the first person I remember seeing after I was hit. He said he thought I was dead. He said it sounded like someone smashing a watermelon. That is a terrible, terrible sound. But I think my racquetball instincts saved my life. I was just able to turn my head just enough."

Starting in 2008, Major League Baseball has made helmets mandatory for base coaches. Good.

It wasn't a good year when it came to baseball and steroids. Seemingly every week, a new name surfaced with a connection to performance enhancing drugs, from Gary Matthews, Jr., in spring training to pitcher-turned-outfielder Rick Ankiel, whose fairytale story was soured greatly when he was named in a steroid controversy. The topic was never more magnified than in the first week in August when Barry Bonds broke Hank Aaron's record for career home runs. Most fans had trouble embracing it, believing that it was achieved dishonestly, illegally, or both. Bonds likely will never play another major league game. He is the best hitter that most of us have ever seen, but for the rest of his life, wherever he goes, he will be known as the all-time home run king, a cheater, and a liar.

And Roger Clemens likely will be remembered, fairly or unfairly, as the greatest pitcher of his generation, the third greatest pitcher of all time, but also a liar and a cheater. His was the biggest name of the ninety-some players mentioned in the Mitchell Report, which confirmed the idea that hundreds and hundreds of players used steroids and other performance enhancing drugs from roughly 1992 on. Clemens vehemently denied the allegations made by his former personal trainer, Brian McNamee, that he had injected Clemens with steroids and HGH a dozen times. Their standoff at a congressional hearing February 13, 2008, provided a most fascinating day of television, but it still didn't clear up exactly who was telling the truth and who was lying. That might be decided someday with a criminal investigation by the Justice Department. Amazing. Just like Bonds, the best pitcher of his era could spend the summer of 2008 attempting to salvage his legacy, his numbers, and his Hall of Fame candidacy, and, more importantly, trying to stay out of jail.

But steroids couldn't detract what the World Champion Red Sox did in 2007. They had the best record in the game (tied with Cleveland) for the first time since 1946, they buried the Yankees early, held them off late, swept the Angels in the ALDS, then came back from a 3–1 deficit to beat the Indians in the ALCS. They swept the rusty, overmatched Rockies for their second World Championship in four years after going eighty-six years without one.

The final out was recorded by closer Jonathon Papelbon, a great pitcher with incredible stuff, who now celebrates post-season clinchers with a Riverdance/Michael Flatley-style jig that is absolutely hilarious. Papelbon has a long and illustrious career ahead of him, but like many young players today, he is completely oblivi-ous to all that came before him in baseball. Papelbon was told the tragic story of Donnie Moore, the Angels' closer who gave up the famous, game-tying home run to Boston's David Henderson in Game 5 of the ALCS in 1986, a home run that helped keep the Angels from going to the World Series for what would have been the first time in their history. Moore killed himself three years later after many personal issues. When told of that Moore had commit-ted suicide after giving up the crucial home run to Henderson, Pa-pelbon asked, "After the *game?*"

The Red Sox won the World Series because Josh Beckett estab-lished himself as one of the great post-season pitchers ever. They won because David Ortiz and Manny Ramirez did what they always do: they hit when it counted. They won with their kids. Jon Lester, twenty-five, a cancer survivor, won the clinching Game 4. In Game 3, the Red Sox became the first team in World Series history to hit rookies 1–2 in the order, and Jacoby Ellsbury and Dustin Pedroia became the first rookies ever to combine for seven hits in a World Series game. A third rookie in that game, Daisuke Matsuzaka, got the win, and hit a two-run single.

I asked our research guy for the last time a Red Sox's pitcher had two RBIs in a post-season game.

"You're not going to believe this," Mark Simon said, laughing. "Cy Young and Babe Ruth."

That's the list: Cy Young, Babe Ruth, and Daisuke Matsuzaka. That can only happen in baseball.

Pedroia is all that is great about baseball. He is barely five feet seven, and was told every step of the way that he was too small to make it to the next level. He swings as hard as he can on every pitch, he thinks he can hit anything thrown his way, he wants every ball hit to him and he loves to play.

"He's a different kind of rookie," Red Sox teammate Curt

Schilling said. "It's different when a rookie shows up with the attitude, 'I'm going to kick your ass, and there's nothing you can about it.' It's really different when that rookie is only five foot two."

"Have you seen his hands?" said Red Sox manager Terry Francona.

"Smallest hands I've ever seen on a baseball player," said Red Sox GM Theo Epstein.

I will report this to George Will and Charles Krauthammer at our next lunch. They'll love it.

Acknowledgments

This project covers twenty-five years, thousands of stories, and owes gratitude to many. First thanks goes to the game itself for providing every day, without fail, what writers want and need most: material.

Thanks to Eddie Crane, who gave me my first job at *The Washington Star*. To Dave Smith, who hired me twice. To my friends from *Sports Illustrated*, specifically Mark Mulvoy and David Bauer. To my colleagues at *ESPN The Magazine*, especially Steve Wulf. To Peter Gammons, who got writers on TV, and to all those at ESPN television, including Jeff Schneider, who put me on *Baseball Tonight*, and Jay Levy, who keeps me on *Baseball Tonight*.

Thanks to all those at St. Martin's Press, who understood the thinking behind this book. Thanks to my editor, Marc Resnick, for whom we wish a World Championship for the Mets.

Thanks to my wife, Kathy, and children, Kelly and Jeff, who helped idiot dad with all their support, especially technical support, in the writing of this book. To my brothers, Andy and Matt . . . my only regret in life is not being able to play the game as well as you did.

And, mostly, thanks to my mom, the aptly named Joy, and my late father, Jeff. My dad taught me to love the game; my mom taught me to love words. My dad loved my mom more than anything, but here's how much he loved baseball. Andy, my oldest brother, played his home games for four years at Catholic University. The right-field stands included a dividing line: Any ball that landed below that line was a double, any ball above was a home run. Andy, a left-handed hitter with power, hit a ball that struck my mother in the shoulder as she was standing on the dividing line. The ball caromed downward, but eventually was ruled a home run.

My father raced to assist my mother, but soon after being assured that her shoulder was all right, he scolded her. "What are you doing?" he asked. "You almost cost the kid a home run."